PUBLICATIONS OF THE TEXAS FOLKLORE SOCIETY
NUMBER XXIX

MODY C. BOATRIGHT, Editor
WILSON M. HUDSON, Associate Editor
ALLEN MAXWELL, Associate Editor

and horns on the toads

PUBLISHED BY
SOUTHERN METHODIST UNIVERSITY PRESS
DALLAS

and horns on the toads

EDITED BY

MODY C. BOATRIGHT
WILSON M. HUDSON
ALLEN MAXWELL

SOUTHERN METHODIST UNIVERSITY PRESS
DALLAS, TEXAS

LIBRARY OF CONGRESS CATALOG CARD NUMBER: 59-15694

PRINTED IN THE UNITED STATES OF AMERICA
BY WILKINSON PRINTING COMPANY: DALLAS, TEXAS

Preface

THIS VOLUME borrows its title from John Q. Anderson's article on the horned toad of the Southwest, with which it opens. Mr. Owens' "Seer of Corsicana" is placed second; "Curanderos of South Texas" comes next because both the Mexican women that Mr. McNeil writes about and the Corsicana "seer" were folk doctors or advisers whom the people visited to learn how to recover from sickness or how to find a hidden treasure or grow rich in some other way. The two articles following are about folk characters who possess in common a kind of creativity which leads in Joe Whilden to imaginative lying and in Grandpa Brown to stories, rhymes, or tricks to raise a laugh at his friends or relatives. Joe is a liar and Grandpa a tease; as depicted by Mr. Faulk and Mr. Hardin they are recognizable as frontier types. In another society Joe might have been a Baron Munchausen and Grandpa a witty satirical poet. Each is original and delightful in his own way.

At this point a scholarly article is introduced, "Southpaws, Psychology, and Social Science," by George D. Hendricks. The next article, by Mr. Paredes, is scholarly also, and it leads into a Mexican-Spanish sequence carrying through Artell Dorman's "Speak of the Devil." In this sequence there is a range from far-distant historical background to specific songs and stories found in the Spanish Southwest.

The rest of the book, with the exception of Richard Lancaster's story from Chief White Calf, has to do with

English-speaking southwesterners. After reading J. Frank Dobie's "Madstones and Hydrophobia Skunks" in *Madstones and Twisters*, Michael J. Ahearn wrote the history of the madstone that has been in the possession of his family for a long time. Everett A. Gillis describes a rural institution as it used to flourish, the singing school. Girlene Marie Williams' "Negro Stories from the Colorado Valley" reads like an illustration of Fred O. Weldon's analysis of the Negro folk hero, who has been formed within a subcultural group in the presence of a larger, dominating group. Cultural conflict is also evident in Mr. Lancaster's "Why the White Man Will Never Reach the Sun," which shows the infiltration of biblical elements into the Blackfoot creation story.

Frontier life and ways are reflected in G. A. Reynolds' essay on "Vigilante Justice in Springtown." In "The Sinking Treasure of Bowie Creek" J. R. Jamison tells a story that was made possible by a kind of unintentional co-operation between the Spaniards who buried the treasure, the Indians who attacked them, the Negroes who dug down to the treasure, the tobacco-chewer in faded overalls who knew all about it, and the well-to-do men of the town who dug deeper with bulldozers and draglines. One of Ruth Dodson's "South Texas Sketches" looks back to frontier life ("Aunt Jane's Scares") and another ("It Cried at Noon") connects with the ghost stories told by Kenneth Porter in the last contribution to this volume.

It is evident that the principal linguistic and ethnic groups of Texas continue to be represented here as in the previous publications of the Texas Folklore Society. A balance is struck, again as in the past, between folklore as collected in the field and articles of a scholarly cast that comment on and illuminate what collectors have brought together. The Society welcomes both kinds of contributions.

The impetus behind folklore studies does not seem to be diminishing in this part of the world. If some of the older members of the Society have become less active, new recruits are being added. It is gratifying to know that nine of the present articles have been contributed by students, five of them undergraduates.

MODY C. BOATRIGHT
WILSON M. HUDSON
ALLEN MAXWELL

Austin and Dallas
October 29, 1959

Contents

and horns on the toads

And Horns on the Toads

JOHN Q. ANDERSON

IN THE anonymous poem "Hell in Texas"[1] appears a list of undesirable things which the Devil created when he took over Texas for "a hell of his own." Prominent in this special creation is the horned toad which the Devil cursed by putting horns on it, and which from that time forward has been in man's eyes a fearful and wonderful creature. So remarkable did the horned toad appear to the early visitors who recorded their impressions of Texas and the Southwest that a whole body of lore has grown up around the harmless little animal. Not only was it misnamed, but the truth about it has remained stranger than fiction, and the two have become so inextricably mixed in the popular mind that they are the same. The tales about the horned toad are familiar: it can "spit blood"; the blood it "spits" is poisonous; it can live for decades sealed up in the foundations of buildings; it can puff itself up like an adder; and it can even smoke cigarettes. Country people used to say that to kill a horned toad would cause cows to give bloody milk.

Not so obvious or dramatic as longhorns, mustangs, coyotes, rattlesnakes, and road runners—all of which have been written about by folklorists—the horned toad has received little attention. Unlike other denizens of the western frontier that have largely disappeared before civilization, the horned toad has not only adapted itself to live with man but continues to flourish. Scientists long since discovered that the horned toad

3

is unique among animals. In the tangled jargon of reports by zoölogists, biologists, and herpetologists are amazing facts which reveal that no one need apologize for telling tales about horned toads. Some of them *are* true.

First, the facts. The horned toad or horned frog, called *Phrynosoma* by scientists, is not a toad, but a lizard of the *Iguanidae* family, kin to the horned lizards of South America.[2] The horned toad is a North American genus of twenty-odd species and subspecies, fourteen of which are found in western and southwestern United States; others are limited to northern Mexico and Lower California. Considerable variety of physical characteristics and habits exists within the family; the species known as the Texas Horned Toad, for instance, lays eggs as most lizards do; other species give birth to their young. A limited subspecies is found only in extreme West Texas.

Living in a habitat of arid to semiarid climate, the horned toad feeds on ants, beetles, flies, and small insects, though it prefers red ants and will lick them up avidly with a toadlike flick of the tongue until completely gorged. With a throat and stomach immune to the sting of red ants, the horned toad of some species is, strangely, vulnerable to ant stings on other parts of its body. It cannot live without water, which it obtains in the form of dew, and in captivity has been observed to lap up greedily quantities of it. A cold-blooded, hibernating animal, the horned toad is limited in activity by temperature. It is, for example, most active in the heat of noon when it scurries over the blistering sand in search of food. By the middle of the afternoon, it searches out a bed of sand and buries itself for the night. On the broiling sand it flattens its body, wiggles vigorously until it is covered over with sand, and there it rests until the heat of the morning sun brings it out again. Below seventy degrees it becomes sluggish and will not eat; consequently, it dies quickly in captivity—it literally starves to death—unless its nest of sand is heated.

The self-burial technique of the horned toad is used in the

fall when hibernating time comes. It buries itself down as far as ten to twelve inches, well below the frost line, and remains there torpid until the spring sun warms the earth again. The Texas Horned Toad, a large and much-studied species,[3] does not bury itself daily but does hibernate from about October until April. Its mating season extends from the spring emergence until July. The Texas species lays twenty-four tough, leathery eggs in a hole up to seven inches deep, a layer at a time, carefully covering each layer with dirt. The mother never returns to the nest and does not take care of the young. Eggs hatch in about forty days, usually in June and July (though a newly hatched horned toad was observed in College Station in November, 1957), and the miniature horned toad fends for itself. The young do not reach full size of about two and three-eighths inches for a year. One truly Texas-sized horned toad reached a record length of four and one-fourth inches.[4]

The Texas Horned Toad has two quite prominent horns on the back of its head; the Regal species of Arizona and Sonora has four. Despite its ferocious appearance, the horned toad is quite docile and easily handled. It especially loves to be scratched. When one side is scratched, it tilts itself as high as the legs can lift it while the opposite side is depressed to the ground. It is subject to a form of hypnosis; three or four strokes with a finger between its eyes cause it to become quiet, close its eyes, and lose some of its reflexes. Often it will offer no defense and not run away but will simply "play possum." On the other hand, it can show fight when angered. Sometimes when captured, it will wiggle and twist its head as if to use its horns; it may open its mouth, hiss audibly, and puff itself up almost to twice its normal size. It has been known to jump toward a person and grasp a finger.[5] Though it may hold on, the bite is not severe. The horned toad does not always show fight toward human beings, but it bristles before dogs, of which it is particularly afraid.

The horned toad's natural enemy is the road runner. One

scientist reported, however, that he found a dead hawk which had swallowed two horned toads whose horns had pierced the craw and caused death.

The most incredible activity of the angered horned toad is the ability to squirt blood out of its eyes. Zoölogist John Van Denburgh in *The Reptiles of Western North America* says:

Especially is this liable to occur on a hot day, when a person grabs a 'toad' rather roughly. Then one or both of its eyes rapidly swell up, the lids meanwhile becoming tightly closed. It is not really the eye that swells, but it seems to be an engorgement with blood of certain spaces behind the conjunctival membrane and beneath the lids. At any rate there is a sudden bursting of blood from between the lids with considerable force, so that several small drops may land at a distance of two or three feet upon one's coat or face.[6]

This astonishing feat can be repeated at least once in a few minutes, if the animal is handled roughly, Van Denburgh continues. Afterward, the eyes seem normal. This blood squirting has been verified by so many scientists that it cannot be questioned.[7] The exact physiology of the act and the reasons for it are still in dispute, however. Some scientists maintain that the act is a defense mechanism, others connect it with the moulting period, and still others associate it with mating. Almost all scientists lose their scientific detachment when describing this strange phenomenon, for as one of them says, this "most amazing performance is without duplicate in the animal kingdom."[8]

Thus scientific facts about horned toads may be summarized, but fact has not prevailed over folk beliefs about the horned toad. The folklore of the horned toad evidently begins with the Spanish conquest of Mexico, when Europeans first saw the curious little animal. Though Spanish accounts were not available, the Mexicans called the horned toad the "sacred toad" because it shed tears of blood, and thus connected it with other animal myths clustering around the Christ. The idea of tears of blood may have passed from the Spanish to the Anglo-Ameri-

cans whose ventures into the West in the early 1800's introduced them to strange animals. Government surveying expedi-
tions in those years usually included naturalists who mentioned the horned toad in reports.[9]

Since the horned toad is indeed capable of ejecting blood,
the folk belief that it "spits blood" is so nearly accurate that it
can hardly be called a myth. The belief that the blood is
poisonous is, of course, superstition, probably connected with
similar beliefs about snakes and toads. Ironically, many young
Texans regard the blood-squirting habit of the horned toad as a
myth, as shown by a survey of seventy-five students at Texas
A. and M. College. Fifty-five young men stated positively they
did not believe that horned toads eject blood, either by spitting
or squirting it out of their eyes. Of the eighteen who believed
the fact, most had actually seen the feat.[10]

A folk belief less spectacular than blood spitting is that
horned toads can exist for years without food or water or even
without air. Such tales often concern horned toads sealed up
in the foundation stones of buildings. Evidently this myth is an
outgrowth of the superstitions connected with the toad proper,
which in literature, fairy tale, and folklore has always been a
creature of darkness and mystery. A French scientist proved
as early as 1777 that the toad can indeed survive for months
without food but dies when deprived entirely of air. The toad's
habit of burying itself during hibernation accounts for the
stories of its ability to live sealed up, and since the characteristics of the toad were transferred to the horned toad on the
assumption that it too was a toad, the horned toad is also
believed capable of surviving when sealed up in concrete.
Among early accounts of its ability to survive without food
and water is that of William Kennedy, an English traveler who
in 1838 wrote that at the end of a tour of Texas,

A sailor in Galveston, who had caged a few of these animals in the crown
of his hat, valued his collection at ten dollars a-piece, and, as an encour-
agement to purchase, assured me that I might convey the prize alive

and well to Europe without any further trouble than supplying them with air.[11]

Reports of horned toads found in cornerstones of buildings have been standard newspaper fare for years. Doubtless the most widely publicized of such horned toad stories is that of Old Rip, who remained in the cornerstone of the Eastland County, Texas, courthouse for over thirty years. In 1928 Old Rip, so called because he outslept Rip Van Winkle, was known to practically every newspaper reader in the United States and in some foreign countries.[12] As the newspapers told the story, in the summer of 1897 when a new courthouse was being built in Eastland, Ernest Wood started downtown to play in the local band at the cornerstone-laying ceremony. Noticing that his son was playing with a horned toad and remembering the story that horned toads could live sealed up in concrete, Wood picked up the animal, took it to town, and handed it to a friend who deposited it in the new cornerstone. In 1928, when the courthouse was being razed to make way for a new one, Wood remembered the horned toad and told Boyce House, editor of the local newspaper. House ran a story which was picked up and circulated by the news services, and on the day the cornerstone was opened about fifteen hundred people gathered to see if the horned toad had survived. The horned toad was indeed in a metal-covered cavity in the concrete. A man picked it up, handed it to the Methodist minister, who in turn passed it on to the county judge, who held it up for the crowd to see. As the toad began to breathe, the crowd grew excited and pressed in for a closer view until an officer of the law seized the animal, mounted his motorcycle, and sped to the edge of town lest the horned toad be crushed by the mob.

Will Wood, who as a boy had been playing with the horned toad when his father took it to put in the cornerstone, brought Old Rip to Dallas for exhibition at a theater — but returned without showing the animal when people poured into Eastland to see the famous horned toad. The theater owner filed suit.

Meanwhile, full-page feature stories appeared in Sunday supplements, foreign newspapers carried the story, and columnist Arthur Brisbane cited Will Wood as saying that the horned toad might have "derived strength" during his thirty-year entombment from the Bible that also had been deposited in the cornerstone. Scientists were sought out by reporters and were quoted both for and against Old Rip's story. Boyce House claims that newspaper space devoted to Old Rip was exceeded only by the coverage of Lindbergh's flight across the Atlantic.

Old Rip was accompanied by a motorcade to a highway promotion convention in Memphis, Tennessee. At Dallas, where the horned toad was taken into custody by the sheriff as a result of the lawsuit, Wood valued the animal at $50,000, and the sheriff approved a thousand-dollar bond signed by an ex-mayor and others. On the tour Old Rip was admired by crowds; forty thousand people saw it in one day at the St. Louis Zoölogical Gardens. In New York a talking moving picture was made of Wood feeding Old Rip with bugs obtained at fifty cents apiece. Climaxing the tour in Washington, Old Rip was shown to President Calvin Coolidge, who because of a mistake in the schedule was kept waiting fifteen minutes before he saw the animal.

Old Rip died in Eastland in January, 1929. Embalmed and placed in a satin-lined coffin, the animal was shown for a fee. As a boy in Hopkins County, Wilbourn Benton (now a history professor at Texas A. and M.) saw the famed horned toad when it was the featured attraction of a celebration opening a paved highway in that area. Benton paid fifty cents to see Old Rip and an extra nickel to touch the animal. He says that a boy who had touched Old Rip could make back part of the admission charge by demanding a nickel from other boys to touch the hand that had touched the famous lizard.[13] Eventually Old Rip was entombed in a concrete mausoleum with a glass top in the lobby of the new courthouse in Eastland, and his likeness appears in the sculptured stars on top of the building.

The most glamorous episode in horned toad lore concerns a

Texas horned toad and Lilly Daché, the famous milliner and
hat designer. In her autobiography, Miss Daché reports that
when she was building her hat shop in New York she read
about a Texas horned toad found in a cornerstone (probably
Old Rip). Thought to have been there 125 years, the horned
toad was still alive and agile and had, the newspapers reported,
brought the house good luck. Miss Daché decided that she must
have a horned toad for the cornerstone of her building. An
obliging friend obtained one which was ceremoniously placed
in the cornerstone along with a copy of the first hat she had
designed. Later, two men who said that they were from the
Society for the Prevention of Cruelty to Animals called on the
designer and soon had her in tears over the unwitting cruelty
she had perpetrated upon the little animal. Miss Daché ordered
the horned toad rescued and then learned that the SPCA visita-
tion was a gag arranged by her friends. As a result, she gave a
fashionable party for the horned toad, and a friend furnished a
glass, bejeweled box for the little animal which was the
honored guest.[14]

Misunderstanding of the nature of the horned toad led to
superstitions and tall tales. Early travelers in Texas and the
West anticipated a strange and different land, and when the
country lived up to their expectations they gladly passed on to
easterners the fiction along with the fact. Kentuckian Jack
Dobell (John Duval), for example, came to Texas in 1835 to
fight in the Revolution, was captured at Goliad, escaped, and
was wandering about in the Lavaca River bottom when he
encountered a horned toad:

In a small grove of timber where I had halted to rest a while [he said],
I saw for the first time a horned frog. I had heard of the tarantula and
centipede of Texas, and supposing the harmless frog was one or the
other I picked up a stick about ten feet long (not venturing to approach
nearer such a poisonous reptile) and mashed him as flat as a pan-cake.[15]

As more adventurers and settlers poured into Texas in the
1840's the traffic in horned toads began. An unknown con-

tributor to *Arthur's Home Gazette* wrote from Texas in 1853:

This Texas of ours is an astonishingly prolific country. . . . in horned frogs, scorpions, tarantulas, and centipedes, we beat the universe. Everybody has seen horned frogs. You see them in jars in the windows of apothecaries. You are entreated to purchase them by loafing boys on the levee at New Orleans — they have been neatly soldered up in soda boxes, and mailed by young gentlemen in Texas, to fair ones in the old States. The fair ones receive the neat package from the post-office, are delighted with the prospect of a daguerreotype — perhaps jewelry — open the package eagerly, and faint; as the frog within hops out, in excellent health. . . .[16]

Texas was still so remote that almost any tale about it would be believed in the East, and wags with a sense of humor sometimes clipped the four- or five-inch claws from the dried pods of milkweed called "devil's claw" and mailed them home as examples of horns from horned toads.

The passage of time only increased eastern interest in the horned toad. In 1901 the *Scientific American* reported that a curio dealer in Pasadena, California, was doing a brisk business in shipping horned toads, both alive and mounted, to the East. He did his business no harm when he reported that some of his live specimens could spurt blood six feet and hit a wall with a resounding splatter.[17]

Twentieth-century westerners, always publicity conscious, have used the horned toad to brag about their differences. In 1941, for instance, *Newsweek* reported the ninth annual "toad gallop" in Coalinga, California, in which 175 horned toads were entered from Arizona, Texas, California, and Mexico. Before 6,000 spectators "Dive Bomber," a "six-inch Texas Horned Toad," beat out "Beef Stew" and "Prissy," who placed and showed respectively for betting customers.[18] It is significant that "Dive Bomber" reportedly measured six inches and was from Texas, since the measurement exceeds the scientists' records of maximum size by two inches.

Easterners were still being taken in by horned toads in 1957, when some Dallas Boy Scouts took several horned toads to the National Scout Jamboree in Philadelphia and disposed of them at ten dollars a head. They frantically wired their mothers for more to be shipped by air express. The Dallas moms met the emergency by capturing more horned toads in vacant lots in 105-degree heat.[19]

Finally, a horned toad has had a significant bit part in a successful movie, Walt Disney's version of Fred Gipson's *Old Yeller*. In the original story, the horned toad appeared only as one of the numerous varmints that Little Arliss was given to carrying around in his pockets. Travis, who tells the story and who knew his horned toads, says, "One time he brought in a horned toad that got so mad he swelled out round and flat as a Mexican *tortilla* and bled at the eyes."[20] In the story as adapted for the screen, the horned toad got a more important role when Burn Sanderson quieted the tempestuous Little Arliss by trading him Old Yeller for the horned toad. For a few seconds the movie camera dwelt on the horned toad (probably a California species), and movie-goers all over the nation and the world perhaps can view, many doubtless for the first time, the unusual little animal.

Thus the Devil did the horned toad a great disservice when he gave it horns that make it look like a miniature prehistoric monster. The fact that around the little creature have clustered tales and lore makes all the more pleasant having a horned toad in the yard or garden. As poet S. Omar Barker has humorously said:

> The horny toad, ill graced but harmless
> Is thought by some to be quite charmless.
> At least he helps eat garden ants up —
> And does not try to crawl your pants up![21]

1. In N. Howard Thorp's *Songs of the Cowboys* (Boston, 1908, 1921), pp. 77-79. On the authorship of the poem, see Mody C. Boatright, "More About 'Hell in Texas,'" *From Hell to Breakfast* ("Publications of the Texas Folklore Society," XIX [1944]).

2. The factual information was taken from John Van Denburgh, *The Reptiles of Western North America* (San Francisco, 1922), I, 364 ff; and Hobart M. Smith, *Handbook of Lizards* (Ithaca, 1946), pp. 287 ff.

3. Van Denburgh, I, 413 ff., cited several studies made in Texas.

4. Smith, *op. cit.*, p. 292.

5. *Ibid.*, p. 295.

6. Van Denburgh, *op. cit.*, I, 392.

7. Van Denburgh cited reports from many scientists confirming their observation of this feat. One researcher reported that as he caught a number of horned toads in one day his shirt became "as bloody as though he had been killing hogs."

8. Lorus J. and Margery J. Milne, "The Horned Toad — Desert Oddity," *Audubon Magazine*, LI (Nov.-Dec., 1949), 366. Smith, *op. cit.*, p. 288, says, "The final touch of the unusual in this genus is the peculiar ability of some species to squirt blood, to a distance of several feet, from the eyes. . . ."

9. Van Denburgh, *op. cit.*, I, 364 ff., cites notations as early as 1833.

10. These students, from forty-nine different counties in Texas, were mostly freshmen who had had no science course in which the facts would have been explained. Forty-seven of them reported having heard of horned toads existing in foundation stones, although most did not believe such stories. Sixteen of the seventy-five reported believing that horned toads could smoke cigarettes, and some said that they had seen them do it.

11. *The Rise, Progress, and Prospect of the Republic of Texas* (London, 1841), I, 135.

12. The information is from Boyce House's *Cowtown Columnist* (San Antonio, 1946), "Old Rip, the Eastland Horned Frog," pp. 3-12.

13. As told to me by Professor Benton, College Station, February, 1958.

14. *Talking Through My Hats* (New York, 1946), pp. 177-78.

15. As related in J. C. Duval's *Early Times in Texas* (Austin, 1899), p. 89.

16. Reprinted in the *Spirit of the Times*, XXIII (May 28, 1853), 172.

17. Charles F. Holder, "A Curious Means of Defense," *Scientific American* (Sept. 21, 1901), pp. 186-87.

18. May 12, 1941, pp. 52-53.

19. Newscast, Radio Station WFAA, Dallas.

20. Fred Gipson, *Old Yeller* (New York, 1956), p. 42.

21. *Songs of the Saddlemen* (Denver, 1954), "The Horny Toad," p. 94.

Seer of Corsicana

WILLIAM A. OWENS

IT WAS a pleasant task that had taken me to Corsicana, a black-land town some fifty miles south of Dallas. I was there to interview with a tape recorder persons who knew the life and lore of early oil fields in and around Corsicana, and to collect tales, songs, photographs of the early days.

"You must see Annie Buchanan," people told me. "She's the most unusual thing you'll find in Corsicana."

"Who is she?"

"A colored fortuneteller. They say she told Colonel Humphries where to drill when be brought in the Mexia field. They say he set her up in business after that. They say—"

With Carl Mirus, a retired oil man, as guide, I went out to Annie's house in the Negro section of South Corsicana. It was an April morning, warm and bright, with a soft Gulf breeze blowing across freshly-plowed cotton fields.

The house, white frame trimmed with bright red and surrounded by a red picket fence, was a mansion among shacks and shotgun houses. A line of cars, some with out-of-state licenses, took up the parking space in the immediate vicinity. Groups of men and women, white and black, waited around the cars and in the yard.

Leaving Carl in the car, I went to Annie's waiting room, another white house with red trim, set apart in a side yard. I passed under a horseshoe over the door and joined the group waiting patiently on folding chairs.

14

I took in quickly the old reed organ, a Coke machine, and a hand-painted sign on the wall: "I will not read to 'women' who 'smoke' are ware 'pants' are 'slacks' here. Positively no 'drinking.' By Mrs. Annie Jackson."

"Where is Miss Annie?" I asked the colored man in the chair next to mine.

"She ain't come yit. You gits yo' card from Mr. Means in the house. You jest go on over."

He pointed to a screen door leading to a screened-in back porch. I went to the door and knocked.

A brown man probably in his sixties, toothless except for a yellow eyetooth on either side, came to the door. When I asked if I could see Miss Annie, he gave me a missionary card on which he scrawled a number.

"I give you number nine," he said. "Miss Annie likes to mix up the white customers with the colored."

Obviously he had moved me ahead of a number of people.

"How long does she read?" I asked.

"She generally quits at first dark."

I took the card and went to where a middle-aged white couple from Paris, Texas, a hundred and fifty miles away, waited. They talked freely, unembarrassedly of having come to see Miss Annie. There was even a kind of reverence in their voices.

"She can tell you things that only you and God know," the man said.

After an hour of waiting, my chances of seeing her that morning began to seem doubtful, and I went with Carl to the Magnolia pumping station, for a demonstration of the latest developments in pipe-line machinery.

When we went back in the middle of the afternoon, the crowd was larger. The waiting room was full. Some of those I had seen that morning had crowded into chairs in a back hallway in the house. At the head of the line was a colored woman in blue flowered dress and white straw hat.

I slid into a chair next to a lovely young white girl who had glanced at me and said under her breath, "Have a seat." She smiled faintly, but she looked worried.

From where I sat I could look into the room where Miss Annie gives her readings. I could not see her, or the person with whom she was talking, but I could hear a deep, rich voice, and I could see a pair of dark brown hands shuffling and reshuffling cards.

The voice stopped, the hands disappeared, and a colored woman came from the room, smiling. Her money obviously had been well spent.

The girl next to me went to the door and said, "Sister, can't you please take me next? I've waited all day."

Her plea rejected, she came back to her chair.

"It's so hard to see her," she whispered to me. "You just have to wait."

I found Mr. Means again and asked his help.

"Maybe you can talk to Reverend Jackson," he said. "He's her husband. I'll see for you."

He returned in a few minutes and took me to the living room. Reverend Jackson, a big dark man with a goatee beginning to turn gray, was lying on a couch watching a cooking demonstration on television.

"What you say you want?" he asked.

"I'm with the University of Texas. We are recording the experiences people have had in the oil fields. It is an educational research program. I would like to record Miss Annie."

Looking as if he didn't really understand what I meant, he said, "I'll see," and went to Miss Annie's reading room.

While he was gone, I had a good chance to study the living room. In the center was a round table with a crystal and rose punch set on it. On the rug around it were baskets and baskets of red, blue, and yellow crepe-paper flowers and masses of green paper leaves.

On the walls were pictures of Lincoln and of several Negro

leaders. At one side a bronze statuette of Joe Louis gazed grimly across the room.

Reverend Jackson shuffled in.

"Miss Annie will see you at eight in the morning if it's for educational purposes," he said.

Assuring him that I had nothing else in mind, I went past the curious stares of the waiting people.

At eight the next morning I took a Yellow Cab with a white driver named J. E. Reed.

"I want to go to Annie Buchanan's," I told him. "Do you know where it is?"

"Yes, sir. I take people out there all the time."

During the short trip he told me stories of Miss Annie's remarkable gift.

Twenty-six years ago his father had lost a cow and calf. He went to Miss Annie for help.

"Go east," she said. "A long way east. Not a hundred miles east, but a long way."

His father went east on the main road ninety miles and found the missing animals in possession of the man who had stolen them.

"I don't know how she done it," the driver said, "but she shore did."

Only recently, he told me, a man from down in the Trinity River bottoms lost his best hound dog. Miss Annie described to him the man who stole the dog and told where he lived.

The taxi pulled up in front of Miss Annie's and I got out, the first customer of the morning. The house was shut tight and there was no one around. My knocking did nothing but disturb an old white rooster and a flock of hens wallowing in the ashes around a washpot.

In a few minutes a colored woman came through the back gate.

"Ain't Miss Annie here?" she asked.

"I guess not."

"I reckon I'd better wait. My little girl's sick. I went to the white doctor and he give me some medicine for her. I just wants to ask Miss Annie whether it's too weak or too strong for her."

"Is Miss Annie good?" I asked her. "Does she help you?"

"She be's mighty good. I don't like to do nothing without astin' her about it."

Then a colored man from Dallas drove up, an ex-G.I. He had driven fifty miles to buy a bottle of Rawleigh's cathartic pills from her. He could have bought the same pills in Dallas, but they seemed to do better when he bought them from her, he told me.

Mr. Means came through the back yard and opened up.

"Miss Annie ain't here," he announced. "She left soon this morning for Marlin."

I reminded him of my appointment.

"She know about it. She say for you just to wait. She's built a new home over there and has to watch the men dig the cesspool. She have to be a man and woman, too. That preacher ain't no account."

The others went to the waiting room. I followed Mr. Means into a house spicy with the smell of barbecue cooking. While he swept the floors and cooked, I followed him around. I learned that his name is U. R. Means and that he and Miss Annie are first kin. I also learned his low regard for preachers.

"Where is Reverend Jackson?" I asked.

"He went to Dallas last night. He ain't a lick of help to her. He's like a kite—always on the sail."

In the dining room, among hundreds of pieces of colored glassware from the dime store, gifts of Miss Annie's admirers, he told me that Miss Annie was upset. The previous Sunday night, while she was conducting services in her church next door, a robber climbed the fence, broke in through a window, sawed a chest open with a handsaw, and took four hundred dollars in cash and all her deeds and receipts.

"She know who done it," he said confidentially. "She waiting till he can be caught with the goods."

He swept the dining room vigorously.

"What's she need with a preacher anyhow?" he demanded. "Her in her sixties and him twenty years younger."

He whacked his broom down the floor of a dark hall, furnished with an iron bed and a wood heating stove.

"She don't know A from B," he said. "She have to make her X. I calls that ignorancy. I don't know why white folks with education comes to her. They say what she knows come from God."

But her inability to read or write had cost her money.

"She ain't got sense enough to keep anything," he said. "Folks gits to her for money all the time."

He recited a list of spongers, including husbands named Buchanan, West, Younger, and now Jackson.

"She say 'Kinfolks is bad luck' when she know about the robbery," Mr. Means told me.

He locked up and went to the store. I joined the group in the yard. A white man came by peddling carp. Colored women bought fish, gutted them on the grass, and washed them at Miss Annie's hydrant.

The white rooster stretched his neck and gave an ear-splitting crow.

"Maybe she coming now," people said to each other hopefully.

A sudden shower of rain drove us to the waiting room. I found myself sitting between a young white man and an aged, crippled Negro. At Miss Annie's there is no segregation. The white man had come from East Texas to ask Miss Annie if there was oil under his land. As he talked, I learned that he was a maintenance engineer on electronic equipment in a chemical plant.

The shower turned to a downpour. The room grew dark. We sat in a circle and talked.

Some Negroes got off on why there is so much meanness in the world. A Negro farmer from the Brazos bottoms summed it up:

"It used to be babies was breast fed. They et nothing but the human. Now first thing when they're born the doctor takes them and puts them on the bottle. That way the animal gits all mixed up wit the human. They gits cow's milk, goat's milk—"

A very dark woman burst out laughing.

"Some of them must git Brahmer," she said.

From that, they turned to talking of the pains and problems that had brought them to Miss Annie.

A white man, a member of the fire department at Corpus Christi, had come to ask her to diagnose his mother's stomach trouble.

A Negro man got up from his chair beside his wife and paced back and forth in the room. Suddenly he stopped and dropped some money in her lap. He frowned at her and spoke in a whisper. She shook her head.

"That ain't enough to make me hursh up," she said belligerently. "When I gits going in there, I'm gonna talk it all."

One huge dark woman who continually showed worn-down teeth in a grin said every so often, "All I wants is a round table."

She was from Calvert; with the money she would spend for bus fare, hotel, and Miss Annie's fees, she could have bought a fairly decent round table.

Then they got around to remarkable cures effected by Miss Annie. Here Mr. Means added his bit.

"She have cured lots of people and holp a lot more," he told the group solemnly.

A tall brown woman said, "My mother had high blood when she come to Miss Annie. Now she's so holp she works two days a week for a white lady."

At one o'clock Miss Annie had not come, and mud had well-nigh stopped traffic in that part of town. Miss Annie might not make it at all. Her Cadillac might not get through.

Mr. Means came to the waiting room.

"I got some barbecue in the kitchen," he said.

Everybody dashed through the cold rain and gathered around in a circle in the kitchen. They ate barbecue sandwiches at two bits apiece and went right on talking. In matter-of-fact tones Negroes and whites exchanged pious remarks, looking up as if some divine secret were being revealed to them.

Reverently they looked at the door to the room where Miss Annie reads to her customers.

"Ain't nobody going in there till Miss Annie come," Mr. Means told them. "What goes on in there belong to Miss Annie and her customers. Miss Annie ain't telling nothing. Folks talks, but not Miss Annie."

It was middle of the afternoon before I got a slipping, sliding ride to town with an arthritic man who had given up seeing Miss Annie that day.

I should have given up entirely on the matter, I suppose, but by now I was completely intrigued by this unusual situation.

Next morning at nine I called a taxi and, with my tape recorder, went back. A crowd had already gathered in yard and waiting room. They looked curiously at me and the tape recorder.

Mr. Means met me at the back door. Miss Annie was at breakfast. Reverend Jackson still had not returned.

"How come you want to see her?" he asked, as if he had never seen me before.

Again I explained, in a voice loud enough to be heard by the people in the yard.

Motioning for me to approach quietly, he let me come to the back door of the hall. He whispered for me to wait while he went inside.

In a few minutes he came back with the news: Miss Annie would see me as soon as she was dressed.

He took me to the living room and told me to set my tape recorder up beside the sofa. He lined up rows of folding chairs at one side of the room. He arranged some sprays of chenille flowers, a black ribbon pompom, and a Bible in a kind of altar on the sofa.

He called the people in from the yard. Silently, reverently they filed in, colored and white together, and seated themselves on the folding chairs. Among them was the white girl I had seen before, her face still troubled, her eyes red from weeping.

Miss Annie came in while I was kneeling beside the tape recorder putting in tape. All I had heard about her had not prepared me.

She is a tall, remarkably well-built woman, marvelously well-preserved for the sixty-three years she claims. Her skin is soft dark brown, her eyes dark, emotional, with a look that seems to pierce ordinary barriers. She was wearing a gray faille suit, pale gold silk blouse, and brown velvet pumps with high heels.

As I rose she looked at me piercingly, and then at the group on the opposite side of the room.

"I giving advice," she said.

I spoke quickly, to ask about her advice on locating oil wells. She answered, her voice loud, full.

"My brother-in-law owned this piece of property. He was buying it, and he lost his wife, and he said, 'Miss Annie, I believe I'll give this property back.' I said, 'Let me look at you and see you.' So I looked at his hand and described the oil. I said, 'Boy,' I says, 'keep it. It'll pay for itself.' I said, 'Heah oil.' He say, 'I thought you had some sense. They ain't no sich thing as oil under the earth.' I said, 'All right, when you give it up, it's gonna be a white man come in here and I'm gonna tell him about that oil.' So sho nuff I told Mr. Humphers. I says, 'Mistuh Humphers, here's the first well.' So that was the first well at Mexia. He got the oil. My brother-in-law's gone in now."

With some assistance from Mr. Means she gave a summary of other places where she had successfully located oil: California, Oklahoma, East Texas, the new Corsicana field, and more than a dozen others.

"Did Colonel Humphries do anything for you?" I asked.

"Yas, suh. He give me $8,500. Yas, suh. $8,500. Mistuh Humphers. He's gone in now."

"What did you do with the money?"

"Paid for this home. Put up this home. And he told me, he says, 'Annie, it's on this place that I will see you. It will be nice for you to stay and white people will be nice to you.' Mistuh Humphers a fine man. Says, 'It'll be nice here in Corsicana.' Says, 'I want you to stay here the longest day as you live.' And I told him, 'Yas, suh.'"

Drawing on what Mr. Means had told me, I asked if Corsicana people had been nice to her.

"I've had so much tribulation and trial since I been here I almost has to leave. I have lots of good white friends—lots of colored ones. But lots of them look you in the face while behind yo' back they're digging a ditch for you."

She handed me a photograph of a handsome, well-dressed white man. I recognized him as Beauford Jester, a former governor of Texas.

"Here's my next one," she said. "It used to be Mistuh Lawyer Jester. So he asked me to read him one morning. I said the first thing I seen he's gonna go on a lawyer and gonna be a railroad governor and from railroad governor he's gonna be United States governor, and after United States governor the second year he'll pass away. So he passed away.

"He said to the girls, 'Now, you give Annie this picture and tell her I want her to keep that the longest day I live.' And he sent a letter. 'Tell Annie I want her to stay in Corsicana.' Next crop I'll be here forty years."

"When did you start giving advice?"

"All my life. I was born that way. My mama was working

for a white lady. That was Miz Annie Stroud at Groesbeck. She says, 'Aunt Marget, is you fixing to born a baby this morning?' She says, 'I don't know.' She says, 'Yes, you is, Aunt Marget.' She's dead now. She says, 'Yes, Aunt Marget, I'm going to phone to Mexia to get a doctor for you.' So she phoned to Mexia to get a doctor and the doctor didn't come. So she phoned to Groesbeck and got a doctor.

"When he got there I was done born. The doctor come in and says, 'I love fresh meat.' Says, 'Y'all done killed hogs.' Says, 'Here's a nice hog heart, hog lights, and chitlings.' Miz Annie say, 'No, that's Aunt Marget's baby.' 'Aunt Marget's baby? Well, I've never seen nothing like that. I've worked on both colored and white and I never seen nothing like that. I'm sixty-nine years old and I never seen nothing like that in my life.' Says, 'Sho nuff.' Says, 'Miz Stroud, would you mind laying a layer of paper on yo' dining room table and put a quilt on that and put a paper on top of that quilt?' She says, 'I'd do anything for Aunt Marget.' 'Now put a sheet on there. Let me examine this thing and see what it is.'

"When he examined me, my feet was back that way and my hands down by my thighs. My haid was down on my shoulders. He says, 'Look here, she's got a mouth full of teeth.' Says, 'Aunt Marget,' says, 'this is a clairvayan.' Says, 'What's a clairvayan, doctor?' 'Some folks call them fortunetellers. She's no fortune-teller.' Says, 'She can tell you things under the earth just like she can on top.'

"Mama says, 'I don't want that thing. I don't want that thing a-tall.'

"So Miz Annie says, 'Well, I'll raise her. Give her to me, Aunt Marget. She can stay around here with me and then you can have her.' So mostly white folks raised me."

She paused for a moment and stared at the plastic and gilt crucifix in her hand.

"Miss Annie," I asked, "when did you first use this gift?"

She passed a hand gently over the figure.

"And so September Mama come in the kitchen one evening. She says, I want y'all childern—we done picked all our best cotton, and I want y'all childern in the morning to get yo' sacks, and, Annie, you git yo' flour sack'—you know I was small—'and I want y'all to go to the field in the morning up here in front of the house.'

"I say to the childern, 'M-m-m.' I already happy. I say, 'M-m-hm-hm.' "

She hummed in a low, resonant voice.

"I says, 'We ain't gonna pick no cotton in the morning.' I says, 'Icicles is gonna be hanging that way. Tree limbs all broke in the yard.' So the next morning Mama got up to cook breakfast and send us to the field. She went to the back door. She says, 'Oh, childern,' says, 'look on the ground.' Says, 'I've never seen nothing like this befo'.' Says, 'That child said that last night, Mama ain't gonna whup me no more, so I started to slap her. So looky here.' She says, 'Childern, come and look,' and the childern run and looked.

"I was setting back in a little room like that little room yonder."

She pointed to the room where she reads.

"Setting down on a little box, jest a-rocking. Jesus spoke salvation to my soul. Says, 'Annie, I want you to give up mother and father, brother and sister, friends and relations and give up the world, and just serve the Lord.' I was so glad I didn't know what to do. I'm so glad it was Jesus fixed me and wasn't man."

Her voice became emotional, the words came faster. I asked how she reads people.

"I tell the future and the past. That's all people's got in the world—future and past. Yo' life is in yo' palm, circling in yo' blood. I read by blood circling—yo' blood circling. It's not by yo' lines, it's yo' blood carried to the palms of yo' hands. I reads hands."

"I've never heard of that kind of reading," I said.

"Lots of people ain't heard of that. That's why I'm getting
lots of them. Lots of them. I never went to school a day in my
life. I built seven churches and a college for my colored people,
but I ain't never went to school a day in my life."

"You read cards also?"

"I read cards too. Yas, suh. The doctor told my mama, says,
'Aunt Marget, never whip Annie, scold Annie about reading.'
Says, 'She'll look them in the face—that's what she's doing
now—and she'll be thu with it. But you go to beating and scold-
ing Annie,' says, 'Annie'll read palms and cards.' And he told
the truth. I sho doing that."

She had another proof of her unusual gift.

"I was walking when I was seven months old. I always
been a wise child. My mama's seventh child."

"A lucky number?"

"A lucky number. It's gotta be."

She turned to the people waiting for her.

"So many good works I've did for the people both white
and colored. Cain't none of them give me nothing but a
good name."

"Can you tell me about someone you helped?"

"A woman come to me one day on the porch out there and
her husband says, 'Miss Annie,' says, 'I've been carrying my
wife to different places and nobody's done her any good and
I've heard about you.' Says, 'My wife haven't walked none in
eight years.' So I told him to go to the store and get some olive
oil. While he was at the store getting olive oil I was praying.
She got up just a-walking and a-shouting and I was a-shouting.
And she walked out and got in the car."

I watched the eyes of people come alive with hope. This
was what they wanted to hear from her, the word of a sage.

"I've helped lots of blind people, people that's blind. I've
holp them. You can put right thick spit in their eyes, and that
heals yo' eyes."

"Do they pay you?"

"People don't give me anything. I don't make no charges. A white feller come here about my income taxes. Says, 'Annie,' says, 'you go up on your readings.' Says, 'People give you five dollars.' Says, 'You ought to charge ten.' So I went up on my readings to five dollars. He says, 'It's worth more than that. You sho tell the truth.' I said, 'My God informed me of the truth. I cain't help but tell the truth because He say no lie you cain't tell.'"

"Do you sing?"

"I sing when the spirit guides me. It comes mostly after I've been reading."

She paused for a moment, then walked across the room and back. She explained that she sang only the songs she made up. "They just comes to me," she said. "I'll put one on."

> Now you cain't do nothing without the Lord,
> Says you cain't do nothing without the Lord,
> Everything you say, Lord, all you do —
> Well, you cain't do nothing without the Lord.
> Yes, Lord, Lord, you cain't do nothing without the Lord,
> Says you can't do nothing without the Lord,
> He created the world and He made everything —
> Well, you cain't do nothing without the Lord.

While she was singing she walked back and forth, clapping her hands. A few of the colored people swayed to the rhythm and clapped hands with her.

When the song was ended, she turned to the flowers and the crucifix. She held the crucifix up to the people. Her voice, her manner changed.

"I'm giving advice," she repeated. "I first demonstrate the dead body of Christ."

The crucifix aloft, a look of adoration on her face, she began a moving testimony of faith, in a voice that reached deep into the consciousness. Light from the ceiling fell on her face, making burnished bronze of forehead and cheek bones, leaving deep shadows around the eyes—creating the effect of a skilfully designed mask.

"When I am in my last hour, my own shining hour, I will ask you to meet me at the River Jordan and cross me over. Thank you, Jesus! Thank you, Father!"

An unrestrained "Amen!" burst from the people.

At times crooning, at times thundering, she told of her most personal relationship with God.

"When I lost my husband, Mistuh West, God said, 'Take missionary cards. Go to the Mount Zion Baptist Church, the Missionary Church, the Church of God.' I took and went. Jesus calls for a church without spot or wrinkle, His Holy church."

From the testimony she went into a sermon as much for all people as for those gathered before her. With repetitions, imprecations rolled forth a flow of words that never paused, never faltered—in a rhythm that stirred, hypnotized the people.

She preached to the men, then the women, and to both as parents.

"Sho nuff, women!" she thundered. "I wouldn't be doing so and so. 'My husband don't treat me like he used to,'" she mimicked in a shrill, piercing voice. "'He don't give me no money. He don't stay at home.' Oh, women, don't you do what that husband do . . .

"Father, mother, just think of the kind of childern you raise on account of sin. Look at yo'selves. Have mercy, Holy Ghost! Oh, fathers, oh, mothers, I'm asking you to check on yo' welfare and yo' lives. When that child done growed up in age and that child say 'I done done something,' you got to give account of that child."

She beat on the Bible. She pointed an admonishing finger at the people.

"I'm asking you to check on yo' lives this morning. Jesus is asking you to live yo' lives. He put it on me, so I'm asking you to check up this morning. Praise the Holy Ghost!"

She took up the spray of chenille flowers and held it to the light. In it she had another message, expressed in symbols.

"Here's a flower . . ."

Her fingers picked out a yellow cluster from the mass.

"... representing Judas who betray Jesus like husbands betray wives—wives betray husbands ... son and daughter..."

She searched out another cluster.

"My Father, this red flower represents Jesus' blood who went down and died on Mount Calvary. Oh, men, oh, women, He made you a light. He made that light to shine."

She separated a pale blue spray.

"That blue flower represent truth around the pulpit. Jesus wants us to shine and tell the truth."

Her hand swept across her improvised altar. The pulpit meant her own living room at the moment.

"That white flower represent pure, the pure in darkness, childern. That black spot on that white flower represent lying around the pulpit and drinking whiskey and beer and wine. That brown spot. That's gossip. Yes, Father, so much gossip in church now people go away from church. Ain't got time to go to church and serve God. You put yo' five dollar in church, yo' two dollar in church, yo' one dollar, yo' fifty cents, yo' two bits ... but you ain't got time to serve God."

She put the spray back on the altar and took up the black pompom.

"I'm fixing to close out now," she said.

Her voice became sad, as if she felt the heartbreak of the world.

"People, this black flower is for the last days. The world is in darkness this morning. The world is in darkness. In darkness, childern! Sho nuff, childern, we in the last days now. The last days. Our last days is our worst days because of the lives we are leading. I'm asking you to check up."

She knelt before her altar. Someone across the room was sobbing.

"I'm going into prayer now. Have mercy, my Father, have mercy. Have mercy, Jesus!"

Almost without thinking I knelt down beside the mass of

paper flowers. I could not see the others, but I could hear their feet shuffling, their chairs scraping on the floor.

"Here it is again this morning that yo' child has come before Thee, the Holy ..."

She took up a rhythm that grew faster and faster. Words poured out, interrupted only by a hoarse roar with each intake of breath. Faster, louder, more stirring the words became. In themselves almost meaningless in repetition, they were terrifying in effect, even to a person who had not come with a troubled spirit.

As I stared into the flowers and green leaves I suddenly saw the curved, mottled hide of a rattlesnake. Old stories of snake cults, snake worship flooded my mind. Her symbolism of flowers was vivid. Could this be a living symbol of evil in Eden? I stared and shivered, waiting for it to uncoil, crawl through the leaves, take a part in the ritual.

There was no movement in the room, only the sound of Miss Annie's voice, higher and louder, working closer and closer toward the point where sense of time, sense of place could be entirely lost.

Unable to bear the fear any longer, I cautiously shifted back to the couch, to a place to leap. Then I dared look again. The rattler still lay coiled among the flowers, but I could see that he was artificial, dead. But I still felt as if I had passed through a chill.

Miss Annie reached a crescendo in her prayer. Her voice was hoarse, but she softened the effect—away from the wrath and terror of an angry God, back to the crooning of a comforting God who could understand the pain, the weakness, the hopes and desires of frail mankind.

With a final "Have mercy, Lord, glory, Father!" she ended her prayer and stood up.

"I'm going in now," she said. She started with measured pace toward her little room.

I looked at the waiting people. Their faces may have been

changed. They seemed so to me. Eagerly they gazed on the door through which no secrets came.

This time no cards had been handed out, no order of preference given.

The white girl stood up, her hands outstretched, the tears flowing down her cheeks. Miss Annie gave her a look that seemed to say, "Come, my child."

Reverently the girl followed Miss Annie into the room and closed the door behind her.

Curanderos of South Texas

BROWNIE McNEIL

SOUTH TEXAS is a region with cultural characteristics that set it apart from other sections of the state. For one thing, there is the mesquite. Now, one might ask how the mesquite tree, as an object of study, can be of interest to anyone but the botanist and what it has to do with folklore of a region. There is no ready answer to that question to be found in science, but fortunately the folklorist can look beyond the realm of science and can merely sense the peculiar characteristics found in the flora and fauna of a region. You may call it *tone* or *atmosphere*, or whatever else you wish. J. Frank Dobie calls it *rhythm*. He says quite correctly that when a writer puts a region into books he has to get the *rhythm* of that region. There is a lot of the rhythm of South Texas in the mesquite.

There is an air of mystery about the mesquite. One never feels that he really knows everything he should know about it. There is something about a forest of mesquite trees that makes one feel as if there is some great dark pervading mysterious force that is lurking about unseen, and he had better watch his step or it will catch up with him and spring on him from behind. Trees that are representative of other regions of the country certainly convey no such deep, dark mysticism. To the eastern mountaineer the pine tree growing alone on a hilltop is a symbol of loneliness, and he sings sentimentally of the trail of the lonesome pine. And in the plantation regions of the South the large and stately live oak, with Spanish moss

32

hanging down, is a symbol of gracious and dignified living, like the patrician society that built plantation houses in the middle of oak groves. An Argentine poet wrote a poem about the *ombu* of the pampas, dwelling at length on its sturdy individualism while observing its tendency to grow alone, a single tree on an otherwise bare plain. Have the trees taken on the characteristics of the man, or has man adapted his way of living to blend with the character of the trees among which he lives? It is quite probably the latter. Whether there is anything scientific to such a belief no one knows, but to the folklorist it is there and is just as real as if it were demonstrated in a laboratory or on a set of graphs. Certainly it is true in South Texas, for the mesquite trees are like man who lives among them, and man is like the mesquite. This is particularly noticeable among the Spanish-speaking people of the region, possibly because they have lived there some one hundred and fifty years longer than the Anglo-American. Or possibly it is the influence of the *indio* upon the Spanish.

In South Texas one senses everywhere the rhythm of *lo mexicano*. One of its prominent characteristics is a belief in the existence of mysterious forces that lurk about waiting for one to become careless and make that fatal error which will bring on doom that is as swift and sure as the inevitable tragedy in a Greek drama. It goes with the region. There are certain persons whom you dare not offend, for they have the power to put curses on you. But just as surely as one may fall victim to the *bruja* (witch), he may engage the services of one whose secret powers are equally as potent in counteracting the evil: a *curandero*, meaning literally a curer or a practitioner of curing. He is what the Anglo-American calls a *faith healer*.

The cult of the *curandero* is deeply rooted among the Spanish-speaking people of South Texas. Some of his remedies and practices which may be traced to the Gypsies of the Middle Ages have descended by oral tradition to the present day. Others are the residue of a vast area of Indian folklore on the

curative powers of herbs of the Southwest and the Central
Plateau of Mexico. But no matter where the cult was practiced
or is practiced today, one ingredient has remained unchanged
as a vital element, and that is the absolute, inflexible faith of
the people who seek such remedies for their ailments. In her
book about South Texas, *El Mesquite*, Elena Zamora O'Shea
says:

Curanderismo is as old . . . as 'La Golondrina,' and 'La Golondrina' is
pretty old. It's about some Moorish king who had been run out of Spain,
and who on leaving the shores of Spain, shed tears as he watched the
swallows returning to summer in Spain . . . how the king's mother told him
to cry like a woman for what he had not been able to defend like a man.

Curanderismo is still as much alive today as it was in the
Middle Ages. It exists in abundance among the people of Mexican origin in South Texas. It would be very convenient to think
that it exists solely among the ignorant and uneducated, and
there is no doubt that this group is inclined to seek out the aid
of the healer more frequently than others, but there are numerous instances of college graduates, supposedly trained to
approach all phenomena with the attitude of the scientist,
seeking out the services of the *curandero* when afflicted with
some ailment.

For many years, the leading figure among the practitioners
of *curanderismo* of South Texas, one whom we might call *el
mero jefe* (the real chief) of the *curanderos,* was Don Pedro
Jaramillo, who lived at Los Olmos, a small community in
Brooks County. Some two or three miles from the city of Falfurrias is a small graveyard in which rest the remains of Don
Pedro. His grave is distinguished from the others by a small
adobe hut that was constructed by the legions of his believers.
It has become a shrine to which some pay daily visits. They
approach it reverently, enter the hut with the same look of
humility with which one would visit the shrine of a saint.
They kneel, pray for a while, light a candle and retire, feeling
that they have paid their respects to one who surely must have

been God returned to earth. Don Pedro has been adequately presented by Ruth Dodson,[1] and I shall not attempt a second review of the subject here. But I will add one more story to the many that are known about Don Pedro. An aged Mexican citizen still living in Falfurrias tells of once being a disbeliever. But he had become afflicted with an illness that made him lose weight and become progressively weaker. The doctors had given up trying to find a cure, and he had finally gone to Don Pedro. The latter gave him crushed leaves of the *lengua de vaca* (cow's tongue), an herb that grows in South Texas. Don Pedro ordered him to brew this into a tea, drink it, and go to bed. He would then fall into a deep sleep during which he would dream that he was dead; but he would not die. These directions the fellow carried out faithfully; he drank the tea, fell into the sleep as predicted, and apparently willed himself back to life. When he awoke he was well and completely cured, and has lived many years since in good health. When asked if he still believed in Don Pedro, the old fellow assumed a look as if I had uttered sacrilege, and murmured: "Si! Era Dios" (Yes! He was God). He is only one of the many Mexican people of Texas who are waiting for the day when the Catholic church will canonize Don Pedro. Miss Dodson relates in her article "Folk-Curing Among the Mexicans"[2] how Don Pedro acquired the power to *recetar,* meaning literally *to prescribe.* In the exercise of his duty as a *pastor* (a shepherd) Don Pedro suffered a terrible accident that left him lying unconscious and alone for many days. It was at this time that God appeared to him and bestowed upon him the power to prescribe. God not only healed him but ordered him to devote himself to helping suffering humanity, which he did for more than twenty-five years.

Don Pedro was a *curandero* among *curanderos.* He not only cured hundreds of people but passed on the power to *recetar* to a favored few who today still practice in South Texas. These carry on his special powers. On each of their altars, an essential piece of equipment for every *curandero,* is a picture of Don

Pedro. It is possible that they may not have an image of the Virgin there, but not to have an image of Don Pedro . . . "Ay no!" one says with pain in her voice, "Es imposible!" One *curandera*, a woman in this case, in South Texas has a special altar for Don Pedro. She prays first to him and then to the Virgin. Don Pedro's fame was made even more lasting and certain when one of the members of the Texas Folklore Society, Professor Frank Goodwyn, who knew Don Pedro personally, gave certain characteristics of his to the *curandero* in his novel *The Magic of Limping John*.

Don Pedro was without doubt the leading *curandero* of South Texas during his time, but he was far from being alone in the practice of *recetando*. Many lesser figures are successfully practicing today. Among them are such names as Don Bazan, Don Nicanor, and Doña Mercedes. (The custom among the Mexican people is to bestow upon *curanderos* the ancient title of *don* or *doña*, which in other ages was reserved for a member of the nobility.) There is apparently no professional distinction made between a man *curandero* and a woman *curandera*, except that, as one man said recently, "The woman *curandera* must be flat-chested and ugly."

Of course, each *curandero* is an individualist, and the *recetas* (prescriptions) that each gives are of his own invention. Enough may be seen, however, of a pattern about their methods to establish several general categories of *curanderos*. The Mexican people express greatest admiration for those whose prescriptions include herbs used in various ways. The prescriptions direct the patient to drink such potions as teas made of orange leaf *(hoja de naranjo)*, sometimes a tea consumed internally followed by a bath in a weaker solution of the same. Some typical herbs used are the *barba de chivato* (billy-goat's beard), *lengua de vaca* (cow's tongue), *uña de gato* (cat's claw), *zapote blanco* (white sapodilla plum).

Doña Graciela of San Antonio has a good reputation and is well accepted among her clientele. Instead of using herbs, she invades the field of fortunetelling, finding lost money and diamonds, and informing people of hidden treasure. Of course, the latter very seldom come to light, but the people keep coming to her. One reason, no doubt, is the eternal hope that this one time she may be right. Then there is always a certain stimulus to the ego to be gained from being the possessor of secret knowledge that may lead to sudden great wealth, even if the secret only lasts for a few days.

Practically everyone who goes to see Doña Graciela is willing to believe that he has a treasure in his back yard. She cannot possibly lose; her clients are already half-convinced when they come to her. She only adds the topping by informing them of the lengthy procedures they must follow in order to unearth the great wealth. Of course, she can inform only by degrees, and so the clients must return for additional information. Somehow they never find the treasure. But "locating" treasure isn't Doña Graciela's only skill. She performs cures that are much easier to believe and far more practical than having people dig up their back yards. She does a tremendous business in helping people pass their driver's license tests. This she is able to do by quite simple means. When a timid soul comes to her with such a problem, she advises him to go on a certain day to take the test, saying, "Don't be afraid. I will be near to protect you." And so the person goes, filled with confidence. And Doña Graciela *was* near, protecting him. He obtained his license, didn't he? What better proof do you want, *compadre?* Doña Graciela may yet reach her full service to mankind.

Another type of *curandera* is the one using a concentrated form of prayer to induce a sort of hypnosis. Doña Maria Chaney is of this type, except that she also prescribes medicines. But either because she is not sufficiently familiar with herbs, or because she prefers not to antagonize the medical doctors in her neighborhood, she confines her prescriptions to patent medicines.

My wife and I recently called on Doña Maria Chaney to

obtain her life story, which she was quite willing to give. We found her in on a Sunday afternoon at her small home in the ranch community of La Bandera, near the village of Palito Blanco in Jim Wells County. We had difficulty locating her because her present name isn't Chaney. She is now married to Felix Valadez, a ranch hand at La Bandera, but she continues to use the name of her first husband, a *gringo* named Jim Chaney. We met Mr. Valadez in the front yard. We introduced ourselves, and I immediately said that we must have come to the wrong house, for we were looking for Doña Maria Chaney. But he hastily informed us that she was his wife and that he was sure she would be glad to see us.

We were ushered into a small room, no more than six by six, and soon Doña Maria made her appearance. There was a ghostly paleness about her face, particularly about her lips, so that at first we did not notice that she was to conduct the interview wearing her pink bathrobe. The room was filled to capacity with a combination of religious objects and colored paper streamers. Many pictures of the Virgin Mary hung about the room; candles were burning in their colored glass containers, and underneath several of these were dollar bills left by some caller in memory of a departed relative. The hand I shook as Doña Maria greeted me seemed to belong to a being from another world.

We did not need to inform Doña Maria why we were there. She announced to us that we had come to obtain the story of her life and that since we had come *de buena fe* (in good faith), she would give it gladly. She knew I was going to write about her; "Y es bueno!" (That is good!) she said. And so she began.

She was born in Vera Cruz, but her exact birth date is not known. She thinks it was about 1903. Her father was Rolo Camara, *capitán de marina* (a sea captain); her mother was Eugenia Camara de Gomez. She never knew her parents, a situation that figures largely in her acquisition of power to heal.

A maid from their home named Gimateca, an *india,* eventually revealed to her the history of her mother and father; they had both been killed during the revolution by a rebel group which raided Vera Cruz. Her father, a non-Catholic, had been a member of a Masonic lodge. When she was fifteen years old, which makes the year about 1918, she accompanied her aunt on a trip to San Antonio. A group in the Masonic lodge called the *Comité Ginestra* had sent them to San Antonio — probably on some mission for the well-being of the young girl, but on the exact nature or purpose of the trip she was vague. The aunt became ill soon after they arrived in San Antonio and was taken to the Santa Rosa Hospital, where after a few days she died. Left alone, "a complete orphan," as she expresses it, in a strange country whose language she did not know, the girl became terribly *asustada* (afraid). A lady in the hospital was kind to her and gave her work cleaning around the place. About this time she developed an ailment in her left hand. It began to twist and become deformed, and the doctors in the hospital were completely mystified as to the cause. Then she began to develop fevers, and still the doctors could do nothing for her.

A Mexican lady who worked at the hospital suggested to her one day that she could take her to a man who could cure her. They went together to another part of town to a place called the *Casa de Espíritus* (house of spirits; this was apparently the name given to the *curandero's* base of operations). The man immediately knew her name, and as a further sign of his curative powers, he was able to produce holy water, although he was not a priest. (How the man was able to manage this she did not say.) The man asked her if she knew any sign by which she could recognize her mother and father, apparently knowing that she had never seen them. She replied that she did not. So he said that he was going to help her meet her mother and father. He placed his hands on her forehead, and she felt a chill come over her. Then she began to dream, although she was not asleep. And in her dream her mother and father appeared to her and asked her why she was suffering so. It was not necessary to suffer. Why didn't she come with them? When she did not come, her mother said that she should stay on earth a while and help cure others who were sick and then she should come and join them. She awoke extremely tired and exhausted, but she knew she had not been asleep. The *curandero* then said that he was going to put her to sleep and within three days she would be cured, but first she had to sleep with her parents for a while. He prepared a tea and had her drink it. She immediately fell into a deep sleep.

"I don't know exactly how long I did sleep," she said. "But when I awoke my hand was cured, and ever since that time I have felt the desire to cure. My first patient was a German in San Antonio, who came to me with a terrible affliction: *el cólico* or *la tripa torcida* [literally: the twisted entrails]. So great was his ailment that he could not pass from either side. I had a lady help me, and together we gave him an *ayuda* [an aid, in this case probably an enema]. We prepared a very hot bath of orange leaf tea and had him remain in it for more than two hours. At the end of this time he was cured. Soon after this a Cuban came to me also with the *tripa torcida*, and the doctors had given him up, and I cured him.

"I once cured a little girl, and her father had bought one hundred dollars in medicine for her. The doctors had said that the girl would die and that there was nothing they could do. So then I cured the girl, and when the father took her back home, the doctors were surprised. The doctors wanted to know my name and wanted to come see me, but the father of the little girl was afraid that they would harm me, and so he would not tell them where I was.

"My first husband was Jim Chaney. I met him in San Antonio and later we were married in Alice. We lived many years together. When he was dying I saw Christ come into the room with a blanket on his arm. He spread out the blanket and covered my husband's face. When I saw this I began to cry, and Christ came over to where I was sitting and put his hand on me, *así* [palm of the hand on the forehead]. I have cured many people. I give *recetas*. They are *recetas patentes* [patent medicines]. I sometimes prescribe S.S.S., sometimes 666 and Hadacol, and I give tea of the *hoja de naranjo* and the *barba de chivato* . . . many people come to me all the time."

At this point our narrator appeared tired, and so we quickly took the hint and declared we must be going. Doña Maria could not let us depart without showing us her naturalization certificate, of which she is immensely proud. The picture affixed to it, taken about 1923, showed a healthy, hefty woman of some one hundred and fifty pounds; this was indeed in severe contrast with the frail creature sitting before us, who could not possibly weigh now more than ninety pounds. But then heavy are the duties of *recetando*, and heavy lies the head that wears the crown . . . in this case, the crown of power to cure. With her strange baths and herb teas and prescriptions for 666, Doña Maria carries on her ancient practice, curing infirmities that have baffled the doctors. Does she really perform such cures? Or is it all a great farce because it has no scientific basis? We cannot deny the facts. All we can say is, *quién sabe?*

Another *curandera*, Doña Maria Perez, practices in Sinton, Texas . . . at 519 South Rachal Street, to be exact. I mention this only to emphasize the almost business-like atmosphere with which she conducts her practice. In a one-story frame house painted a brilliant yellow, looking as if it had been added to frequently, room by room, Doña Maria keeps office. One waits a long time to see her, for her patients are numerous, and on a typical Sunday afternoon — the busiest time of the week for *curanderas*, by the way — one must wait his turn. At least, there is an air of being strictly-business up to a certain point, and beyond that one is lost in the more ethereal ways of the mystic. She is most unpredictable. She may dispatch a patient with a brief, rapid-fire series of questions about the ailment, or she may keep him for hours conversing in low muttering tones, unintelligible even when one approaches the open door on some feigned pretext to try to figure out what is going on. But faith cannot be hurried, and one waits.

And so we waited on this warm Sunday afternoon in June in her yard, God's eternal waiting room. We sat in the shade of an ebony tree on a bench made of two discarded railroad ties placed across some large stones. A light breeze was blowing from the Gulf not far away, and it was quite pleasant in that wonderful shade. My wife read. Son Bob amused himself with the red burningbeans (from the ebony) lying about on the ground. A brisk rub of a bean on the seat of his pants, then he would apply it to his arm, following this with an exclamation at the mild burning sensation. He was soon bored with this and began to flip pebbles with his thumb. And still we waited. A flock of bantam chickens was sitting out the afternoon almost hidden in a dense clump of shrubs close by. A pebble landed in the thicket and the bantam rooster responded with the proper alarm to his ladies: "Cut-CUT-cut-cut-cut!" The second *cut* was high-pitched and heavily accented, the last three tripping rapidly down the scale. The game was on. A barrage of pebbles, single-fired, was dispatched in their direction, not to hit but to land near by to evoke more alarms. Soon they were routed and took cover in another thicket, but just before he dived into its shelter the little rooster reared back and gave out with a pretentious little crow of false victory. We called out "Ole! Ole!" and admired his bravery. A smothered laugh, barely more than "Humm," came from the porch, and we remembered the woman who had been sitting there for a long time. She was short and fat. Her facial features were *pura india*. She and her husband had brought her mother over from "Jorge West" to be treated for a dislocated hip. She had been sitting for a long time with a completely motionless face, and we had forgotten that she was there. It was quite plain that faith is sometimes slow.

Finally the poor ailing *señora* was helped out the door, and then it was our turn. One does not soon forget those eyes of Doña Maria. They are of the blackest midnight hue, but more than that, they possess a fierceness that would make *El Mio Cid* himself tremble with fear. Certainly she has the power to heal, if not by faith, then by scaring the ailment out of her patient with fiery glances from those eyes. And, in fact, the curing of *sustos* (frights) is one of her specialties. Recently she cured a girl in Sinton who was declared *loca* (crazy), but she was not crazy according to Doña Maria, only *susto* in an advanced stage. She prescribed for the girl several doses of *aceite de come* (an oil derived from a seed) and a bath in a tea made of a compound of herbs that she put together. After taking the first dosage the girl began to improve. Three days later she was cured and was no longer *susto*. If a person has only headaches, Doña Maria says, and is not particularly *susto*, she cures him by placing a piece of cactus across his forehead. The thorns, however, are first removed from the cactus, and it is peeled. This latter is particularly important in that it allows the juice of the cactus, the vital force in curing the headache, to flow freely over the forehead.

Doña Maria laments the standardized techniques that modern social trends have forced upon her. People these days don't want to take the trouble to follow the old prescriptions, and besides they are too scared of snakes to go into the woods looking for herbs. So she is forced to prescribe the patent medicines obtainable at the neighborhood pharmacy. She has had to give up prescribing some of her favorite herbs, such as the *laurel cimarrón* (different from the mountain laurel) and the *canela del monte*.

The interview could not have closed without my asking something of her life story and how she received the power to heal. "Yo nací en una zalea" (I was born on a goatskin) was her first reply. Additional questioning revealed the fact that this event occurred around 1882; "Yo no estoy muy presente"

(I am not very sure), she said. She knew it was near Delfina, Texas, a small community near Brownsville. Her father, Manual Perez, worked on the King Ranch as a woodchopper, and they were always poor. She still uses her maiden name, although for many years she was married to Gregorio Rosas and lived with him on the Willie Dougherty ranch near Edinburg.

Doña Maria is a disciple of Don Pedro Jaramillo and received her power to cure from him. In due homage to this great figure of *curanderismo,* on the wall immediately above her chair she keeps his photograph, which shows a dignified old fellow with a white beard fully two feet long. When she was in her thirties she had become a *partera* (midwife), and faithfully served the Mexican women in her area for some years. One day she was descending a steep stairway on the outside wall of a house. She doesn't know what caused it, but she fell and was knocked unconscious, remaining so for many days. She knew that she was afraid in her mind, but she could not wake up enough to persuade herself not to be so. Her parents took her to Don Pedro. He gave her herbs to take and told her not to be afraid, and since that time she has never been afraid. It was during the period of recuperation that she felt the desire to give the cure to others.

Curanderismo has been around for a long time. It is neither science nor pseudoscience. It is one of those purely folk arts which are still with us in this age of machines and corporate living. It is a vestige of the Middle Ages that seems to hang on and survive in defiance of an industrialized civilization. It will probably be with us for a long time to come.

1. "Don Pedrito Jaramillo: The Curandero of Los Olmos," in *The Healer of Los Olmos and Other Mexican Lore* ("Publications of the Texas Folklore Society," XXIV [1951]), pp. 9-70; and *Don Pedrito Jaramillo, Curandero* (San Antonio: Casa Editorial Lozano, 1934). The latter is in Spanish.
2. In *Tone the Bell Easy* ("Publications of the Texas Folklore Society," X [1932]), pp. 82-98.

Joe Whilden, One of the People

JOHN HENRY FAULK

JOE WHILDEN is a man born in Bastrop, Texas, in 1892, as he says just after the last great Indian battle on the North American continent, which took place in Travis Heights, just south of the Colorado River running through Austin. This last great Indian battle was, according to Joe Whilden, fought by Stephen F. Austin, and Austin, Texas, was at that time called Waterloo and wasn't the capital. Joe forgets that he has also said that his daddy built the capitol, laid the cornerstone. "Daddy was a rock mason and the only man they could get to lay a cornerstone. Folks was ignorant in that day and didn't know how to lay cornerstones." So Joe's daddy laid the cornerstone of the state capitol back sometime before 1892, the year Joe was born, and Stephen F. Austin fought the last great Indian battle on the North American continent. The people wanted to change the name of the town from Waterloo to Austin, but Austin said, "No, all I want is the Stephen F. Austin Hotel named after me."

Should you interrupt Joe at this point and say, "Well, I don't think it was built until after Austin was already the capital of Texas," Joe won't answer in words, but will just look at you with a kind of pity and indignation that you are not aware of the facts of life, that you are utterly ignorant of what happened.

Joe lived when Stephen F. Austin (who died in 1836) had the Austin Hotel (built in 1924) named after him. The city council met and forced Austin to let them name the city after him. They said to him, "After you whipped them Indians in

45

Travis Heights they quit fighting and you deserve to have
Austin named after you."

Joe says that he remembers when he was just a little boy
his mama and daddy used to bring him from Bastrop on a
steamship up to Austin, Texas.

"Joe," I would ask, "where did the steamship come from?"

"All the way from the ocean, come all the way up the
Colorado River."

"Over sand bars and all?"

"Wasn't no sand bars in the river then. Wasn't no sand in
it to make bars. It was deep. A man could swim a horse any
place in it then except over the fords."

"Well, how did they bring the steamship over the fords?"

"I don't know," Joe would admit. Then he'd look at me as
if I were interrupting him in a very discourteous manner.

I would apologize by saying, "Would the steamboat go on
up past Austin?"

"No, there was a dam there. That steamboat would have
gone all the way to Marble Falls, I reckon, if it hadn't been for
the dam up above Austin."

Joe likes to talk about historic people. He can't read or
write, but he knew O. Henry, who left Austin for the last time
—for a federal prison—in 1898. Joe explains, "Most folks are
balled up on O. Henry. His name was Old Henry, John Old
Henry."

"Oh, you knew him, then?" I asked.

"Knowed him well. Papa hauled wood to him, but he got to
where he wouldn't let nobody haul him his wood but me and
he'd give me up to two bits extra to go get me some candy;
I was just a boy, then. That was when they had circuses on the
capitol grounds."

I said, "I didn't know that they ever rented state property
to hold circuses on."

"Yes, Ringling Brothers, Barnum and Bailey would come
there and hold their circuses on the capitol grounds. I was

settin' there one time, about ten years old, when they had a great big elephant I'll never forget. I don't remember the lady's name, but she's standin' no further away from me than from here to that cot; it wasn't over ten foot. That elephant retched over with his trunk, took that six-week-old baby out of her arms and stuffed it in its mouth. Didn't chew, just swallered. We thought maybe if we could get to him fast enough maybe the baby wouldn't be dead. Elephants ain't got chewin' teeth; they just swaller. And so they got a 30-30 rifle and a machine gun. Shot that elephant seventeen times right between the eyes with a 30-30, and the elephant just kept swingin' his trunk and looked at 'em. Didn't even dent his head. So they had to take a blow torch and cut him half in two. And they found the baby — whole, swallered it whole, but it was dead."

I don't know exactly how—I'm not artist enough to reconstruct what Joe had built. Honestly, everybody listening to him thought he was going to say the baby was alive, but the baby was dead. "Course it naturally would have been."

"Why, Joe," I said, "you can't put your fist down an elephant's throat. Its gullet's too small." You have to prompt him like that, you have to kind of play against him with expressions of disbelief to cause him to sail off the ground. In order to sail, to really get up into the atmosphere, Joe's like a plane that has to take off against the wind. If you just swallow everything he says he finally gets bored and shuts up, but if you'll just play along, saying, "Oh, Joe, I can't believe this happened" — he'll rise. He rises on each gust of wind; each gust of disbelief raises him a little higher.

"Well, I remember when I'se working out at Manchaca with a bunch of Messicans on the Katy railroad. A boy got killed. A load of cross ties fell on him and crushed him; so we buried him out there about fifty foot off the Manchaca Road: nobody knowed who his folks was er anything. About a week later I'se going by the grave late one afternoon. I remember the hame chain broke on the mules and I pulled the team up and stopped to fasten it, and I heard somebody calling — calling from that grave. I went over there and listened and I heard this feller—I recognized his voice—sayin', 'Let me out, let me out.'

"Well, I drove on down the road to Tom Beckett's place and pulled up where he was chopping stove wood and said, 'I think that feller's still alive up there in the grave. Don't you reckon we ought to dig it up?' He said, 'Aw, he wouldn't be.' And I said, 'Well, if you got a shovel, I'm willin' to dig if you are.'

"He went back up there with me; we stopped the mules and got out, and went over there and could still hear him. 'Let me out. Let me out,' he kept saying. And you could see the grave just kinda risin' and fallin', just kinda risin' and fallin'. Tom Beckett said, 'Well, I reckon we ought to dig.' And so we dug, got that feller out and he was just as live as I am now. In fact he shook my hand for thirty minutes and said, 'Thank you so much, I don't know what I'd a *done* if you hadn't let me out.' "

"Joe," I said, "I don't believe a man could live six foot under the earth in a coffin for a week. I just don't believe that's possible."

"That feller thanked me every time he seen me after that for years. That's all I know."

One of the memorable events during Joe's life was the cyclone that struck Austin about thirty-five years ago. According to Joe the cyclone divided north of Austin, one prong of it hitting the Colorado River near Deep Eddy. It sucked the Colorado River dry for a half mile each direction — so dry that a person could walk around on the bed of the river till the waters ran back together. The other prong of the cyclone hit a bluff and bounced over Travis Heights or it would've wiped all of South Austin off the map. When a cyclone hits a bluff it'll bounce for a mile and a half up in the air and then come right back down as soon as it gets a chance.

"Joe, what causes cyclones?" I asked.

"Well, Johnny, hit's just like air in a pipe." (He's never at a loss for an explanation, scientific or otherwise.) "It's like air in a pipe. You can pump air into a pipe, stop up one end of it and pump air into the other. That pipe's gonna give way and blow up. Well, there are pockets in the air that way, and sometimes them things'll get so tight, jest swell and swell, till finally one of 'em gives loose and it throws air in a circle and it'll start circlin' and there's your cyclone for you. And you better stay out of its way if it's comin' in your direction.

"Well, when that cyclone come along that hit Travis Heights, I'se out at Penfield. [Penfield is the site of the Woodward Body Works, but it was called Penfield during World War I, and that's the South Austin name for it until this day.] And that thing come past St. Edward's College. I seen it comin'. A red-headed feller working with me yelled, 'Cyclone comin'!' and he broke and run plumb the other side of Barton Springs. And then he seen that prong of the cyclone sucking the Colorado River dry at Deep Eddy, and broke and run back—run almost back to Penfield." All this three- or four-mile run in the time it took the cyclone to move maybe three hundred yards from St. Edward's College over to Woodward Body Works, where Joe was working.

"It was dippin' down and around," Joe said, "and you'd say it looked like trash. But it was really houses and trees way up in the air. They way it skipped some places was curious. There was a stack of sawdust right next to a water trough. The cyclone picked up that trough, didn't spill a drop of water out of it, twirled it way up in the air and didn't even stir that sawdust settin' right next to it. That's what a cyclone'll do.

"My nephew, Paul Whilden, was standin' out in the back yard and his mama said, 'You'd better come in the house. There's a cyclone comin'.' Paul's holding his little baby brother, named I. P., and not more'n six months old—never did learn to walk till he's three. Paul was a-holdin' him in his arms in the back yard watchin' that cyclone come. The thing whipped down and sucked that baby's diaper off and never touched the baby nor Paul. Baby was jest as naked as the day he was born when that cyclone took off again, before Paul knowed what was happening. And his mama said, 'I told you not to stand out there when a cyclone was comin'.'

"Well, they had an old dominecker rooster that made a run for the henhouse when he seen the cyclone—animals know when cyclones is comin'. While this old dominecker was stretched out flat a-running, the cyclone caught him and took every feather he owned—picked him jest as clean as the palm of your hand; wasn't but one feather left and that was a tailfeather—one tailfeather. And that old rooster died of embarrassment. He wouldn't go round the other chickens after that.

"The cyclone reached into a shed, a harness shed, where my sister had a banty hen settin' on twelve eggs in a little ole shackly box. It sucked that box and that banty hen and her eggs all out together and just twirled 'em. Paul said he seen 'em go and said it looked like an airplane propeller jest a-whirlin' yonder and he said, 'Well, that's goodbye banty hen and eggs.' That cyclone jest set 'em down as easy as a tabby cat carrying a kitten near Onion Creek under a big mattress that it blowed outa somebody's house. It was sorter humped up over the box to leave way for air and walking out. It kept that banty hen warm and kept that hail — you know it hailed awful hard during that cyclone—from hittin' her, I reckin, because she brought off eleven chickens outa them eggs jest two days later. Their feathers was kinda twirley around on 'em—the fuzz was twirled around where they had twirled around inside of them eggs.

"Another funny thing about that cyclone was the way it hit old man Hardkoff's dairy. He was milkin'—it hit late in the afternoon about four or five o'clock. He had all his cows' heads—twenty-four Holstein cows—in stanchions. It jerked them cows' bodies off the heads—the heads jest flopped down, twenty-four heads—and he never did find what went with them cows, never did find a single piece of ary a carcass. Heads just layin' there in the stanchions.

"And it took a watch out of old man Adcock's—he was workin' there at Woodward Body Works—it took a watch out of his overhall pocket and slipped it into another feller's pocket. This feller jest run his hand in his coat pocket, said, 'Well, I declare, here's your watch and chain.' They thought it'd killed old man Adcock, but after he come to he looked for his watch, started beatin' around on the front of 'im and found it where the feller had put it.

"None of what I'm telling you got into the papers. They didn't put the best part of that cyclone into the papers."

When Joe's daddy didn't come up to Austin from Bastrop by steamboat he'd drive his team and mules and stay in the wagon yard down at the foot end of Congress Avenue. According to Joe, men don't have voices any more like they had in those days. Now they have to have radios, have to have telephones, can't get word around without 'em, but his daddy didn't have to have either one to communicate with folks in distant spots. Joe said, "Papa had an awful loud voice and in that day they had mule-drawn street cars that run up and down Congress Avenue and all the way out to Hyde Park. Papa would get in the wagon yard and start puttin' axle grease on his wagon wheels. You unbolt the hubcap and lean the wagon wheel off a little piece, you know, and then grease the hub—put axle grease on it. Well, Papa would start to do that and the mules would step up a step and he'd yell, 'Whoa!' and that whoa would stop every mule car in Austin, Texas, plum out almost to the dam on West Sixth Street and plum out to the gin on east Sixth Street and out to Hyde Park. The city authorities got to where they wouldn't let him grease his wagon when he come to town because he'd stop the street car mules."

My own daddy was the cow caller of South Austin when our cows would get out. He would get up about 4:30 and invite me to go out to milk with him. I milked the cows every morn-

ing and every night from the time I was eight years old until
I got out of the university, but never was strong at calling them.
When Daddy called them, people in Travis Heights a mile
away could hear him. Joe was right.

Joe said, "Why, when Jim Ferguson made a speech, great
goodness alive, if somebody 'ad a give him one of those new-
fangled microphones that everybody's talkin' over now, he'd
a-tore it up and throwed it away. You can't hear a man's naked
voice no more; you got to hear it over them microphones even
in a little room. Jim Ferguson'd stand up there in Wooldridge
Park and when he cut loose with his naked voice, people could
hear him way past the block that Wooldridge Park covers. He
and other great men in those days had something to say.
Nowadays what people say is just like the machines they use
to talk over."

Joe thinks the world is going steadily down the road toward
hell. In the first place, man's body isn't protected as it used to
be by real medicine. People go in now for all kinds of crackpot
medicines. As a matter of fact, Joe will sell you a bottle of lini-
ment that you can rub on your chest and it'll knock out pneumonia just—just like that. He'd a-been dead many a time if
Carrie hadn't a-rubbed his chest with this medicine.

About satellites, Joe said, "Now they think they are goin'
to shoot a thing around the moon, but they won't be able to
do that. You can get these perfessers to tell you the moon is
this far and that far up there, but you grind 'em down to it and
back 'em against the wall and they won't tell you jest how far.
They ain't been there, and they ain't no way to measure some-
thin' you ain't been to. Them things won't stay up. God's not
gonna allow it. Johnny, I've got a feelin' God's kinda tired of
the way man's carryin' on anyhow. He's gonna put a stop to it.
He's gonna put a stop to it one a these days."

Dad was a lawyer in town but he kept a herd of Jersey cows
and Joe and his wife lived out in our back yard in a little
house that Daddy built. It was wired for electricity. I'd seen

people screw a light globe out of its socket when the switch wouldn't work, and that's what I did for the globe in Joe's house. But he wasn't satisfied. He figured that electricity was still flowing out through the socket and wasting and would soon get the room so full of electricity that if you struck a match in it it would blow your house up. So he had us take the wiring out. I was in high school then and very pompous about my knowledge. I said, "Aw, Joe, if the globe isn't burning up electricity, it can't waste out the end of the wire."

"It does, too, I studied it," Joe answered flatfoot. His study had to be from some other source than the written word, for he couldn't read, can't read yet, and never has pretended to read. A man don't have to read as long as he can go into Bloom's Store or Wukasch's Store and just call for Levi Garrett's snuff.

Joe had a brother named Zee, who was a fighter. He'd fight a man at the drop of a hat, Zee would. He belonged to a group that I don't know what's happened to sociologically. Zee was the first man I ever saw have a fist fight with another full-grown man. Zee loved to fight. When he got a little drunk, he would go around looking for trouble. If he didn't find it, he'd make it. Zee was working out north of Georgetown in a beer hall—no, he wasn't working there, but he was courting a lady that graced that establishment. Daddy had gotten him out of trouble repeatedly, always in trouble for fighting. Zee was also a strictly dishonest man. He is now in the state penitentiary doing a life term. When Joe describes Zee, he describes him as a completely naïve, fresh, soft personality. Everything with Joe is white or black. This is his testimony.

"Zee borrowed my car to go up to Georgetown to see this lady, and she'd jest keep after him all time, 'Come back some more, stay up here later.' He'd say, 'No, I've got to get my night's sleep and get up and work tomorrow.'" Joe never mentions the occupations Zee was engaged in. The truth is he never hit a lick of work in his life. But let Joe go on.

"She'd just keep after him and everything, and she'd say, 'Stay up here and you can drive me back down to town where I'm stayin' at.' Zee would say, 'Well, I have to go to work in the morning, and besides you might have a husband that you ain't mentioned.' She'd say, 'No, I cross my heart I ain't got a husband.' Well, shore nuff a feller come in there one night, took a double-barrel shot gun, and started shooting at Zee and missing him, and Zee managed to knock the gun out of his hand and take it away from him. And the feller said, 'I'll cut yore heart out.' He snatched up a knife he found somewhere and started at Zee with it and when Zee seen he was going to be cut all to pieces, he jest happened to touch the trigger of the gun and it went off and it hit that feller pretty broadside. Zee could shoot pretty good. The shot put a hole through that man that you coulda stuck a hat in, and you wouldn't had to roll up the brim —just stuck it through.

"They arrested Zee, put him in the Williamson County Jail and the sheriff said, 'We'll let you off if you'll peddle dope for us.' The governor was sellin' dope around. He sent word to Zee, 'I'll let you off if you'll peddle dope.' Zee said, 'No, I'd rather stand trial. I jest killed a man in self defense.' And they said, 'We'll get some folks here to say you're lyin' and say you shot him in the back.' And they wouldn't let Zee testify, wouldn't let him testify a-tall. Hired all them fellows to say he shot that knife man in the back runnin' toward his car." (Which happened to have been a fact. The man was unarmed.) "They sent Zee to the penitentiary. Zee coulda got out of it if he'da peddled dope for the sheriff."

In 1940 Roosevelt was running for his third time, and I was a very ardent Roosevelt supporter. Pappy O'Daniel had risen on the Texas horizon, and his way of thinking fitted Joe's perfectly. Joe doesn't require reality. He doesn't require fact. O'Daniel in his Bible-thumping, Sunday morning praying over the radio and talking about his church-going gave Joe somebody to grab hold of in place of vanished Jim Ferguson. Pappy

O'Daniel had become pretty much a mouthpiece for big inter-
ests fighting Roosevelt. Now Pappy O'Daniel's paper—he put
out a thing called *O'Daniel's News*—carried a picture of Roosevelt wearing a crown and calling himself King Franklin I. Joe
had read the picture, presumably, for when I solicited his vote
for Roosevelt, he said, "I ain't a gonna do it. Not after he said he
was gonna be king."

"Aw," I said, "that's tommyrot. Of course he never said a
thing like that."

"He done it too, down here at the foot of East Avenue.
I was standin' within ten foot of him, and he stood up there
and said, 'I am President now but elect me again and before
I'm done with it I'll be the king and my old woman'll be queen
and my children will be whatever they call sons and daughters
of kings.' By golly, he told me that."

Roosevelt never came to Austin, never made a speech there
in his life. Facts have no effect on Joe. "Why, I coulda retched
out and touched him on the toe of his foot."

I was on a Rosenwald Fellowship collecting folk material
with a recording machine when Pearl Harbor was bombed on
Sunday morning—afternoon in Austin. That night Alan Lomax,
who was folk archivist in the Library of Congress, phoned me
and said: "I want you to go out and get six representative
people in your community to record a message to President
Roosevelt. These messages will be made into a historical docu-
ment. We want the people to express their reactions to this
outrage."

On Monday afternoon I went to Joe's house with my recording machine and said, "Joe, did you hear the news? They
declared war this morning."

Joe said, "Yeah, I heard about it; know all about it. I
know them Japanese; they're heatherns. They ain't Christians;
every one of them is heatherns. That's why they done it Sunday
morning. They knowed our boys was all in church over there.
And they bombed us—laid for us. They coulda done it any

other day, but a heathern'll do that—catch you at church and jump you."

I said, "Well, here's your opportunity to speak to President Roosevelt. You've been telling me how Roosevelt needs to consult wise men." (Joe used to get outraged about Roosevelt's having professors in the cabinet—"old long-haired perfessers gonna tell me how to plant a field, tell me what to plow, just what to put in. I'll give any one of them—I'll give him forty acres and give him the mules and the seed and let him have the crop free." Joe never had anything but a rent house in his life. But it made no difference.)

"Here's your opportunity," I said, "to tell President Roosevelt exactly how you feel, now that our country's under attack and we've gone to war at long last. You are going to be speaking directly to him as your neighbor. You are a neighbor of his telling him exactly how you feel about the situation."

I set the microphone up for him. At that time we didn't have tape recorders; we recorded on records. If a cutting head had to be lifted up after it was put down, that part of the recording was spoiled. I instructed Joe that after I got the record started and raised my hand, he was to lean back and say, "President Roosevelt," or "Mr. President," or whatever he wanted to start with and then just talk out of his heart. "Let our President know your feelings," I said. "Tell him what you want to do to help win the war and give him whatever advice you want to give him." (You have to see Joe's face. He has a kind of bulbous nose, with huge pockmarks in it and almost a possum look in his eyes except they are set a little farther apart than a possum's and a little crossed and full of self-assurance, and he always has a lip full of snuff).

I started my machine and signaled Joe to start. He said, "President Roosevelt..." and not another word. I urged him to go on, giving him a signal to continue, but he just remained silent. Finally I took the cutting head up and I said, "Why didn't you go on? You spoiled a record."

"Didn't hear him answer." Joe had to learn a little bit about a recording machine; then he was free with advice to Roosevelt. "It ain't commonly knowed," he said, "but them Japanese build their houses outa shucks and paper almost altogether. They're just splinter wood. Now you wait till a good north wind is blowin' and have somebody light a rag soaked in kerosene oil and throw it into the north end of them islands. The fire will run Japs out like a cedarbrake fire scattering armadillos. Now, Mr. President, while the fire is being set at the north end of each island, have soldiers with clubs stand at the south ends and club them Japs as they run into the water. We could weed a lot of 'em out thataway."

Grandpa Brown

WILLIAM HENRY HARDIN

PRESENT-DAY chambers of commerce of the various metropolitan centers of Freestone, Limestone, and Falls counties would probably be most reluctant to admit that malaria was ever prevalent in those areas stretching between the Trinity and Brazos; however, the early years of the D. H. Brown family were spent mainly in recurrent moves farther and farther west to escape the "chills and fever" encountered in this region. Henry Brown married Rachel Stovall in the late eighties. They began their struggle with life as tenant farmers in the Trinity bottoms. A large family was reared on submarginal farming tracts, with the discouraging, back-breaking work periodically interrupted by another move farther west in an unceasing search for improved health and better living conditions.

By our current standards these two people married when they were both children: Grandma Brown was sixteen, Grandpa eighteen. During more than sixty years of married life, the tribulations of the world did not appreciably erode their veneer of childlike enthusiasm for living—with each other. When Grandfather died, Grandmother followed him within six months.

One of Grandfather's chief delights was to tease Grandmother; and, despite angry protestations and some display of pique, it seemed that she enjoyed being teased fully as much as he enjoyed teasing her. He would go to great pains to provoke her or "get her goat," and his stories of such incidents through-

out their lives were always highly amusing to everyone who
heard them except Grandmother. Regardless of how many times
a story was retold, she always co-operated appropriately by
"huffing up" and acting mad just long enough to bring the
fullest flavor to the account.

The Brown children were all "crowded together like peas
in a pod" as Grandmother expressed it, referring to the short
periods separating their ages.

"A youngun will be birthed in the spring," Grandfather once
remarked. "And it will be way next fall before the next one
shows up!"

One of the frequently told stories of the East Texas era of
their married life, consistently received with delight, concerned
Grandmother's determination to die. This was when the eldest
child, my mother, was about eight years old. The stresses of
childbirth, chills and fever which had not responded to the
favorite tonic, and the hard work of a tenant farmer's wife had
worn Grandmother out. In today's terminology she would probably have been described as suffering from a nervous break-
down or even combat fatigue. She finally went to bed and
stayed there for an extended period. The doctor had tried
everything in his bag of cures without any remedial effect: calo-
mel, epsom salts, and his favored iron and quinine tonic were
all useless. So one day he told Grandfather that no medicine
could help Grandmother; the only thing that would cure her
would be some mental shock that would shake her out of her
apathetic state.

Grandfather struggled along trying to cheer Grandmother
up, but she kept sinking lower and lower. Finally she decided
she could live no longer. At the ripe old age of twenty-five
"she was ready to cash in her chips and take a spell of rest
eternal," as Grandfather told the tale. She dramatically called
her husband and all the children to her bedside late one afternoon just before sundown.

"Henry," she sobbed to Grandfather, "I've labored long in

the Master's vineyard. I'm tired and weary and I'm gonna die. I just can't go on."

He stammered, "Aw, Rachel, you'll snap out of it in time. The old chills and fever have just laid you low. Just all run down." He caressed her forehead with his hand tenderly and added, "Tell you what we'll do. We'll send Jim down to the store and pick up a bottle of that pink stuff. That'll straighten you out."

"No," she moaned, determined to have her way. "I just know I'm gonna pass away. But there is just one promise I want you to make me. Please! You will promise, won't you?"

"Well," he countered, "what is it?"

"I want you to let Sister Ada raise the kids. She's a good Christian woman, and you can depend on it she'll raise them right."

"Not only NO, but HELL NO!" Grandfather exploded. "I won't let that dried up skinflint raise *my* kids. I wouldn't even let them go over there and stay all night!" With a calculating gleam in his eye he continued, "As a matter of fact, I've already picked out another woman!"

Grandmother glared at him speechlessly for a few minutes and, without further conversation, Grandfather returned glare for glare. Then Grandmother rose from her deathbed and, while the remainder of the family did the necessary evening chores around the place, she cooked supper—a herculean task that had been beyond her strength for weeks. While she subsequently suffered the occasional illnesses that are the lot of the average person, she never again resigned herself to dying. In fact, she seemed to be inspired by some inner conviction that by hook or crook she would outlive Grandfather.

Grandmother's sister, Ada, and her husband, Ed, were two of the in-laws that Grandpa disliked "best," and of course his comments upon them always served to arouse Grandmother's ire and sense of protectiveness just as effectively as if Grandfather were kidding Grandmother herself. She could always be depended upon zealously to defend any of her relatives against his assaults.

"Ed Heaton could sit down on a dime and still give back a nickel in change," Grandfather often declared. "But before he'd turn loose of the nickel, Old Liberty would be crying for mercy."

Aunt Ada and Uncle Ed lost their first child and, while Aunt Ada was grieving over its death, Grandfather insisted that Uncle Ed came up to Aunt Ada, placed his arms around her shoulders and tenderly consoled her by saying: "Don't cry, honey; we'll get another one!"

This particular couple fell heir to a lot of Grandfather's raillery. Uncle Ed got killed in an accident on the Cotton Belt. The railway was at fault and a very liberal settlement of the claim was made out of court. Grandfather said that Aunt Ada, when receiving the check from the railway claims adjuster, had remarked: "Ed shore was a fine man and I'm going to miss him. You know what? I'd give back half of this here money, just to have Ed alive again."

Grandfather was generous to a fault and he detested penury of every sort—particularly that of Uncle Ed. One year Grandpa raised only one hog through to killing time. That was a tough year. The shotes got into a patch of young cockleburs and, of course, it was a lucky thing that even one of them survived. Several of the neighbors came around on the day that the one remaining hog was butchered, and Grandfather gave away so much meat that all that remained of his hog was some spare ribs, the head, the spleen, and the chitterlings. If it had not been for Grandmother's foresight in canning up a lot of vegetables the past summer, as well as laying in an abundance of dried black-eyed peas and pinto beans, the Brown clan would really have suffered in getting through the next crop. Peas were always a "must" in the Brown family. They always thrived in spite of drought, flood, or storm and supplied the core around which a working man could subsist. One of Grandfather's standard sayings when starting on a trip was: "If I don't get back, be sure and plant a big pea patch!"

Grandfather told another tale on Uncle Ed. Several of the men of the neighborhood, along with Grandfather, butchered Uncle Ed's five hogs for him and, because Uncle Ed was ailing at the time (not able to do any work but sufficiently active to stand around and closely supervise the operation), they cut the meat up, salted it down, ground out the sausage, and rendered the lard. For lunch Uncle Ed had brought out a bunch of corn pone left over from a previous meal and stipulated that the men could supplement this bread by toasting off the spleens (called "long tongue"). When all the work had been done, each of the workmen received as compensation for his labor one hog's head, bestowed by Uncle Ed with this remark: "Oh, go ahead and take the whole thing. We don't like them here anyway—meat tastes too strong." This episode irked Grandfather so much that he composed a commemorative poem—which provoked Grandmother fully as much as it provided pleasure to Grandfather:

Owed to Ed

Come all you farmers and I will tell
About a man that you all know well.
He's a Baptist deacon on Onion Creek,
And so damn tight his eyeballs squeak.

Came the first norther in Oh six
All the folks from the branches and creeks
Pitched right in with neighborly will
To help Old Ed his hogs to kill.

Ed was sickly as could be
And could not get up the energy
To stick a shote or scrape a hair,
But he spouted advice everywhere.

We dressed out the meat and cut up the lard —
All except Ed worked long and hard.
A scrumptious feast when the noon bell rung
Was made out on pone and fresh long tongue.

Tired as a dog, Brown finally went back
To his hungry family in the old log shack.
His heart was heavy and his feet were lead;
Ed had paid him off with a damn hog's head!

Grandfather resented the tendency of his "favorite" in-laws to think that anything they had was better than the belongings of anyone else. Uncle Ed had the best mules, and Aunt Ada's cows were thoroughbreds. Her floors were cleaner, her quilts were more original and warmer to sleep under, and her bread rose faster and cooked off lighter than anybody else's. Uncle Ed chopped the best wood, plowed the straightest furrow, raised the best hogs, corn, cotton, or what have you. Even his bees made sweeter honey!

Grandfather told this tale of Uncle Ed's entry into heaven:

Old Saint Pete was drowsily sipping on some Heavenly Metheglin when he was rudely snapped to attention by a loud pounding at the golden gate out front. Pete got up and parked his glass of Metheglin on the edge of a big harp standing close by. The racket out at the gate was getting louder and louder.

"Take it easy, Greasy, you got a long way to slide," grumbled Saint Pete as he slowly clumped out to the gate. He got there and suspiciously peered through the golden bars and saw Ed.

"Who're you, and what do you want?" Pete queried.

"BROTHER Ed Heaton," was the reply. "And I crave to gain entrance to the Elysian fields of Paradise, and bask eternally within the smile and grace of my Lord and Savior."

Saint Pete canted his head to one side and really looked Ed over because he sure knowed Old Ed for what he was. Then Saint Pete studied awhile longer, but pretty soon made up his mind. He sadly shrugged his shoulders and opened the gate to let Ed in, saying as he did so:

"Oh, well, come on in! BUT — I'm warning you — you won't like it here. This place will never measure up to the Heatons'."

Another thing about Uncle Ed that irritated Grandfather was his "store boughten" teeth. They were very expensive dentures and Uncle Ed took delight in revealing this information to all and sundry. He would leave the dentures lying around on the mantel over the fireplace, or on the library table in the living room, where all visitors could see them and be properly appreciative of their sterling qualities. Eventually, the temptation became too great and one day Grandfather swiped Uncle Ed's teeth. Before he relented and returned them, Uncle Ed ate soup and "softened vittles" for over a month, bemoaning the lot of a good Christian man who was cruelly toothless. This episode occurred in the very early years of Grandfather's married life.

Grandfather was never a man to avoid killing two birds with one stone if and whenever possible. Grandmother was a small woman but she had a terrific thirst. One of her greatest pleasures was drinking cool water out of a glass dipper from the old cedar water bucket that hung in the central breeze-way (dog trot) of their home. Her thirst was so intense that she always placed by her bedside a large glass of water which she drank during the middle of the night. This midnight practice was most annoying to Grandfather, so one night after the lamp was blown out he sneaked out of bed and slipped Uncle Ed's false teeth into Grandma's glass of water. Grandpa loved to tell about how she awoke and fumbled around in the darkness for her glass of water and how her irritating loud gulps came to an abrupt halt when the false teeth slid with a "chonk" down against her lips. Grandmother was momentarily very angry and never did seem really to appreciate the humor of this episode, but it certainly cured her intense craving for water during the night.

While Grandfather was a farmer and the usual barnyard odors never seemed to impress him unfavorably, he was particularly rabid on the question of soiled diapers. He objected violently if the baby was changed in his presence, and the offending diapers had to be taken outside the house immediately. He had installed a tow sack on the backyard fence as the place for these items to be stored prior to washing.

Perhaps some of his antipathy to Aunt Ada was associated with the dirty-diaper motif. Aunt Ada was just a year older than Grandmother and they had always been very close to each other. In fact, they acted as midwives back and forth when their babies were born, and the frequency of the birth of their children usually made it possible for either one to act as a wet nurse for the other's children. Many times one of them would care for the babies of both families while the other worked in the field.

Another reason for the hostility between Aunt Ada and Grandfather, according to Grandmother, was probably the fact that they were so like each other in their bent toward practical jokes. One of these involved dirty diapers. Once when Aunt Ada was waiting on Grandmother after a childbirth, Grandfather became particularly incensed over an odorous diaper and threw it outside on the red ant hill in the front yard by the chinaberry tree. The red ants really were stirred up over this disruption of their peace and quiet.

"Imagine a grown man acting like that over a little baby's diaper!" exclaimed Aunt Ada disapprovingly, and she and Grandfather harangued back and forth considerably over the matter.

"You can get used to anything," Aunt Ada taunted.

"I'll be damned if I'll EVER get used to THAT!" Grandpa yelled.

"I'll just bet you could," she countered.

"There ain't any sense betting away all your small change, because I damn well won't!"

And thus their harangue went on and on for a long time, until they had Grandmother frantic with tears and they had to shut up. Aunt Ada only dropped the matter verbally, how-ever. She took a particularly "ripe" dirty diaper and sewed it inside the ticking of Grandfather's pillow, and she installed another specimen underneath the upholstery of the buggy. This latter action was especially effective because Grandfather was using the buggy every day to attend a "protracted meeting" which was in progress.

Grandfather ranted and raved about the hidden odor, first noticed when he went to the revival meeting and again later when he went to bed. He was embarrassed by his friends' giving his buggy a wide berth, and at home he searched under the bed, behind the trunk, and everywhere except inside his pillow. After a couple of days he quit complaining about the objectionable odor, so Aunt Ada surreptitiously freshened the supply. This renewed Grandfather's protests for a day or so. Finally, Grandfather quit griping about the odor. Aunt Ada revealed the joke to him in the presence of Uncle Ed and some visiting neighbors, still insisting that even Grandfather could get used to dirty diapers. Everyone there—except Grandfather —thought it was an awfully clever joke and, of course, Grandfather had to pretend to be a good sport about it.

No one could prove that he was not being a good sport about this trick of Aunt Ada's; however, a short time later she did misplace her spectacles (another of her sources of joy which she could brag about unendingly), and Uncle Ed had to read her *Baptist Standard* to her for a couple of months. Stranger still, when she finally found the glasses they were propped in an accustomed spot against the old Seth Thomas clock on the mantel where she just "knowed" she had searched for them in the first place. It was also at about this time that a big rat strangely managed to crawl back into a recess in the springs of Aunt Ada's bed and die. The odors arising from its putrefaction led eventually to discovery of the pungent corpse, and while no hint was passed that Grandfather had had anything to do with the rat's having selected this particular spot to depart for its ancestral reward, his quip to Aunt Ada that "anyone can get used to anything in time" did not have the effect of soothing her injured feelings.

Grandfather had very positive ideas about life and death. He was an enemy of ostentation of any kind. When one of his sons, Albert, died, his grave was heaped with an array of expensive wreaths. While Grandfather appreciated this indication of

Uncle Albert's popularity among his fellow-men, he felt that the display was needlessly expensive and that the same sentiments could have been as adequately expressed otherwise.

"When I die," he said, "they can just cover my grave with dogwood flowers." He meant, of course, that it would not be necessary to buy expensive and ostentatious floral wreaths. Grandmother really censured him for this statement, pointing out that, unless he happened to die within the very brief period of the year during which the dogwood is in bloom, dogwood flowers would probably be the most expensive wreaths imaginable.

"You'd better just be careful of your druthers, or you will wind up dead with NO flowers on your grave!" Grandmother admonished him, but he was not particularly perturbed over such a prospect. It created an opening for him to retell his story about how he wanted to die. He needed little coaxing or stimulation to tell this one—only an audience.

How'd I druther die? Well, it's like this. First I'd want to be deadly sick for a long time, and though you kids might be scattered around over the country like a mad woman's knittin', I'd want all of you to get back home here to see me die.

Then, I'd want Rachel, and all you kids, and all my dear relations to gather around my deathbed. Rachel, here, would be sobbing sighs and wiping off drops of tears as big as water buckets, and she'd remember to be sorry that she laughed at me when I sat down in the bull nettles down on Owl Creek.

Sister Ada would have to get here some way or other, her big, popped, bleary eyes all swoll up—looking like a left-over fried egg in a slop bucket — and in her sweet syrupy voice she'd bemoan how she wished she hadn't been SO mean to me in my lifetime. I'd look up soulfully at her.

"Aw, Sister Ada, don't weep," I'd say right sympathetic like. "Set yore mind at ease. I know you couldn't be different. You weren't responsible for your wicked heart. You were born with it."

And you kids would have sufficient time to properly appreciate what a wonderful, wonderful daddy you have been privileged to have — you'd be sorry you didn't always scratch my feet as long as I wanted you to every time.

I'd just lie there on my deathbed and relax and enjoy your sorrow.

Then, after I'd got everybody properly appreciating me, I'd want to get well, so I could remind all of you how silly you looked hanging around my deathbed like that.

On another occasion Grandfather averred that he did not intend to die, but would just live to be a hundred years old and then turn into a gray mule. However, it did not work out that way. He was not quite eighty when he came down with pneumonia late one fall. His last instructions before dying were, "Rachel, if I don't come back, be sure and plant a big patch of peas in the spring."

But before planting time had come, Grandmother had joined him in that Great Beyond where we may be sure Grandfather is in ecstasy "getting the goat" of someone within the heavenly throng.

NOTE: Most of the stories told here were heard from David Henry Brown himself over a period of twenty years' close acquaintanceship with him. Of course his tales have been embroidered upon by the various children —the ones contributing the most to these tales from an embroidery standpoint being Beth (Brown) Hardin, Denton; Jack Brown, deceased, Lubbock; and Thelma (Brown) Growdon, Melrose, New Mexico. William Henry (Bill) Hardin may have been guilty of minor infractions in this respect also.

Southpaws, Psychology, and Social Science

GEORGE D. HENDRICKS

All left-handed people owe the Devil a day's work.
—Texas Superstition.

His saul has ta'en some other way,
I fear, the left-hand road.
—Robert Burns, "Epitaph on Holy Willie."

Archeology, sociology, psychology, and folklore are related sciences. Each in its own way concerns what is behind, without, and within the human being. Each encompasses the cause and effect of every human action—be it of the mind, heart, or hand. In external appearance, man is a symmetrical animal; but he does not act symmetrically. His master hand dominates his physical actions, assisted by his helping hand. All four of the above mentioned sciences are inextricably concerned with this human phenomenon of lateral preference.

An expert sociologist would know the extensive ramifications of the right-handedness of the modern world. A mere amateur could list the normally right-hand artifacts. Among these would be scissors, the comptometer, door knobs that open to the right, sewing machines with right-hand controls, and the standard pipe thread and electric light socket which tighten to the right. The right hand carries the melody on the piano, directs the bow upon the violin, and strums other stringed instruments. Time is measured out with the top right-hand sweep of the clock's hands, and calendars read from left to right. The standard buck of pressing machines in commercial cleaning shops is larger on the left so that the right

69

hand can manipulate sleeves and pants legs upon it. And any teacher of manual arts knows the difficulty of translating textual instructions for a left-handed student.

Etiquette dictates many right-handed mores, not the least of which is the manner of setting a table and eating. The standard greeting is the shaking of right hands. Oaths are always taken with the right hand. A man usually tips his hat with his right hand.

Psychologists have determined that the right-handed person is also right-eyed, right-legged, and right-footed. The modern world has been made to his order. His eyes read nearly all languages from left to right.[1] The same is true with figures. Lighting normally is from the left to benefit the right-handed writer, and the standard tablet arm chair is designed for him. In his automobile he shifts gears with his right hand, he adjusts most of the dials and buttons on his dashboard with his right hand, and he controls the accelerator and brakes with his right foot. He tightens the nuts, the screws, and the wheel lug bolts on his car with a right-hand turn. He looks for signal lights on the right side of the street; and he follows right-lane traffic whether in air, on land, or in the water.[2] And railroad engineers look for signals on the right side of the tracks.

Some 96 per cent of the modern normal population is right-handed. Were they born right-handed? Or did they adjust themselves to their environment? Why are the remaining 4 per cent left-handed?[3] Wherein are they "different"? Why is it that 12 per cent of abnormals such as criminals, insane, and feeble-minded are left-handed?[4] Does this greater percentage indicate that being left-handed is "abnormal"? What kind of training should be given left-handed children? It is from such somewhat moot questions that superstitions and prejudice arise, and it is upon such material that folklore thrives.

Anthropologists such as Sir Daniel Wilson, Gabriel de Mortillet, W. Johnson, W. Wright, D. Brinton, Margaret Mead, Ira S. Wile, S. D. Porteus, and D. Wilson have established several facts and presented corresponding theories concerning left-handedness.[5] Neolithic and Paleolithic man's flint instruments were chipped for left-hand as well as right-hand use. Stone Age man had no distinctly right-hand tools, no social pressure required him to be right-handed, and the theory is that his population was in equal percentage sinistral. Then, from 4,000 to 2,000 B.C. when Bronze Age writings, plows, carts, and potter's wheels were invented, dextrality began to prevail. Finally, from 2,000 B.C. to the present, the Iron Age implements have become more and more dextral. Among North American Indians, tools and implements indicate little lateral preference; and among modern primitives such as Australians, Africans, Bushmen, Bantus, Pygmies, and Hottentots, an equal number engage in work with marked left-handed preferences. With the passage of time and with the advancement of machinery, dextrality has increased and sinistrality decreased correspondingly.

Exactly how the preference for dextrality evolved in the human race is still a matter of conjecture. Plato advanced the theory that right-handedness was developed in the infant by the way the mother held it in her arms. He reasoned that the mother would hold her child in her stronger right arm, thus pressing its left arm to her body and leaving its right arm free. The fallacies in this reasoning are, of course, obvious. Any observer will note that a right-handed mother will hold her infant in her left hand in order to tend it with her right. Thus, if Plato's theory were true, it would follow that every other generation would be left-handed.

For the want of a better surmise, present-day psychologists such as Abram Blau have accepted Thomas Carlyle's theory of primitive warfare. Carlyle became much concerned about handedness when his own right arm became paralyzed. He mentioned in his diary, in 1871, that because the heart is on the left side, the ancient warrior turned that more vulnerable side away from his foe and held a shield over it with his left hand.

This arrangement furthermore placed his right hand wielding the sword or club nearer his opponent's heart. Carlyle further supposed that primitive left-handed warriors were eventually killed off because of their disadvantage.

In ancient warfare the leader's assistant usually fought on his left, thus helping to protect his more exposed and more vulnerable flank. To this date, when U.S. Army officers march officially or walk informally together, the lieutenant is always on the captain's left. The *lieutenant,* according to his title, is to "take the place of" his superior officer in his absence. He is to move from the *left* and assume the position of command (Italians and Englishmen call him the "left-tenant").[6]

Whether or not there is any direct connection, other modern military customs, tactics, instruments follow this precedent. The most common one is the right-hand salute. Also, at the command "Forward," all troops standing at attention shift their weight to the right (and presumably stronger) side. Then at the command "March!" they step off on their left feet with a full thirty-inch pace. In counting cadence, they all shout *odd* numbers as their *left* feet strike the ground.

Handles for épées, rapiers, dirks were grooved to fit the right hand. Rifles were later tailored for the dextral, the breech bolt being on the right side. Every time a left-hander fired the '03 Springfield rifle, he had to reach over and across the gun to cock it with the left hand, thus completely blocking his line of sight toward his enemy and usually upsetting his own balance. Modern artillery instruments are certainly dextral. Dials setting angles in mills on the transit, the aiming circle, and the range finder are convenient only to the right hand. The gunner corporal stands on the right side of the howitzer, sets the angle of deflection, and pulls the lanyard with his right hand. The number-one gunner, though he stands at the left side of the howitzer, sets the angle of elevation and elevates the tube with his right hand. From first-lettered units on down, military organizations are usually deployed tactically from left to right, so that they read on a situation map as they would normally be printed in an alphabet. Our military world is, and always has been, a right-handed world.

Though the beginning of this evolutionary process of racial dextrality was perhaps accidental, once the preference was established it was so cumulative as to become a tradition. Infants learned to use right-handed tools by imitation, and adults taught their use by formal precept and example. More important, however, was the social pressure upon the individual to conform to the resulting code of human conduct and cultural law evolving from dextrality. The right became the normal, good; the left became the abnormal, bad.

The very philology of laterality itself is a mirror of the concomitant prejudice against the left-handed and for the right-handed. The Latin *laius* meant literally *on the left side*. Figuratively it meant *awkward, foolish,* or *stupid* when applied to a person; *inconvenient* when applied to a time. The Latin *sinister* meant literally *on the left hand;* figuratively it connoted *unlucky, adverse, injurious, awkward, pernicious.* The English borrowing retained the pejoration. The Latin *rectus* meant literally *to the right side;* figuratively it meant *straightforward, honest, desirable.* English derivatives retain the figurative amelioration. Latin *dexter* meant literally *right* or *on the right;* figuratively it meant *skilful.* Again the English derivatives retained the ameliorations. A dextrous man is skilful. A person equally skilful with both hands is not ambisinister, but instead ambidextrous. French *gauche* translates simply *left* or *to the left,* but in English a gauche person is very clumsy. French *adroit* translates simply as *right* or *to the right;* but in English an adroit person is straightforward, honest, admirable, skilful. No one ever offers advice to go *left* down the middle, and no one ever says that *left* here is the exact spot. Instead, it is always "Go *right* down the middle" and "*Right* here is the exact spot."

Lord Chesterfield wrote, in 1749, to his son, "An awkward address, ungraceful attitudes and actions, and a certain lefthandiness (if I may use that word) loudly proclaim low education."

In Texas at least, to say that someone has two left feet describes him as being extremely awkward. I was much surprised to find that there is a corresponding medical term in use describing children whose awkward motor control cannot be attributed to any organic neurological defects. Galen is said to have recognized the condition when he wrote that some children are "ambilevous." This word translates as *doubly left-handed*, according to psychologist Blau, and ably characterizes the disorder. In Blau's words,

> These children show a lack of skill and coordination in both hands comparable to the left hand of a definitely right-handed person. The normal smoothness of muscular coordination is absent and movements are jerky, inept, and bungling. The movements of feet and body in general are often coarse and awkward.[7]

I had always heard of left-handed compliments as being undesirable. But this research revealed such things as a left-handed friend, conjecture, god, policy, opinion, work, wisdom, favor, blessing, business, and ordination. All of these are questionable, doubtful, spurious, or sinister. A left-handed dream is ill omened. A left-handed chance is a cruel, unfortunate blow. Left-handed monkey wrenches, fountain pens, and spokes are nonexistent but negativistically useful in ridiculing the ludicrous or insignificant. "The lad's takkin no moore notice on him than if he'd bin th' left-hand spoke ov a cart wheel," wrote a man named Brierley in *Marlocks* (1867).[8]

In heraldry, a bar sinister was one drawn across a shield the reverse of the usual manner, not from upper left to lower right, but the opposite. It was popularly but erroneously supposed to indicate illegitimacy. To marry with the left hand was to contract a morganatic marriage. In medieval Germany princes were permitted to marry commoners, and the ensuing progeny were regarded as legitimate, though they could not reign or inherit fortunes. In such morganatic marriages the bridegroom gave the bride his left hand instead of his right during the ceremony.

Along the wharves of the New Orleans port I have heard seamen mention a common superstition. A sailor never boards an ocean-bound ship with his left foot first; to do so would invite a disaster. Furthermore, if a sailor sneezes on the port side immediately after boarding the vessel, the voyage will probably be unlucky; if he sneezes to the starboard, favorable winds can be expected.

In addition to signifying awkwardness, inexactness, and bad luck, the attributive expression *left-handed*, in the folk idioms of the past, also pertained to infirmity, stupidity, improvidence, dishonesty, and downright evil.

Beaumont and Fletcher spoke in their play *Captain* of a certain infirm character as ". . . one of a left-handed making, a lanck thing."[9] A man named Taylor published, in 1636, a guide to British travelers cataloguing the country taverns and describing rural routes. "In Chertsey," he warned, "there is a decayed left-handed bridge over the river: I wish it mended." A person named Tyron wrote, in 1683, a treatise on the *Way to Health,* advising that ". . . most men inclining to the left-handed way, are thereby precipitated into all uncleanness."

Joseph Wright records in *The English Dialect Dictionary* an interesting entry apparently concerning a stupid daughter. The supposedly chagrined father said, "I niver seed noabody moore *left* to th'r sens then oor Claudia was when she married [sich] a fella."[10]

Money thrown "over the left shoulder" was money squandered. In Samuel Richardson's *Clarissa* (1748), there was an improvident character whose financial affairs warranted close scrutiny, ". . . an account of what will go over the left shoulder; only of what he squanders, what he borrows, and what he owes, and never will pay."

A nineteenth-century English proverbial couplet says that left-handed work is dishonest, slovenly, and fruitless:

> Left-handed wark, though paid in part,
> Ends aye in naked back or broken heart.[11]

And James Stevens translated, in 1707, *Quevedo's Complete Works*, which offered this profound advice, "Tis not safe trusting a Left-Handed man with money."

The adjective *left* meant, at its worst, *downright evil*. As late as 1884 a person named Grant, in a group of *Lays*, remarked of a character that "He was so far *left* as to commit sin." Shakespeare's Falstaff admits, "I, I, I myself sometimes, leaving the fear of God on the left hand and hiding mine honour in my necessity, am fain to shuffle, to hedge, and to lurch . . ."[12]

And *left*, as a substantive, formerly signified a mean, worthless, evil person. In a 1425 writing entitled *Seven Sages* there is a line concerning a certain ". . . wyf, that cursyd *lyfte*, [who] brewed the childys deth that night." Or the substantive *left* could designate evil in the abstract, as in Langland's *Piers Plowman* (1377): "Conscience hym tolde, that wronge was a wikked luft."

Just as *left* symbolized evil, so did *right* symbolize good. In the Bible much evidence testifies to the efficacy of the right hand:

I have set the Lord always before me: because he is at my right hand, I shall not be moved. (Psalms 16:8).

Thou wilt shew me the path of life: in thy presence is fulness of joy; at thy right hand there are pleasures for evermore. (Psalms 16:11).

Fear thou not; for I am with thee: be not dismayed: for I am thy God: I will strengthen thee; yea, I will help thee; yea, I will uphold thee with the right hand of my righteousness. (Isaiah 41:10).

For I the Lord thy God will hold thy right hand, saying unto thee, Fear not; I will help thee. (Isaiah 41:13).

. . . Ye shall see the Son of man sitting on the right hand of power, and coming in the clouds of heaven. (Mark 14:62).

It is Christ that died, yea rather, that is risen again, who is even at the right hand of God, who also maketh intercession for us. (Romans 8:34).

The risen Christ was to sit at the right hand of God, it was widely known. He was, of course, from a theocratic viewpoint, next highest in honor.[13]

Following in this tradition of dextrality, Virgil has Aeneas say in the *Aeneid*, "Dextra mihi deus" (My right hand is to me as a god).[14] Aeneas was, of course, a fictitious folk-hero, one who acted aright and redressed wrongs. In eighteenth-century Ireland there was a real folk-hero, an insurgent leader whose *nom de guerre* was Captain Right and whose actual identity was a most carefully kept secret. As a matter of fact, over a period of years the title was used by more than one person.[15]

Thus it is seen that the words *left* and *right* have symbolic associations in both religious and profane circles. According to G. A. Gaskell, in most religions the left hand symbolizes the externally passive incoming energy of the soul, while the right hand symbolizes the externally positive outgoing energy—that which *does* the evolutionary force from within outward.[16] This idea is in keeping with dextrality. The right hand is the stronger, the doer, the giver. It is analogous to the scriptural advice in Matthew 6:3-4:

> But when thou doest alms, let not thy left hand
>   know what thy right hand doeth;
> That thine alms may be in secret: and thy Father
>   which seeth in secret himself shall reward thee openly.[17]

It is also analogous to the customary Hebraic manner of blessing offspring, as seen in Genesis 48 in the story of Manasseh and Ephraim, the elder and younger brother respectively. It seems that their grandfather Israel, who was to give his blessings to these two sons of Joseph, apparently got mixed up and violated the custom of placing the right hand upon the elder and the left hand upon the younger boy; but it turned out that he knew what he was doing:

> And Israel stretched out his right hand, and laid it upon Ephraim's head, who was the younger, and his left hand upon Manasseh's head, guiding his hands wittingly; for Manasseh was the firstborn. . . .

And when Joseph saw that his father laid his right hand upon the head of Ephraim, it displeased him; and he held up his father's hand, to remove it from Ephraim's head unto Manasseh's head. . . .

And his father refused, and said, I know it, my son, I know it; he also shall become a people, and he also shall be great: but truly his younger brother shall be greater than he, and his seed shall become a multitude of nations. (Genesis 48:14-19).

The division between profound religious belief and superstitious paganistic hokum is often a razor's edge. I would hesitate to categorize either the above allusion to the blessing of offspring or the following several allusions pertaining to death, Christmas, and marriage; but I think they all come close to that razor's edge, and which side of it they are on depends upon the individual's viewpoint. The Mordvin of the Finno-Ugric cult is quite serious when he washes the corpse of his deceased beloved. He then holds a sickle by the blade and cuts a portion of grain for a sacrifice. All of this he is careful to do with his *left* hand; then he throws the grain backward over his left shoulder. He continues the ceremony backward, contrary to the sun's motion, with his clothes on inside-out, placing other offerings upside-down on the grave. According to Mordvin tradition, *this* world is right-side-up, straightforward, and right-handed; the *next* world is upside-down, backward, and apparently left-handed.[18]

The missionary Graan once wrote that in heathen times Swedish Lapps celebrated Christmas in a peculiar manner. After several preliminary functions, the climax of the festivity occurred when every man in the village would pass by a receptacle and deposit within it three spoonfuls of fat with his *left* hand.[19]

In the Perthshire highlands of Scotland it was once thought that the bridegroom should wear a left shoe without a buckle or latchet, "to prevent witches from depriving him, on the nuptial night, of the power of loosening the virgin zone."[20] It is said that the same superstition and custom are current in Syria.

In Texas there is a superstition that a bride should never step over a doorsill with her left foot but should always use her right one instead. According to Philip F. Waterman, this is probably a universal superstition with a certain amount of logic behind it.[21]

It is also a general American and European superstition that if the moon is looked at over the left shoulder, the result inevitably will be insanity or death.[22] The left shoulder also figures in a superstition of the Nubas of East Africa. It is their belief that they will die if they enter their priestly king's domicile. The only way to prevent death is to bare the left shoulder and get the king to lay his hand on it. The king, like atomic power, is the source of both good and evil; he must be isolated for his own good and for the sake of others. The left shoulder, the weaker side and more susceptible, is the one to inoculate.[23]

So far, the right side has been presented as advantageous; the left, disadvantageous. But there are always anomalies and exceptions, and there are two sides to every question. Ovid wrote in *Fasti* (IV, 883-34): "... tonitru dedit omina laevo, Iuppiter ..." mentioning "thunder on the left" as a favorable omen. Pliny also shared this belief. In Christopher Morley's novel entitled *Thunder on the Left,* the phenomenon is also considered lucky. This superstition has an explanation: the Roman augur always faced south, and the east was of course to his left. Omens from the east, whence the sun rose symbolizing the generation of life as opposed to the dying sun in the west, were always considered auspicious.[24]

Few left-handed heroes have come down through the annals of history. Their absence makes an occasional one all the more striking. The author of the book of Judges mentions one such hero of the Israelites, repeating and apparently emphasizing his left-handedness. The Israelites had been persecuted by the wicked King Eglon of Moab.

But when the children of Israel cried unto the Lord, the Lord raised them up a deliverer, Ehud the son of Gera, a Benjamite, a man left-handed: and by him the children of Israel sent a present unto Eglon the king of Moab.

But Ehud made him a dagger which had two edges, of a cubit length; and he did gird it under his raiment upon his right thigh.

And he brought the present unto Eglon king of Moab: and Eglon was a very fat man. . . .

And Ehud put forth his left hand, and took the dagger from his right thigh, and thrust it into his belly:

And the haft also went in after the blade; and the fat closed upon the blade, so that he could not draw the dagger out of his belly; and the dirt came out. (Judges 3:15-22).

Ehud then made a dramatic escape.

Perhaps there is some merit in Carlyle's theory that the left-handed primitive warrior was at a disadvantage. This would especially be true if his enemies were right-handed and more numerous than he. But it would also work the other way. There is adequate testimony of the prowess of the left-handed warriors and athletes, both of olden and of modern times. In 1622 a man named Massinger wrote, "I wud not giue vp the cloake of your service to meet the splay-foot estate of any left-ey'd knight aboue the Antipodes, because they are vnlucky to meet."[25] There is also scriptural evidence. The Israelites were at war with the Benjamites. The latter came near to winning when they unleashed a crack regiment composed entirely of left-handed warriors, "seven hundred chosen men left-handed; every one could sling stones at an hair breadth, and not miss." (Judges 20:16). These slew many times their number.

Indeed, most athletes prefer not to compete with any opponent who is of opposite laterality. His style, technique, and strategy are different and therefore more difficult to cope with. This is especially true in boxing and fencing. In football a left-footed punter is sometimes at a premium. More spectacular is the southpaw in baseball. For one thing, when he makes a hit, his momentum is already toward first base, whereas the right-hander has to release the bat, regain his balance, and start from a dead standstill. This one difference affords the left-handed batter probably a three-second advantage and better chance to chalk up a run. Mickey Mantle is ambidextrous at bat. When he faces a southpaw pitcher, he bats right-handed; and when he faces a right-handed pitcher, he bats left-handed. And so far his left-handed batting averages as well as his right-handed batting.

Perhaps it is an advantage to be left-handed in bowling. One of my students tells me that, according to bowling rules of etiquette, when several bowlers are in position at the same time, the bowlers on the alleys to the right bowl first. This is not true, however, if there is a left-handed bowler among them. "Left-handed bowlers are considered somewhat freakish, so they are always allowed to bowl first in this situation," he concluded.

A left-handed polo player may not be considered freakish, but he is certainly considered unpredictable and dangerous. For years the Polo Association of America tolerated the left-handed player so long as he stroked back-handed on the right side of his horse. Apparently too often he would forget this special restriction and would (in his natural style) charge and collide head-on with a right-handed opponent, who would, of course, be on the same side of the ball as he. The result was usually broken bones of both men and horses. Finally the association outlawed all left-handers.

In automobile racing it is definitely advantageous to turn to the left. All automobiles are constructed so that the torque of the engine pulls counterclockwise. This causes the weight of the machine to nose downward when the vehicle turns leftward and thus help prevent capsizing from centrifugal force. A sudden turn to the right at high speed is much more dangerous, as the opposite is the effect: the front of the vehicle tends to rear up and turn over to the left. At all official race tracks, all curves and turns are made to the left.

The left is not always disadvantageous, as has been shown in sports, in warfare, in primitive religions, and in paganistic superstitions. There are, in fact, indications of whole primitive sinistral cultures. There are pictures of Sardinians with shields on the right arm and swords in the left hand. There exist pictures of Egyptians plowing fields, branding cattle, and harvesting grain in such a manner as to indicate left-handedness. In the Metropolitan Museum of Art, there are pictures of Knoters reaching back to the fifth century B.C. which show men with spears held in the left hand and shields on the right arm. Ira S. Wile uncovered, in 1934, a legend that Alexander the Great once discovered a country in which everyone was left-handed. These legendary strangers tried to convince Alexander that greater honor was due the left hand because it was nearer the heart.[26]

It appears, even in modern times, that being left-handed is not always necessarily a handicap. In 1945, Christie Jeffries questioned 127 school principals as to whether left-handed teachers were handicapped. Eighty-one said *no,* twenty-two were noncommittal, twenty-four said *yes.* Of these last, only seven gave anything like logical reasons. Four of the principals were left-handed themselves; they all answered *no.* One of them remarked that "I believe left-handedness about as important as false teeth."[27]

Mary M. Wilcox Jones was apparently fed up with hearing educators suggest that retarded reading skills went with left-handedness. She therefore inaugurated a testing program in the Beebe Junior High School in Malden, Massachusetts in 1942. The fifty-seven left-handed students tested made an average score higher than the 569 right-handed children. Miss Jones's conclusion: "There are, therefore, 92 chances in 100 that . . . the mean of the left-handed children will, on the average, score slightly higher than the mean of the right-handed children."[28]

What to do about left-handed children has always concerned parents. When a Kafir child's left hand becomes too active, the parent scalds it in steaming sand so that the child is forced to use his right. Zulus teach their children never to reach for or offer anything with the left hand, nor to eat or count with it.[29] In the dextral culture of the Kafirs and Zulus, social pressure is evidently powerful. In our own it is likewise powerful, but we know more about psychology than they, and there is much speculation among our educators concerning the effect of changing the laterality of a child. There is also wide divergence of opinion. Some authorities, like Norbert Wiener, claim that "As a consequence [of changing laterality] the processes associated with speech and writing are very likely to be involved in a traffic jam and stuttering is the most natural thing in the world."[30]

More recently, however, reliable studies have disproved causal relationship between shifting of handedness and stuttering. For example, in 1940 E. M. Daniels gave handedness and speech tests to 1,548 college students, among whom there were 20 stutterers. Only one of 34 left-handed and 4 of 138 ambidextrous students were stutterers. Of 77 students who had shifted laterality, only one stuttered. The other fourteen stutterers were right-handed.[31] Another study is noteworthy. A four-year campaign to "cure" left-handedness in the schools of Elizabeth, New Jersey was recently launched. The left-handedness of 250 cases was reduced to 66, and not a single instance of defective speech resulted.[32] Modern psychiatrists, however, believe that, had further pressure been brought to bear upon the remaining 66, some form of psychotic neurosis would have developed.

Perhaps the most extensive and most significant treatise on the subject is Abram Blau's *The Master Hand* (1946). Blau says that handedness is an acquired trait, not inherited. He says that a man is left-brained *because* he is right-handed (i.e., a man is not right-handed because he is left-brained).[33] The use of the hand develops *first*. If necessary (as in the case of accidental injury to the hand), the laterality can be shifted without injury to brain, speech, or emotional stability.

Blau has a most interesting theory as to the causes of the

persistence of left-handedness in spite of the dextrality of our culture. He lists three:

1. An inherent deficiency. A physical defect in the right member enforces use of the left.... [This does *not* mean that the preference itself is inherited.]

2. Faulty education. Left-handed parents unconsciously are models.... Many parents actually encourage sinistrality in the mistaken belief that this will prevent an emotional disorder.

3. Emotional negativism. This is probably the most common type of sinistrality—the product of an emotional contrariness [the will *not* to learn] in early childhood.[34]

An appreciable number of reliable studies have shown that the incidence of left-handedness among antisocials is about three times greater than among normal members of society.[35] These antisocials include criminals, mentally deficient, truants, psychotics, neurotics, psychopaths, delinquents, and incorrigibles. Even among epileptics sinistrality is much greater than among normal people. But Blau warns that sinistrality is not the cause of these abnormalities, not even a symptom of them. Instead, the fact that an antisocial individual may be left-handed may be a symptom of early childhood emotional negativism, which in turn may be the symptom of the underlying basic cause of his maladjustment, usually some emotional crisis due to parental or other social offense or neglect. There is probably more truth in the statement that man is as he is because things are as they are than in its opposite.

All left-handed people are not criminals, not even potential criminals. Neither are they all "unusual," "different," "queer," "screwballs," "freaks," "witches," or "bewitched." Most of them are "abnormal" only in the sense that 96 per cent of the "normal" population are right-handed. Sinistrality is a phenomenon about which there is still much to be learned. It will be up to the anthropologist, sociologist, psychologist, and folklorist of the future to discover more hidden truths and falsehoods about sinistrality.

1. In *The Oxford English Dictionary*, a "left-handed tongue" is one written from right to left, as Hebrew or Arabic.

2. As many other right-handed persons have done, I have met with considerable difficulty readjusting to exceptions to the above preceding statements. A Plymouth automobile has two wheels with lugs that tighten to the *left*. After about fifteen minutes of tremendous muscular exertion and some verbal exasperation, I found that I had been tightening instead of loosening the bolt, when I discovered the letter "L" stamped on it. And it took all of three weeks in England for me to become accustomed to left-lane traffic.

3. Among the different studies which I have encountered and which I shall cite later, this percentage varied from 2 to 13; but 4 per cent was the most often cited.

4. Authorities vary also here, giving from 10 to 30 per cent. Most seem to agree, however, that the percentage of abnormals who are left-handed is approximately three times greater than the percentage of normals who are left-handed.

5. The findings of these scientists are summarized by Abram Blau, *The Master Hand* (New York, 1946), pp. 57-60. The references cited are as follows: Sir Daniel Wilson, *The Right Hand: Left-Handedness* (New York, 1891); Gabriel de Mortillet, *Formations des Varietes, Albinisme et Gauchissement* (Paris, 1890); W. Johnson and W. Wright, *Neolithic Man in Northeast Surrey* (London, 1906); D. Brinton, "Left-handedness in North American Aboriginal Art," *American Anthropologist*, IX (1896), 175; Ira S. Wile, *Handedness, Right and Left* (Boston, 1934); Margaret Mead, *Growing Up in New Guinea* (New York, 1930); S. D. Porteus, *The Psychology of a Primitive People* (New York, 1931); D. Wilson, *Anthropology* (New York, 1885).

6. The same is true of *all* ranks. The lower ranking officer or enlisted noncommissioned officer always walks on the left.

7. Blau, p. 148.

8. Cf. Joseph Wright (ed.), *The English Dialect Dictionary* (New York, 1902), III, 569.

9. Cf. "left-handed" in Sir James A. H. Murray (ed.), *A New English Dictionary on Historical Principles* (Oxford, 1901). Unless otherwise indicated, quoted citations may be found in this reference.

10. Wright, III, 569.

11. From Salmon's *Gowodeau*, I, 90-91. Cf. Wright, III, 569.

12. *Merry Wives of Windsor*, II, ii, 25.

13. An analogy is perhaps in order at this point. A similar political principle seems to have obtained in the amphitheater of the French National Assembly of 1789, when the nobles still commanded sufficient respect to be granted honorable places to the right of the president. Of course, the radicals moved to the *left*, as far away from the nobles

as possible. What few moderates there were, were squeezed into the *center*. Thus, in their origins, these political terms were somewhat accidental. It is believed that Carlyle, in *The French Revolution* (1847), was perhaps the first to speak of "the extreme left." Derivatives like *leftist* and *left-wing* did not become generally current until after the application of Marxism about 1920. Cf. William Rose Benét, *The Reader's Encyclopedia* (New York, 1949), II, 622.

There is perhaps some linguistic analogy at work with these words: right/good as left/bad. Martin Agronsky once commented on the radio, during the height of the recent Senatorial investigations for subversives, that a new baseball term like "port field" would have to be substituted for "left field." The recent association of Communism with the term *left* is enough to taint it, but mere word analogies have perhaps even more potent ways of influencing emotionally charged words.

14. *Aeneid*, X, 773.

15. Cf. Clarence L. Barnhart, *New Century Cyclopedia of Names* (New York, 1954), III, 3361.

16. G. A. Gaskell (ed.), *A Dictionary of the Sacred Language of All Scriptures and Myths* (New York, 1924), p. 337.

17. Proverbial statements are often contradictory. John Florio wrote, in 1578, in *First Fruites*, "One hand washeth the other, and both the face." The contradiction here is only on the surface, as there is another underlying moral intended.

18. John A. MacCulloch, *The Mythology of All Races* (Boston, 1927), IV, 72-73.

19. *Ibid.*, IV, 67.

20. Sir James G. Frazer, *The Golden Bough* (London, 1922), III, 300.

21. Philip F. Waterman, *The Story of Superstition* (London, 1929), p. 107. According to Waterman, "The sanctity of the doorway is attested by a great number of customs and superstitions. There are special ways of crossing a threshold in order to do so auspiciously — for example, one should step over it with the right foot in place of the left, the reason being that, in the lore of superstition, the right side of the human body is frequently supposed to be more potent than the left."

22. Maria Leach, *Dictionary of Folklore, Mythology, and Legend* (New York, 1950), II, 644.

23. Frazer, III, 132.

24. The Greeks, whose seers always faced *north* for signs, considered omens from the left unlucky, for the same reason. It all depends upon the viewpoint. Cf. G. R. Crooks and C. F. Ingerslev, *A New Latin-English School-Lexicon* (Philadelphia, 1869). Reference is made here to "laevus" and "sinister." See also *The Natural History of Pliny*, translated by John Bostick and H. T. Riley (London, 1855), II, 85.

25. *The Oxford English Dictionary* gives this reference as *Vir. Mart.* IV, ii.

26. Incidentally, there is a reason given (which I have heard in Texas) that the engagement and wedding rings are always worn on the left hand because it is nearer the heart. For references concerning information in this paragraph, see the following: J. H. Breasted, *A History of Egypt* (New York, 1931); A. Erman, *Life in Ancient Egypt,* translated by H. M. Tirord (London, 1894); Ira S. Wile, *Handedness, Right and Left* (Boston, 1934). These are summarized by Blau, p. 65.

27. Christie Jeffries, "Are Left-Handed Teachers Handicapped?" *Education Digest*, X (January, 1945), 38.

28. Mary M. Wilcox Jones, "Relationship Between Reading Deficiencies and Left-Handedness," *School & Society*, LX (Oct. 7, 1944), 238-39.

29. Blau, p. 63.

30. Norbert Wiener, "Cybernetics," *Scientific American*, CLXXIX (Nov., 1949), 18. See also Kenneth L. Martin, "Handedness, a Review of the Literature of the History, Development, and Research of Laterality Preference," *Journal of Educational Research*, XLV (March, 1952), 527-33.

31. E. M. Daniels, "An Analysis of the Relation between Handedness and Stuttering," *Journal of Speech Disorders*, V (1940), 309.

32. Kenneth L. Martin, pp. 527-33.

33. Blau, p. 169.

34. *Ibid.*, pp. 182-83.

35. *Ibid.*, p. 88. Blau lists five such studies and their findings: C. Burt, *Mental and Scholastic Tests* (London, 1921); E. A. Doll, *Anthropometry as an Aid to Mental Diagnosis,* Publications No. 8, New Jersey Training School for Feeble-minded Girls and Boys, Vineland, N. J., 1916; H. H. Goddard, *Feeblemindedness* (New York, 1914); H. Gordon, "Left-handedness and Mirror Writing, Especially among Defective Children," *Brain*, XLIII (1921), 313; E. Stier, "Linkshändigheit, besonders in der Armee," *Deutsche Med. Wchnschr.*, XXXV (1909), 1587.

The Bury-Me-Not Theme in the Southwest

AMÉRICO PAREDES

IN "Bury Me Not on the Lone Prairie" the dying cowboy begs his friends not to bury him in unconsecrated ground. He wants to lie in the churchyard of his own town, not on the wind-swept plains, where the buffalo and the coyotes will disturb his grave. The song is a cowboy version of an English tune, "The Ocean Burial." But "The Ocean Burial," it would seem, is not solely responsible for the presence of the bury-me-not motif in the ballads of the Southwest. The same theme is found among another people who also inhabit southwestern United States, the people who gave the American cowboy his working gear, his cowpony, and much of his professional vocabulary.

The importance attached to burial in holy ground stems from medieval European customs. No one could be buried in consecrated ground except with the service of the church, and this office was refused to excommunicated persons, to people guilty of notorious crimes, to unbaptized persons, and to persons against whom a verdict of *felo-de-se* had been found. So the right to be buried in the churchyard of his own village must have been highly valued by the medieval European. Conversely, being buried in unconsecrated ground was a form of punishment, entailing serious consequences in one's after-life.

In songs such as "Bury Me Not on the Lone Prairie" and "The Ocean Burial" the dying man apparently has every right to be buried in his own churchyard. But he dies far from home and cannot be granted his wish. Not so in the bury-me-not ballads of the Spanish-speaking peoples of the Southwest. In these the dying man says, "Bury me not in holy ground." The motif is treated in a diametrically opposite spirit.

The bury-me-not-in-holy-ground motif is at least four hundred years old in the Spanish-speaking tradition. Coming to the New World from Spain, it is found throughout Spanish America, from Argentina to New Mexico. It was propagated by means of a Spanish *romance* which is dated as of the sixteenth century, "El Mal de Amor" ("Love Sickness"). In the *romance* a little shepherd goes along a mountain side, his coat wet with tears. He is dying of a broken heart because his love is not returned. He does not wish to lie in holy ground.

Adiós, adiós, compañeros,	Farewell, farewell boys,
las alegrías de antaño.	And the joys of yesteryear.
Si me muero deste mal	If I die of this malady
no me enterréis en sagrado;	Bury me not in holy ground;
no quiero paz de la muerte,	I want no peace in death
pues nunca fuí bien amado;	For I never was beloved;
enterréisme en prado verde,	Bury me in the green meadow
donde paste mi ganado,	Where my flocks graze,
con una piedra que diga:	With a headstone saying,
"Aquí murió un desdichado . . ."	"Here lies an unhappy wretch."

The lines became quite popular and seem to have been introduced wherever a singer forgot the ballad he was singing, especially if it served to heighten the effect of a dying scene. Thus we find desperadoes, dying queens, unfaithful wives about to be murdered by their husbands, and lovers slain by their rivals — all asking not to buried in holy ground but in a green meadow where the cattle graze. In a Portuguese ballad, "El Romance del Conde Preso" ("The Captive Count"), the hero wishes to be buried in the green meadow where the villagers do their marketing, with his head sticking out of the grave.

Whether the detail of the head in "El Romance del Conde Preso" is to be taken seriously or in jest is hard to determine.[1] But this particular version came to be regarded as comic and passed into the *relaciones* or humorous ballads. In "Don Gato"

the cat dies and is buried in a green meadow where the cattle
graze. His head sticks out of the ground, the hair very neatly
combed. "Don Gato" found its way to Spanish America, where it
is one of the best known of the *relaciones*.

But the bury-me-not motif also came to America in other,
more serious ballads. There is evidence that it arrived early,
and that it spread at an early date to those remote parts of New
Spain that are now the American Southwest. In New Mexico the
"no-me-entierren" motif is found in its pastoral form, side by
side with variations which appear to be native to Spanish
America. Aurelio Espinosa has collected a ballad in New Mexico
which says,

Chiquita, si me muriere	Love, if I should die,
no me entierres en sagrado;	Bury me not in holy ground,
entiérrame en campos verdes,	Bury me in green fields
donde me pise el venado . . .[2]	Where the deer may step on me.

From California Espinosa has a fragment on the same theme.

Entiérrenme en campos rasos,	Bury me in bare fields
donde me pise el ganado.[3]	Where the cattle may trample me.

Here the green meadows have become bare fields, and the
lonely grave will be trampled upon by the hooves of cattle.
These last appear to be American variations on the old Spanish
theme.

For the motif had been taken up by the vaquero of Mexico
and the gaucho of South America, who often found their graves
on the lonely *llanos*, far from churchyards. For them the formal
language of the Spanish ballad acquired new meaning. The
lonely graves on the prairie, especially those on the Kansas
Trail, must have affected the American cowboy in a similar
way. But the vaquero and the gaucho, following the little shepherd who was both their artistic and their professional ancestor,
sang about wanting to be buried on the prairie.

Death on the horns of a bull was an occupational hazard; so
the cause of death was changed from a broken heart (or some

comic mishap, as when Don Gato falls off the roof or Don Coyote dies from the toothache) to goring. Besides being in unconsecrated ground, the grave would be trampled by cattle. In many versions, often in the best ones, the green meadow also disappears. In "El Hijo Desobediente," the Mexican ballad about Felipe the Disobedient Son, the grave is in the wild, lonely badlands, as befits the grave of one accursed.

In adding to the bury-me-not theme the motif of filial disobedience, Mexican balladry made the ultimate reason for death the punishment of sin. Filial disobedience is the main moral problem of Mexican ballads concerned with family relations. It is a sin that is usually washed in blood. In "El Hijo Desobediente" Felipe and another young man quarrel at branding time. As they threaten each other with their irons, Felipe's father arrives and attempts to calm his son. In language reminiscent of the Cid Felipe threatens to run his father through with his sword, though what a vaquero is doing with a sword the ballad does not explain.

Quítese de aquí, mi padre,	Stand out of the way, my father,
que estoy más bravo que un león;	I feel fiercer than a lion;
no vaya a sacar la espada	Or I may draw my sword
y le parta el corazón.	And run you through the heart.

Felipe's father curses him, and the curse works as curses always do in ballads. A black bull comes down from the mountain, a bull that had never before come down. He gores Felipe. In some variants the actual goring is discarded; we get the impression that Felipe is dying even as the black bull comes down the mountain. The black bull becomes a symbol through the elimination of the original climax.

After willing his possessions Felipe asks that he be buried in unconsecrated ground. There is a harking back to ballads like "El Romance del Conde Preso" in Felipe's request that his arm be left sticking out of the grave, clutching a gilded paper on which will be written his name and his crime.

A suggestion of the sense of sin and atonement which is so strong in "El Hijo Desobediente" is found in American cowboy songs such as "The Streets of Laredo" and "Bury Me Out on the Prairie," in which the young man asks to be buried in the green valley or on the prairie because he has done wrong. On the other hand, there is at least one Spanish-language ballad which is closer to the spirit of the American cowboy songs than are the usual "no-me-entierren" ballads. In "El Corrido de Kiansis" the *caporal* returns to the Border and tells the mother of a vaquero that her son died on the Kansas Trail. She replies that her son's body must not remain on the prairie.

Vaya ustéd y traígame a mi hijo,	Go and bring back my son,
que no lo he visto llegar,	I have not seen him arrive;
y llevarlo al camposanto	We must take him to the
donde lo quiero enterrar.	churchyard,
	Where I want to bury him.

It seems then that the two bury-me-not traditions in the Southwest, arriving from different directions but having a common source in medieval Europe, have inevitably crossed paths and, existing side by side, have reacted upon one another. It is not strange that the Mexican vaquero and the American cowboy should have found some things in common when both rode the Kansas Trail. Not the least must have been the thought of death and of burial far from the rites of their religions. The lonely graves along the trail would have been frequent reminders of that.

1. There are, however, traditional songs of Albania and Serbia in which an immured woman asks that her breast be left out of the wall so she may suckle her child. See Stavro Skendi, *Albanian and South Slavic Oral Epic Poetry* ("Memoirs of the American Folklore Society," XLIV [Philadelphia, 1954]).

2. Aurelio M. Espinosa, "Romancero Nuevomejicano," *Revue Hispanique*, XXXIII (April, 1915), 479-80.

3. Aurelio M. Espinosa, "Los romances tradicionales en California," *Homenaje Ofrecido a Menéndez Pidal* (Madrid: Librería y Casa Editorial Hernando, S.A., 1925), I, 312.

Cante Jondo and Flamenco in Andalusia and Hispano-America

WALTER STARKIE

Tengo un dolor no sé donde,
Nacido no sé de qué;
Sanaré yo no sé cuando,
Si me cura no sé quién.
—Andalusian Folk Poem

IN *Travels through Spain in the Years 1775-1776* by Henry Sinebourne, published in Dublin in 1779, there is an interesting reference to a Gypsy dance called *Manguindoy*, which he saw performed by Gypsies near Cádiz. "Among the gypsies there is a dance called the *Manguindoy* which is so indecent that it has been forbidden under severe penalties. This dance and likewise the *Fandango* have been introduced from Havannah and are apparently of negro origin." The word *Manguindoy* comes from the Caló words *manguindó* and *manguindoñé*, which are used for Gypsy beggars of both sexes. Thus *Manguindoy* is a begging dance, which the Gitana dances for the stranger in order to extract some *parné* or money from him. I have seen the Gitanas in the caves of Guadix or Benalua de Guadix dance a similar lascivious begging dance which is exactly as described by the celebrated eighteenth-century traveler. This dance was in what the Gypsies call *Zorongo* style and was danced by the girl with exaggerated *zarandeo* or undulation which they compare to the *cernedor* or grain-sifter.[1] I had seen the same kind of dancing among the dancing girls of Tetuan, Tunis, and Kairwan. It is, however, essentially Gypsy, for in Rumania, Bulgaria, and Macedonia among nomadic tribes I had seen the wild *Tanyana* danced by an old hag for the chief of the tribe as a

ritual of the full moon. I have described it in my book on
Hungary and Rumania, *Raggle-Taggle*. In the *Tanyana* the
dancer imparts so intense a vibratory movement to her hips
that she passes into a kind of trance and is possessed by the
duende or demon of the dance. The *Tanyana*, in spite of its
feelings and contortions, is part of a solemn ritual of the moon,
and the Gypsies watching it sing the song of the moon, a tribal
invocation to the God of Nature, celebrating the incestuous
union of the Moon-witch Goddess and her brother the Sun:

> The Men: Lado! Lado! Mroi Ganga!
>   (Leda! Leda! Be my refuge!)
> The Women: Pala! Pala! Mroi Pola!
>   (Sun! Sun! Be my pride!)[2]

The Gypsy, like the Jew and the Arab, was absorbed by
Andalusia, and there is no place in the world where the Romanichal found closer racial affinity than in the Tartessian land
which possesses the oldest civilization of the Mediterranean;
as a proof we find there the finest Gypsy type physically
and morally in the world. The Gypsy, moreover, has brought
customs of his own to Andalusia, such as fortunetelling from
the lines of the hands, which existed in Persia, but was lost
among the Arabs until reintroduced by the Gitanos. The Devil
of the Gypsies, *Beng*, is derived from *Bheka* (frog) in Sanskrit,
but probably the Romanichals were originally serpent wor-
shipers, for there is no doubt that they treat the reptile with
great respect and try to ward off its evil influence. The Andalusians have adopted this taboo so universally that if a stranger
does happen to mention the word *snake* in an Andalusian house
the company immediately exorcize its evil influence by calling
out, in chorus, "Lagarto!" ("Lizard!").

The Gypsy has accentuated the underlying melancholy of
the Andalusian, for whereas the Arab does not think of death,
and the Jew shuns using the word for it, the Gypsy revels in
talk about funerals, and always brings the subject of death into

his singing. In his *coplas* the old mother is waiting for news of the son who has been killed in the bull ring, or the jealous husband has knifed his young wife. The Gypsy singer is obsessed by the death theme, and it is strange to find the name *alegrías* (joys) given to a certain class of songs improvised in *Flamenco* style, which are full of the deepest sadness. The Gypsy, as the Spaniards would say, *tiene la alegría de estar triste* (rejoices in being sad). The Hungarians, who likewise are so susceptible to Gypsy improvisation when it is done by a *Cigany primás*, who plays to their face, say: *Sirva vigad a Magyár* (the Magyar revels in being sad).

Origin of Cante Jondo

Cante Jondo or "Deep Song," as its name suggests, is a song of deep sadness. It has been very well defined by the Spanish writer and Academician Federico García Sánchez as "the drama of humanity in chains." The words are the equivalent in Andalusian dialect to *Canto hondo*, song from the depths of humanity, song of the gaol and the brothel; that is to say, the song of the Gypsy pariahs who live on the fringe of human civilized society. The term was applied to the tribal singing of the Indian Gypsies who brought from the East a new musical style which was embodied in ancient Andalusian folksong.

Falla maintained that the Gypsy tribes who settled in Granada were those who introduced the new element into primitive Andalusian music called *Cante Jondo*. But he adds emphatically that *Cante Jondo* "was not created by any single one of the races which contributed to its development: it was a musical style growing out of an Andalusian foundation, which fused with Byzantine liturgical, Arab, and Gypsy elements."[3]

The term *Cante Jondo* was given to a group of Andalusian folksongs whose prototype, according to Falla, is the *Siguiriya Gitana,* from which other forms, such as the *Polo, Martinete, Debla, Caña,* and *Soleares,* are derived. Some experts like the Andalusian poet Carlos de Luna call the *Caña* or the *Debla* the grandmother of the *Cante Jondo*. The styles of song included in *Cante Jondo* must be distinguished from the more modern groups of lighter style called by the name *Flamenco*, which include *malagueñas, granadinas*, and *rondeñas*—special styles traditionally associated with Málaga, Granada, and Ronda, where there existed celebrated creators of Gypsified song.

Cante Jondo has analogies with types of melodies found in the East. The position of smaller intervals in the scale is not invariable, and their production depends upon the raising or lowering of the voice due to the expression given to the word sung. This leads to the alteration of four out of seven notes of the scale. Thus only three notes are fixed. There is also *portamento* of the voice, that is to say, a style of singing which produces infinite graduations of pitch between two notes. Another Gypsy element in *Cante Jondo* is the repetition of the same note to the point of obsession, accompanied by an *appoggiatura* from above and below. This, according to Falla, is characteristic of certain forms of enchantment.

The Gypsy Zambra

We should always remember that music for the Gypsy was forever part of a ritual. His *Zambra* is always a solemn performance, where there is gravity and melancholy as well as fierce gaiety and *joie de vivre*.

The word *Zambra* is the same as the Arabic *Sâmira*, which was used by the Moors for revelry by night or a party at which people told stories. It is used today, especially in the caves of the Sacro Monte at Granada, for a collective Gypsy dance. The Arabs were a carrying race and carried the music of Persia and Byzantium to Andalusia, and the celebrated singer and poet of Bagdad, Ziryab, nicknamed "the Blackbird of Song," became as famous in Cordoba at the court of the Emir Abder-rahmann II as he had been at the court of Harun al-Rashid. Cordoba and Seville became the two great centers of literature and music under the triumphant Moors, and there was a saying that when a writer died he bequeathed his books to Cordoba, and when a musician died he donated his music instruments to Seville.

According to Rafael Mit Jana there were two kinds of music among the Moors in Spain, cultivated music called *Alah* and popular, lighter music called *Qrihah*. The compositions in *Alah* style were so complicated and full of arabesques that only virtuosos could sing them. Those of *Qrihah* style were scorned by the artists and "highbrows" and were fit for drunken revelers and frivolous women.

The music of Moorish Spain after the final expulsion of the Moors from Granada in 1492 was preserved by the exiled race in North Africa in Tetuan, Xauen, and today those ancient songs celebrating the beauties of the Alhambra in the days of Muza and Boabdil are still called *nuba ghernata*—music of Granada. The word *nuba* means a suite of short songs and instrumental pieces that resembles in structure the European suites of Corelli, Bach, and other composers. The Moslem suite possesses significant parallels to the classic suite: its *daira* or prelude, its instrumental overture, its melodies in slow tempo followed by faster rhythmic tunes and by its rapid finale are equivalent to the Prelude, Allemande, Saraband, Minuet, and Giga in Bach.[4]

The Moslem and the European suites keep the same keys and develop in the same way, alternating slow and rapid pieces, but their difference lies in the fact that the classic suite is purely instrumental, whereas the Moslem suite consists of singing and dancing. In the past, however, in the Western countries vocal music was combined with dancing and wandering minstrels who used to perform with dancers and singers. With the Moslems, however, there always existed a rigid conservative tradition which dominated their music as well as their lives ever since the far off days when the minstrels sang in the Alhambra or the Albaicín at Granada. The Moslems associate music with magic, and in their gatherings each individual associates the words and melody of each song with the hours of the day and the season of the year. A Moorish concert lasts many hours, from midday until the following morning. During that time many Moorish *nubas* are performed before an audience of ecstatic *aficionados*. So strong is the symbolic and magic significance of this music called *nuba ghernata* that there are certain sects who are devoted to these musical songs, in spite of the prejudices of the orthodox Moslems who disapprove of them.

Gypsy Music Styles

The variety of styles of song in *Cante Jondo* and *Flamenco* music is bewildering: to find a parallel, we have to turn to Indian music, in which the Hindus associate music with every season of the year.

Music was divided into *Rāgs* which were special melodies, and the word *rāg* according to Fox-Strangeways meant "color or emotion," and it was customary to illustrate it by a *Rāgmāla* or picture of the subject of the music.[5]

Flamenco

Now that we have considered the words *Cante Jondo*, let us explain the word *Flamenco*, which expresses an essential element of Andalusia. Some used to say that the word meant "Flemish" and was applied originally to the band of Flemish courtiers who accompanied the Emperor Charles V when he came to Spain. The word was used in a scornful sense of the nomad bands of Gypsies, who had come from Germany, and the people called these Oriental wanderers Germans and Flemings. Rodriguez Marín says that the word was applied to the Gypsies because by their physical appearance (slender legs and prominent buttocks) and bright-colored garments they resembled the flamingo. A third interpretation derives the word from a compound Arabic word, *fallah-mengu*, which signifies "peasant in flight," and the word was applied to the Gypsies, because the people believed that they were descended from the expelled Moors. A recent interpretation by the Arabist Patrocinio Barriuso derives *Flamenco* from two Arabic words, *fellah* and *mangu*. *Fellah* means "husbandman" and *mangu* means "to sing." *Flamenco* thus would mean the singing of the country people, that is to say folksong.[6]

Flamenco then came to be used of the music played and sung by those who imitate Gypsy manners, and the word began to cause a furor in Spain in the days of 1876 when the first production of the opera *Carmen* with Bizet's tawny, sensuous music made Gypsified fashion the rage. Any piece of music vaguely resembling *Cante Jondo* or possessing a touch of Gypsy about it was called *Flamenco,* and the word today is applied to anything that is bright or vivacious.[7]

When considering the Gypsy element in Andalusian music we must remember that the Gypsy does not create—he perpetuates. The Gypsy arrived in South Spain as a foreign wanderer and he absorbed the music of the Andalusian and sang, played, or danced it, adding his own peculiarities and idiosyncrasies. The difference between the singing of the Gypsy and the genuine Andalusian is that the Gypsy does not let the note prolong itself, but interrupts and amputates it. The Andalusians describing this peculiarity say, "Los Gitanos muerden el cante" ("The Gypsies bite the song"). The words as sung by the *Gitano* trip over one another and accentuate the fierce individualism of the Romanichal.

The Jewish Influence

The influence of the Jews must be added to that of the Arabs, for there is an exact parallel between the two philosophers who symbolize the two Oriental cultures—Averroës the Moor and Maimonides the Jew.

The Sephardic Jews considered as "Deep Song" those melodies which they could sing in their synagogue without fear of the Inquisition. According to Medina Azara the songs were sung on Jewish feast days, and the word for feast day in

Hebrew is *Jom Tob* (good day), and this popular pronuncia-
tion became *Jondo*.[8] Thus what today is called *Cante Jondo*
was in Jewish language "Festival Song," and the people who
sang it were believed to be the cantors or singers in the
synagogue.

Some Spanish musicologists, such as my friend García
Matos, deny the influence of the Sephardic or Spanish Jews on
the music of *Cante Jondo* and *Flamenco,* but I myself have had
many opportunities of hearing the Jews sing their traditional
Spanish songs in such places as Rhodes, Salonica, and Constan-
tinople, and I was struck by the similarity these songs have
to *Flamenco* music.

In a comparison of the Gypsy singing of South Spain with
Moslem and Jewish singing in the East of Europe, it is important to note the strange ritualistic cry *ay-ay* repeated again and
again against the frenzied accompaniment on the guitar. It
produces on me the effect of a keener's wail. When I was in
Yugoslavia among Gypsies I heard some of those from the Moslem region near Mostar and Sarajevo sing primitive songs
accompanied by the one-stringed *gusla* wherein the singer cried
out *oy-oy* repeatedly before beginning the song. Then he concluded the song with the same cry of *oy-oy*.[9]

Gypsy Dancing

Many of the Gypsy singers in South Spain are also dancers,
for singing leads to dancing in the *juerga* or spree. Just as in
the case of the Hungarian, the Rumanian, or the Russian Gypsy
performer, in Spain the members of the *Cuadro Flamenco*
sing one song after another full of melancholy. The *Martinetes*
and the *Siguiriyas* are full of descriptions of gaols, *crimes pas-
sionels,* and vendettas. After singing such songs, the dancer
parodies the melancholy of the singer.

The characteristic *Baile Gitano* which one may see in the
caves at Granada, the home of the Gypsy dance, is a tragi-
comedy. At one moment it is comic and at another tragic; at

times it is classical in its grace, and at another it is grotesque.
It is more intense and wilder than the ordinary Andalusian
dance. One may see the Gypsy dancers in all their "abandon"
at the "wakes" and baptismal and marriage feasts which the
Romanichals hold in the caves. The dancing of the Spanish
Gypsies always reminds me of the Gypsy dancing I have seen
in the East of Europe.

In this alternation of the tragic and the comic, as in the
Oriental dances, great importance is given to graceful movements of hands and arms. The whole performance develops
according to a ritual—a combination of playing, singing, and
dancing in which the audience take part. The cries of *ole* from
the audience animate the performer to produce rapid undula-
tions of his body and stimulate him to give himself entirely
up to the spirit of the rhythmic orgy. Watch the Gypsy girl:
she in her turn is possessed by the demon—the *duende,* who, as
the Gypsies say, has entered her body through the soles of her
feet. She is like one in a trance, and her golden skin has faded a
shade paler. The rhythm of hand-clapping (*palmas sordas*)
and of finger-cracking (*pitos*) has hypnotized her into magic
movement: her nostrils are dilated. She is a writhing column of
fire, a marble Aphrodite suddenly springing to life. The audience shouts *ole* and *Faraona,* for to them she is Pharaoh's
daughter.

The Gypsy Guitar

Meanwhile the Gypsy guitar player has his ear cocked,
ready to catch the slightest "nuance" of the singer, and with
his eyes half closed in his masklike face he is a sculptural figure.
His *sonanta* (as the Gypsy calls the guitar) seems to shadow
the voice of the *cantaor,* underlying with its mellow chords
the harsh Gypsy tone, and embellishing the pauses with rapid
interjections played *punteado.* He produces melody and harmony on his instrument: at one moment he makes it sound like
an organ in a distant church, at another he caresses the instrument lazily and languidly suggests the *Zambra* in the garden

of a Moorish harem; then with rhythmic tapping he leads into a harsher tribal music, following in the wake of the fairy trail laid by the Gypsy singer who is now "biting the song," as the *Calés* say in Triana, in a male voice full of rugged fierceness *(una voz machuna de temple brusco)*. And while the singer forces the notes higher and higher toward the climax, his partner, with his guitar, produces a metallic tone similar to that of the singer, and when the latter's voice falters or his inspiration begins to flag, the guitarist broadens out into a bewildering series of *falsetas* or variations; for his function is like that of the czimblaon player in Hungary who, according to Liszt, supplies the rhythm, indicates the acceleration or slackening of time. So close is the relationship between the singer of Andalusian music and the guitarist that the guitar has been called the "conscience of Andalusia." It is the guitarist who creates the atmosphere for the singer and the background which enables him to find scope for inspiration. He can produce both melody and harmony from his instrument and, even if he is a poor Gypsy guitarist in a tavern, he has his own rhapsodic style which he plays according to tradition.[10]

The Zambras *in the Caves*

The Gypsy *Zambra* in the caves at Granada has an ancient history, for it goes back to the days at the end of the fifteenth century when Ferdinand and Isabel captured the Alhambra. During the Eucharistic procession that was held on Corpus Christi after 1492, it was customary for the Moorish population of the city to dance their *Zambras* in the streets in honor of the feast. Then Gypsy dances, and dances from other provinces of Spain, were performed after the religious procession. These dances became very elaborate in the sixteenth and seventeenth centuries.

In the eighteenth century Charles III, after prohibiting in 1765 the *Autos Sacramentales*, or religious allegorical plays that were performed on Corpus Christi, also vetoed the dances in the processions on that day. Nevertheless it was the same King Charles III who in 1763 had introduced a new law whereby the Gypsies became "New Castilians" and settled down in the cities and town, adopting the habits of sedentary people. And as they were famed throughout Andalusia for their skill in dancing, they contributed to the creation in the eighteenth century of what is known in the world as Spanish musical style. It was in the second half of the eighteenth century when the popular spirit with its racial traditions, which Spaniards sum up in the significant word *casticismo* (genuine or true to caste), became consecrated in the short musical play-type known as the *tonadilla*.

The *tonadillas* (miniature operettas that took twenty minutes to perform) with their street cries, folksongs, and tavern Gypsy dances, were the musical counterpart of the sparkling one-act *sainetes* of Ramón de la Cruz which portrayed the Madrid of Goya.

The Gypsies now began to dance in the taverns of the cities and in the courtyards of palaces the *Fandango, Manguindoy,* and other old Spanish dances which had been imported into Cádiz from Havana and Cartagena de las Indias. In those later years of the eighteenth century, too, the bullfight was emerging into its present position as the national spectacle of the country with its hosts of *aficionados* drawn from the humble as well as from the wealthier classes. In 1796 there appeared *The Art of Bullfighting* by the celebrated matador Pepe Hillo, who, according to the poets, used his sword as pen and dipped it in the bull's blood rather than in ink to write his treatise. Pedro Romero, Pepe Hillo, Costillares, and their followers became, like the ten rulers of Plato's Atlantis, the creators of a caste devoted to the cult of the sacred bulls.

And this caste system with its innumerable ramifications, which is summed up by the significant word *castizo,* included the Gypsies, who brought to the art of bullfighting qualities analogous to those they displayed in singing, guitar playing, and dancing. With their lithe elegance, their swiftness, their intuitive knowledge of animals, and their courageous skill in an emergency, they soon became past masters in this national art, as well as in all the arts that are included in the word *Flamenco,* which has puzzled scholars and folklorists for the past hundred and fifty years.

It is significant that the Gypsies have preserved customs and art forms which the Andalusians themselves had forgotten. Many of the ancient dances did not disappear but were preserved under other names, and the Gypsy was instrumental in maintaining the *castizo* or genuine tradition.

Take as an example the *Bolero,* which was not an old dance, for it only goes back to the middle of the eighteenth century, the period of the *tonadilla.* The *Bolero,* however, is a variant of the ancient *Seguidillas,* and its invention was attributed by some authorities to a man of noble stock from La Mancha, the home of *Seguidillas,* Sebastian Cerezo, and by others to a Sevillian coachman, Antón Boliche. What the inventor did was to adapt to the rhythm of the *Bolero* many of the attractive elements from the old *Fandango, Bolo,* and *Tirana.* It was even said that in the *Bolero* could be found traces of the *Chacona* of Lope de Vega's day.

Our main authority on all folklore and dances in those formative years of the early nineteenth century is Serafín Estébanez Calderón (El Solitario), whose *Escenas Andaluzas* is a mine of information. Much of the information acquired by Prosper Mérimée for his works on Spain was derived from Estébanez Calderón, who was a patient and long-suffering guide, philosopher, and friend of the author of *Carmen.*

El Solitario tells us that even the *Zarabanda,* against which the church had so fiercely fulminated in the seventeenth century, was still sung and danced by Gypsies in South Spain under the name *Ole* and *Tirana.* The *Canto Andaluz,* he says, begins with the prolonged *Jípios* and *Ayes,* which rise and fall in unending sequence, but the singer "goes deep down," which

is an exact translation of the term *Cante Jondo.* As the singer,
he says, utters his *ay,* he moves his head and turns up his eyes,
as if he were following mentally not the measures of the music
but the undulating line of his cry. This undulating movement
contrasts with the Aragonese, who in his *Jota* takes up a fixed
attitude in front of his woman partner, for in the *Jota* we hear
the clash of arms, and we see, as the poet Salvador de Rueda
said, "the plumes and panoplies of war." Estébanez Calderón
stresses the dignity of the Andalusian Gypsy dances, which show
off the performer and seem to say to us, "I am strong, I am
agile and I have charm."

The Influence of America on Andalusian Music

Estébanez Calderón is most insistent that originally there
was no sensuality or suggestiveness in the *Baile Flamenco,*
and the genuine Gypsy performed the dances as though they
were part of an ancient religious rite. But the Andalusian dance
changed in America, and the national tendencies were exaggerated in the exciting milieu of Cartagena de las Indias or in
Cuba, when the Spaniards came into contact with the exotic
dances of the colored peoples. Then when the Spanish dancers
returned to Andalusia, their dancing reflected the American
influence by a double exaggeration, stressing on the one hand
the languid passiveness of the individual dancer in an exciting milieu, and, on the other, intensifying what was originally
only a slight tendency to eroticism in the Andalusian dance.

When we read Estébanez Calderón's warnings against the
American corruption which crept into *Flamenco* dancers in
1838, can we wonder if today, over a hundred years later, it is
difficult for an *aficionado* to discover a *Gitana* who will perform
for him the genuine *Baile Jondo* (Deep Dance) that corresponds in dancing to *Cante Jondo* (Deep Song)?

The Deep Dance springs from that primitive but exclusive
refinement which we find in ancient races like the Andalusians
and the Indian Romany. It is individual and it corresponds to

the subconscious desire of the *Gitana* to create for herself a new world of sensations. It shows the passionate violence of desert dwellers, the desolate mysticism of the Jew, the sensuousness of the Arab, and finally the pantheistic religion of the Gypsy.

The *Gitana* who has been in contact with the American populations for generations loses her ascetic qualities and becomes languid and self-indulgent, and in order to cast her spell over audiences that respond more easily to the direct primitiveness of the Negro dancing, she is forced to exaggerate and even deform the dances that were her patrimony as *Faraona,* Pharaoh's daughter.

In Spain the singer of *Cante Jondo* and the dancer perform for an ecstatic audience of *aficionados,* people who understand the real thing. These are bitter critics and refuse to accept what is not pure and genuine in style. They disapprove of performances given to large audiences in great cities and they prefer to retire to some tavern on the banks of the Guadalquivir with its wooden partitions where they may share a bottle of Manzanilla with the artists.

After a long interval of expectancy, which sometimes may last for hours, the singer, the guitarists, and the dancer discover the *duende* that will enable them to give free rein to their inspiration and express the rare essence that still survives in the pure art form called *Cante Jondo.*

As Manuel Maschado, the king of *aficionados,* said of Andalusia:

> Cádiz salada claridad; Granada
> agua oculta que llora;
> Romana y mora, Córdoba callada:
> Málaga cantaora;
> Almería dorada:
> Plateado Jaén: Huelva,
> La orilla de las tres carabelas.

1. Walter Starkie, *Don Gypsy* (New York, 1936), pp. 313-14.
2. Starkie, *Raggle-Taggle* (New York, 1933), p. 247.

3. Manuel de Falla, *El Cante Jondo* (Granada, 1922).

4. Starkie, *Don Gitano* (Barcelona, 1944), pp. 66-67.

5. Starkie, "The Gypsies as Minstrels," *Journal of the Gypsy Lore Society,* Series III, vol. XII (1933), no. 2.

6. P. García Barriuso, *La Música Hispano-Musulmana en Marruecos* (Larache, 1941), p. 59.

7. Starkie, *In Sara's Tents* (New York, 1953), p. 93.

8. Medina Azara, "Cante Jondo y Cantares Sinagogales," *Revista de Occidente,* XXX (1930).

9. Starkie, "The Gypsy in Andalusian Folk-lore and Folk-Music," *Proceedings of the Musical Association,* session LXII, Nov. 15, 1935, London.

10. Starkie, "Cante Jondo, Flamenco and the Guitar," *Guitar Review,* no. 20, 1956.

The Personification of Animals in the *Relación* of Mexico

DONALD M. LANCE

Versos muy extravagantes
divertidos, fabulosos,
de reéir y pasar el rato
para todos los curiosos.

"VERY ODD VERSES, entertaining, fabulous, something to laugh about and pass the time, for all curious people": perhaps this was to be the ultimate role of ballads presenting animals speaking, marrying, and cavorting around as human beings. There is also, however, historical evidence that some of these ballads were composed (or first sung) for the express purpose of satirizing, or subtly portraying, the actions of certain real people.

The motif of the personification of animals in balladry in the Spanish language seems to occur primarily in one type of ballad. Vicente T. Mendoza calls this type the *romance de relación* or simply the *relación,* because it does not differ greatly from the *romance* of Spain or the *corrido* of Mexico yet does not fit exactly into either of these categories or other categories.

The principal difference between the *relación* and other ballads in Mexico and Spain is in literary style. The *relación,* often a parody, usually tells of fabulous and incredible actions, such as fantastic battles. The characters in the *relación* may be either human or nonhuman. The *relación* shares the narrative form of the *romance* but loses the austerity and sophistication of the *romance* in the presentation of its subject matter. In order for the *relación* to present these fantasies, it must be reduced in form to a simplicity of statement, a style with more lightness, grace, and freedom than other ballad types.

The *relación* does not appear to have existed prior to the seventeenth century. One of the first references to this ballad type was made by Serafín Estébanez Calderón, who predicted in his *Colección de Escritores Castellanos* in 1830 that the *relación,* like other Arab traditions, would gradually die out. How wrong he was is shown by the appearance of recently recorded *relaciones* in two books—*Cancionero Popular de Extremadura,* published in 1930 by Bonifacio Gil García, and *El Romance Español y el Corrido Mexicano,* published by Mendoza in 1935.

The *relación* originated in the western portion of Spain, mainly in the provinces of Castilla, Extremadura, and Andalusia, and was found in more abundance in the area surrounding the cities of Salamanca and Bajadoz and the Ronda and Alpujarra mountain ranges near the cities of Medina and Jerez. No approximate date is given by Mendoza for the traveling of the *relación* to Mexico. It appears in Mexico primarily in the area from Zacatecas to Oaxaca, probably having been brought into the territory through the port of Acapulco.

The personification of animals in ballads is briefly mentioned in various works on balladry of other cultures; however, the treatment is quite brief and is included as parts of other topics. While we may not draw definite conclusions from this fact, we should not be led to believe that this theme is of no consequence as a separate study in areas other than Spain and Mexico. Perhaps the theme did not exist to such an extent as others or did not live so long as it did in Mexico and Spain.

As has been noted, this motif in Mexico and Spain appears primarily in one certain type of ballad. This is not true in other areas.

William J. Entwistle states in *European Balladry* that the presentation of animal histories in ballads is peculiarly German and constitutes an important sector of the balladry of Germany and the lowlands of Europe. He found these stories more abundant in countries of German influence, such as Lusatia, Czechoslovakia, and Poland. Entwistle also points out that some ballads using this theme are "simple allegories, others are not so much parodies as etherealizations of human activity."

Entwistle also mentioned finding this motif in the Greek klephtic ballad. These ballads originated as chronicles of the *klephts,* or outlaws, in the Greek mountains during the period of Turkish domination over Greece in the sixteenth and seventeenth centuries. Many of these ballads would portray elements of nature helping the *klephts* in some way. In one of the ballads referred to by Entwistle, three partridges speak, telling of the chances had by a certain eagle, who in reality was a *klepht.*

In *A Book of Danish Ballads,* Axel Olrik mentions a Danish ballad of this type which originated in South Saelland about 1330 and which does seem to be based on historical facts. In the ballad a small bird sang his complaint to a linden tree. The bird was supposed to have been Sir Jens Due of Tessebölle, who was betrothed to Ann Nielsdatter. In the ballad a falcon comes and drives the small bird away. The falcon was reported to be the wealthy Falk of Vallö, whom the lady subsequently married.

In English and Scottish balladry many occasions are found in which animals or birds speak or act as human beings. In many cases the animals are actually people who have been transformed into animals by some supernatural agency—a fairy, the fairy queen, or a magician. These really should not be considered in the category of personified animals even though the beings are essentially animals at the time. There are as many ballads in which nonhuman beings actually act or speak as human beings, either to each other or to human beings, such as "The Three Ravens" or "The Twa Corbies," "The Carnal and the Crane," "The Bonny Birdy," "Broomfield Hill," "Lady Isabel and the Elf-Knight."

The animal personification motif is also found in many

ballads in the United States. Many of these were brought over from England; some are still in almost the same form and wording as the versions remaining in England. Arthur Loesser, in *Humor in American Songs*, gives American versions of three ballads that he lists as being in the Sourwood Mountain theme of American hillbilly folk ballads. The texts are still quite close to the British versions. The ballads are "Bird Song," "Barnyard Song," and "Froggie Went A-Courting." The last is also known as "The Gentleman Frog" in Great Britain. Loesser mentions several others that are considered American, the most popular of which is "The Boll Weevil Song."

However popular or significant these animal ballads may have been in their time and circumstances, their special meaning vanished as their time and sources grew more remote. Whether or not the ballads originally had personal, social, political, or other overtones, many of them lived on because of their entertaining nature.

Whether the use of animals in these ballads was or was not intended to be appealing primarily to children, many of them did ultimately become nursery songs. The fact that the *relación* has animals actually doing the acting may be the reason for their extreme popularity with children, Mendoza suggests. He cites Roderico Caro's statement in *Los Días Geniales* that in his time the children sang a particular animal ballad with much gusto and many laughs.

However seriously ballads personifying animals may be studied, there are those who do not consider them valid balladry. Referring to the *relación*, Merle S. Simmons states in *The Mexican Corrido* that "the significance of this group . . . is nil insofar as understanding the Mexican scene is concerned, but their value to a study of the Mexican *pueblo's* psychology would be considerable." Simmons' primary reason for not seriously studying them in relation to the *corrido* is that the ballad style is not essentially that of the *corrido*.

In reading and interpreting the *relaciones* printed in *El Romance Español y el Corrido Mexicano,* one finds many of them quite similar in content to various ballads, nursery songs, and game songs that are still heard in the United States.

Below are presented, with comments, translations of several of the *relaciones* about animals from *El Romance Español y el Corrido Mexicano.* These are not, by any means, all of the ballads using this theme, nor are they necessarily the most popular ones. Mendoza also included several fragments, which are not presented here. Those given below were chosen primarily for their relation to known American songs.

One of the *relaciones,* "La Rana," has an incremental lyric similar to that of "There's a Hole in the Bottom of the Sea." Although none was actually found, there may be some connection between the two ballads. The ballad in English has a frog on a log in the hole in the bottom of the sea; the ballad in Spanish has the frog singing under the water. "La Rana" comes from the Valley of Mexico and has been heard in Taxco, Mexico, as well.

Estaba la rana cantando debajo del agua;
cuando la rana se puso a cantar,
vino la mosca y la hizo callar.

> The frog was singing under the water.
> When the frog began to sing,
> The fly came and made it be quiet.

Callaba la mosca a la rana
que estaba cantando debajo del agua;
cuando la mosca se puso a cantar,
vino la araña y la hizo callar.

> The fly quieted the frog
> That was singing under the water;
> When the fly began to sing,
> The spider came and made it be quiet.

Callaba la araña a la mosca, la mosca a la rana
que estaba cantando debajo del agua;
cuando la araña se puso a cantar,
vino la araña y la hizo callar.

The spider quieted the fly, the fly the frog
That was singing under the water;
When the spider began to sing,
The rat came and made it be quiet.

In subsequent verses are added the cat, the dog, the stick, the fire, the water, the bull, the knife, the man, and finally:

Callaba el hombre al cuchillo, el cuchillo al toro, el toro al agua,
el agua al fuego, el fuego al palo, el palo al perro,
el perro al gato, el gato al ratón, el ratón a la araña,
la araña a la mosca, la mosca a la rana
que estaba cantando debajo del agua;
cuando el hombre se puso a cantar,
vino su suegra y le hizo callar.

The man quieted the knife, the knife the bull, the bull the water,
The water the fire, the fire the stick, the stick the dog,
The dog the cat, the cat the rat, the rat the spider,
The spider the fly, the fly the frog
That was singing under the water;
When the man began to sing,
His mother-in-law came and made him be quiet.

Another equally interesting ending which was related is:

. . . y cuando yo me pongo a cantar,   And when I begin to sing,
ningún desgraciado me viene a callar.   No wretch comes to quiet me.

Professor Mendoza says that the predecessor to this ballad may be the following song which he obtained from *Cantos Populares Españoles* by Francisco Rodríguez Marín, from Spain:

Ésta es la bota   This is the bottle
que buen vino porta   That brings good wine
de Cádiz a Rota.   From Cádiz to Rota.

Aquí está el tapón   Here is the stopper
que tiene la bota   That is on the bottle
que buen vino porta   That brings good wine
de Cádiz a Rota.   From Cádiz to Rota.

Éste es el cordón
que amarró el tapón
que tiene la bota
que buen vino porta
de Cádiz a Rota.

Aquí está el ratón
que royó el cordón
que amarró el tapón
que tiene la bota
que buen vino porta
de Cádiz a Rota.
etc. . . etc. . .

This is the cord
That fastened the stopper
That is on the bottle
That brings good wine
From Cádiz to Rota.

Here is the rat
That gnawed the cord
That fastened the stopper
That is on the bottle
That brings good wine
From Cádiz to Rota.

Besides ballads like these using incremental repetitions, there are songs utilizing the opposite effect, a diminishing one. Many schools still make use of "Ten Little Indians" as an exercise in counting. A *relación* with a similar effect is listed by Mendoza as being a traditional song of Mexico: "Los Diez Perritos" ("The Ten Little Dogs"). The predecessors to this *relación* seem to be combinations of counting exercises and medical remedies for the cure of bubos, or glandular swellings. These were found in Portugal. Only the titles were translated into Spanish by Mendoza—"Fórmulas para la cura de los Bubones" ("Formula for the Cure of Bubos"), "Las Nueve Glándulas Hermanas" ("The Nine Glandular Sisters"), and "El Bubón y sus Nueve Hijas" ("The Bubo and His Nine Daughters").[1] The version from Mexico:

Yo tenía diez perritos
y uno se murió en la nieve,
ya nomás me quedan nueve,
nueve, nueve, nueve, nueve.

De los nueve que tenía
uno se comió un bizcocho,
ya nomás me quedan ocho,
ocho, ocho, ocho, ocho.

De los que quedaban
uno se clavó un tranchete,
ya nomás me quedan siete,
siete, siete, siete, siete.

I used to have ten little dogs
And one died in the snow;
Now I have left only nine.
Nine, nine, nine, nine.

Of the nine that I had
One ate a biscuit;
Now I have left only eight.
Eight, eight, eight, eight.

Of those that I had left
One was cut up by a heel knife;
Now I have left only seven.
Seven, seven, seven, seven.

De los siete que quedaban
uno se quemó los pies,
ya nomás me quedan seis,
seis, seis, seis, seis.

Of the seven that I had left
One's feet burned up;
Now I have left only six.
Six, six, six, six.

De los seis que me quedaban
uno se mató de un brinco
ya nomás me quedan cinco,
cinco, cinco, cinco, cinco.

Of the six that I had left
One killed himself in a leap;
Now I have left only five.
Five, five, five, five.

De los cinco que me quedaban
uno se cayó de un teatro,
ya nomás me quedan cuatro,
cuatro, cuatro, cuatro, cuatro.

Of the five that I had left
One fell off a theater;
Now I have left only four.
Four, four, four, four.

De los cuatro que me quedaban
uno se volteó al revés,
ya nomás me quedan tres,
tres, tres, tres, tres.

Of the four I had left
One turned upside down;
Now I have left only three.
Three, three, three, three.

De los tres que me quedaban
uno se murió de tos,
ya nomás me quedan dos,
dos, dos, dos, dos.

Of the three that I had left
One died of a cough;
Now I have left only two.
Two, two, two, two.

De los dos que me quedaban
uno se murió de ayuno,
ya nomás me quedan uno,
uno, uno, uno, uno.

Of the two that I had left
One died of hunger;
Now I have left only one.
One, one, one, one.

Y ese uno que quedaba
se lo llevó la tostada,
ahora ya no tengo nada,
nada, nada, nada, nada.

And that one that I had left,
He went to the devil;
Now I have none.
None, none, none, none.

The third *relación* which is a kind of exercise suggests the type of song often heard among the undergraduates of colleges in the eastern part of the United States, in particular "Sing Me Another One." The singer sings a rather ridiculous verse, and the rest of the group joins in the refrain. The *relación* which Professor Mendoza included is entitled "Los Animales" ("The Animals"). The version below comes from the state of Aguascalientes; another version was collected in the state of Guanajuato. The refrain is simply the single line "¡Ay, eso si es verdad!" ("Ah, that certainly is true!") and is given between each of the verses.

Yo vide una poblanita	I have seen a little Puebla girl
que salió de una barranca	Who came out of a ravine
con su vestido amarillo	Wearing her yellow dress
y su zapatilla blanca.	And her little white shoes.
Yo vide una garrapata	I have seen a tick
tejer una servilleta	Weave a napkin,
y yo me encontré un zancudo	And I met a mosquito
apretando una carreta	Pulling a cart.
Con las costillas de un piojo	With the ribs of a flea
tengo que formar un puente	I have to make a bridge,
y por el pico de un gallo	And over the beak of a rooster
tiene que pasar la gente.	The people have to pass.
Ví un sapo con botines	I saw a toad wearing leggings
que iba a montar a caballo,	That was riding a horse;
también ví pasar un gallo	I also saw a rooster go by
unciendo dos jabalines.	Yoking two javalinas.
Yo vide una mariposa	I have seen a butterfly
con sus dientes de marfil,	With its teeth of ivory.
le conté más de tres mil	I counted more than three thousand
aparte de los colmillos.	Except for the fangs.
Allá en la barranca blanca	There in the white ravine
mataron un español,	A Spaniard was killed.
le echaron las tripas fuera	They took out his intestines
y ¡Alabado sea el Señor!	And, Praised be the Lord!
Yo vide una chiva prieta	I have seen a black goat
en su silla bien sentada	Seated comfortably in her chair
con la pierna bien cruzada	With her legs well crossed
y a la sombra de un laurel.	And in the shade of a laurel.

A theme that appears in animal ballads in several countries is the marriage of animals. The most widely known animal marriage balled in the United States and Great Britain probably is "Froggie Went A-Courting." Entwistle also mentions five ballads about animal marriages in Germany.[2] Mendoza presents two *relaciones* with this theme—"El Casamiento del Piojo y la Pulga" ("The Wedding of the Flea and the Louse") and

"El Casamiento del Huiltacoche" ("The Wedding of the Huiltacoche").

"El Casamiento del Huiltacoche" is included not so much for its musical structure as for its literary background. This particular ballad can be traced back to the province of Extremadura, Spain. The version given below is that collected in the state of Michoacan, Mexico.[3] No translation has been found for the word *huiltacoche,* but a reference to a *huiltacoche* in the *relación* "Versos muy Extravagantes" indicates that it is some kind of bird.

— Hoy se casa el Huiltacoche
con una urraca famosa. —
Le dijo al madrugador
el pájaro ruiseñor
y el Huiltacoche agregó
cuando encontró al chuparrosa:
— Quiero que me hagas favor
de ir a conocer mi esposa. —

Estaban en el estrado
cuando llegó el zopilote,
con su sombrero de lado,
pidiéndoles un cigarro,
no dado sino comprado
y hasta se quitó el sombrero
y dijo a su compañero:
— Hoy se casa el Huiltacoche. —

Estaban en las tortillas
cuando llegó el aguililla,
y en companía de la ardilla
le dijo a la chuparrosa:
— Yo no he sido escandalosa
y por donde quiera he andado,
si quieres, vamos al monte. —
Y allá le dijo el zinzontle:

— Hoy se casa el Huiltacoche. —

La tonina toca el harpa
y el jilguero el clarión;
la tonina que bien canta,

"Today Huiltacoche marries
A famous magpie,"
Said the nightingale
To the early riser.
And Huiltacoche added
When he met the hummingbird,
"I want you to do me the favor
Of meeting my wife."

They were in the drawing room
When the turkey buzzard arrived
With his hat tilted to the side,
Asking them for a cigarette,
Not given but bought,
And he even took off his hat.
Then he said to his companion,
"Today Huiltacoche marries."

They were eating
When the chicken hawk arrived
And in the company of the squirrel
Said to the hummingbird,
"I have not been bad
Wherever I have traveled;
If you like, let's go to the woods."
And there the mockingbird told
  him,
"Today Huiltacoche marries."

The dolphin plays the harp
And the linnet the horn.
The dolphin, who sings well,

borracha toda la noche,	Drunk the whole night long,
como iba a ser la madrina,	As she was going to be the bridesmaid.
hasta subió en el coche	She even climbed into the coach
y dijo a la golondrina:	And said to the swallow,
— Hoy se casa el Huiltacoche. —	"Today Huiltacoche marries."

The other animal marriage ballad presented by Mendoza
has six variations, each coming from a different state. Versions
of "El Casamiento del Piojo y la Pulga" were found in Zacatecas,
Veracruz, Mexico City, Querétaro, and Tamaulipas; and one
version was listed without its area of incidence. Each version
has essentially the same verse structure and similar situations.
The needs of the flea and the louse and the animals supplying
the needs vary from one version to another, but the story is
told in the same manner each time. A representative version is
the one from Zacatecas:

El piojo y la pulga se quieren casar	The flea and the louse want to get married,
y no se han casado por falta de pan.	And they haven't married for lack of bread.
— ¡Bendito sea Dios que todo tenemos!	"God be praised! We have everything
pero de harina, ¿'hora sí qué haremos?—	Except flour. Now, what shall we do?"
Contestó el borrego desde su corral:	Answered the lamb from his corral,
— Hágase las bodas yo doy un costal. —	"Have the wedding; I'll give a bag."
— ¡Bendito sea Dios que todo tenemos!	"God be praised! Now we have everything
pero de manteca, ¿'hora sí qué haremos?—	Except lard. Now, what shall we do?"
Contestó el cochino desde su corral:	Answered the hog from his pen,
— Hágase las bodas que manteca aquí hay.—	"Have the wedding; here is lard."
— ¡Bendito sea Dios que todo tenemos!	"God be praised! Now we have everything
pero de quien guise, ¿'hora sí qué haremos?—	Except the cook. Now, what shall we do?"

Dijo la gallina desde su corral:
— Hágase las bodas que yo iré a guisar. —
— ¡Bendito sea Dios que todo tenemos!
pero de quien sople, ¿hora sí qué haremos?—

Contestó el jicote desde su panal:
— Hágase las bodas que yo iré a soplar. —
— ¡Bendito sea Dios que todo tenemos!
pero de padrino, ¿'hora sí qué hacer?—

Contestó el ratón entono ladino:
— Hágase las bodas yo seré el pedrino. —
Se hicieron las bodas y hubo mucho vino;
soltaron al gato, se comió al padrino. . .

¡Ah qué taraguda! lo que sucedió:

se desató el gato, todo se acabó.

Said the hen from her coop,
"Have the wedding; I'll go cook."

"God be praised! Now we have everything
Except someone to fan. Now, what shall we do?"

Answered the hornet from his nest,
"Have the wedding; I'll go fan."

"God be praised! Now we have everything
Except the groomsman. Now, what shall we do?"

Answered the rat in a smug tone,
"Have the wedding; I'll be groomsman."

They had the wedding and there was much wine;
The cat was untied; he ate up the groomsman.

Ah, what a calamity! Here's what happened:
The cat got loose; all was ended.

Mendoza prints two *relaciones* which are similar to the tall tale or the "whopper" found in American folklore. The following one, "El Piojo," is from the state of Jalisco:

El lunes me picó un piojo
y hasta el martes lo agarré.
Para poderlo lazar
cinco reatas reventé.

Para poderlo alcanzar
ocho caballos cansé,
para poderlo matar
cuatro cuchillos quebré.

Para poderlo guisar
a todo el pueblo invité,
de los huesos que quedaron
un potrerito cerqué.

On Monday a flea bit me
And I didn't catch it until Tuesday.
In order to rope it,
I broke five lariats.

In order to overtake it,
I tired out eight horses.
In order to kill it,
I broke four knives.

In order to cook it,
I invited the entire town.
From the bones that were left,
I fenced in a small pasture.

Yéndome yo para León me encontré un zapatero y ya me daba el ingrato veinte reales por el cuero.	As I was going to Leon, I met a cobbler; And the ingrate would give me only twenty *reales* for the hide.
El cuerito no lo vendo, lo quiero para botines para hacerles su calzado a toditos los catrines.	The hide I'll not sell; I want it for leather To make shoes For all the dudes.
El cuerito no lo vendo, lo quiero para tacones, para hacerles su calzado a todos los m. . . mirones.	The hide I'll not sell; I want it for heels To make shoes for all the . . . onlookers.

The *m* . . . in the last line was given without comment but seems to be a ruse of the singer. The singer probably gets to the *m* . . . and hesitates to look around for the gaping mouths of his gullible onlookers before saying *mirones*.

Perhaps the most bizarre of the *relaciones* presented by Mendoza is the one to follow, "Versos muy Extravagantes" ("Very Odd Verses"). The ballad was arranged by Jesús Silva Aceves and published as a broadside, a copy of which is on file in the Biblioteca del Museo Nacional of Mexico.[4] The same story also appears in the "Corrido Vacilador" ("Leg-Pulling *Corrido*"). Higinio Vázquez Santa Ana includes a portion of this *corrido* in *Canciones, Cantares, y Corridos Mexicanos*.[5] The ballad printed by Vázquez Santa Ana has the same story and details as the *relación* but is divided into definite eight-line verses. As the *relación* is quite long and at times irrelevant, only a few representative selections are presented here:

Iba llegando un coyote a la gran ciudad de León, cuando salió un zopilote	A coyote was arriving At the great city of Leon When there came forward a turkey 　　buzzard,
que andaba de comisión ye le dijo en la calzada: — Oiga amigo, ¿A dónde va con esa mujer casada? Ahora me la pagará. — Se lo llevó con el juez	Who was on duty, And told him on the highway, "Listen, friend, where are you going With that married woman? Now you're going to pay for it." He took him to the judge

al dar vuelta en una esquina:
era éste un gato montés
que estaba en una cocina.
Una pobre golondrina
al saber, pues, lo acaecido,
se fue volando del nido,
en busca de una torcaza
porque no tenía marido.

. . . .

Descalzo y con un huarache,
llegaron apareaditos:
una ardilla y un tacuache,
llegaron con sus hijitos;

. . . .

Como decentes personas
todos llegaron en coche:
un zinzontle, una paloma,
un gorrión y un huiltacoche;
ese mismo día en la noche,
pusieron un gran fandango;

. . . .

Como era tan concurrida
todita la reunión,
se fueron a una función
y todita la pacota
y bailando La Mascota

pasaron todos por León.

Just around a corner;
The judge was a wildcat
Who was in a kitchen.
A poor swallow,
Upon knowing what befell,
Went flying away from the nest
In search of a dove
Because she had no husband.

. . . .

Barefoot and with one huarache
They arrived in pairs:
A squirrel and a possum
Arrived with their children.

. . . .

As upstanding people
All arrived in coaches:
A mockingbird, a dove,
A sparrow, and a *huiltacoche;*
That same day in the night
They had a great ball.

. . . .

As there were so many people
In the gathering
They went away to a party;
And all the group,
Dancing *La Mascota* ["The Mascot"]
Passed through Leon.

*Y con ésta me despido
de los cuales, sin rivales;
aquí se acaba el corrido
de relación de los animales.*

1. Vicente T. Mendoza, *El Romance Español y el Corrido Mexicano* (Mexico, 1939), p. 739.
2. William J. Entwistle, *European Balladry* (Oxford, 1939).
3. Mendoza, pp. 195, 209.
4. *Ibid.,* p. 724.
5. Higinio Vázquez Santa Ana, *Canciones, Cantares, y Corridos Mexicanos* (Mexico, 1931), p. 94.

Rails Below the Rio Grande

JOHN T. SMITH

RAILROADS have consistently exercised a compelling fascination over the minds of most people. This interest in railroads is particularly noticeable in the United States, but it occurs elsewhere as well. The lure of railroads and trains is really a complex of feelings and emotions. Some enjoy the thought of traveling and conquering space on fast transcontinental streamliners. Others are lured by the sight and sounds of railroads; particularly was this true during the age of the steam locomotive, now rapidly disappearing. Still others are absorbed by the romance of work and construction which went into the making of the railroads.

American interest in railroads is quite adequately demonstrated by the vast body of folklore that has grown up around the various phases of railroading. This body comprises materials of all kinds—legends, tales, and ballads. Perhaps the classic example of railroad folklore is the legend and ballad of John Luther Jones, better known as "Casey Jones," who met his death at the throttle of a fast Illinois Central passenger train in April, 1900. In general, the American public has been and still is fascinated by the romance of the rails.

South of the Rio Grande, railroads are still relatively new. In Mexican ballads, the attitude of the people is quite different from that of their neighbors to the north. This essay examines four Mexican *corridos* which treat the railroad theme. A study of these *corridos* will show that the Mexican does not regard the railroads of his country with the feelings of romance cherished by Americans in general.

The rail lines were rather late in arriving in Mexico. Although the first line was begun in 1837, it was not completed until 1873, when Juárez began to improve the internal conditions of his land.[1] Railroad building expanded rapidly in the eighties and nineties under the Díaz dictatorship. By 1900 more than nine thousand miles of rail had been laid.[2] Mexican capital had little or no part in this railroad construction; most of the lines were laid by American builders. As a result, many areas of the country were not touched by rail; instead, there was a series of lines connecting Mexico City with the United States.[3] Modern improvements have been slow in coming to Mexican railroads. Today many lines still use steam exclusively, and there is much antiquated equipment in sharp contrast to the diesel-powered streamliners of American lines.

The attitude of Mexicans as reflected in their balladry is often hostile. In general, they looked upon the railroad as a form of foreign exploitation that disturbed their peaceful way of existence. Evidences of this attitude can be seen in the four *corridos* printed below. This difference in attitude is crucial to an understanding of why the railroads do not possess the charm and excitement for the Mexican folk singer that they have for the balladeer in the United States.

The first of these pieces relating to the railroad is a short, eight-line poem entitled simply "La Locomotora." These eight lines are in reality a part of a long love song with many verses. The poem pictures the locomotive and train as an unwelcome invasion of and intrusion upon the old ways; the narrator much prefers the carts of his home—"but, oh, I enjoy more the carts/ from the sad valley where I was born."

In this expression there is certainly nothing of the warmth felt toward trains by nearly everyone in the United States, young and old. "La Locomotora" is the resentful expression of one whose privacy has been disturbed by an unwelcome appearance of the railroad, "the locomotive with conductors with watches and caps." The second four-line stanza of this *corrido* has nothing in it that bears upon the railroad directly.

The second of the four *corridos*, "Entrada del Ferrocarril a Guadalajara," expresses even more forcefully the resentment of the populace toward the coming of the railroad, a symbol of exploitation by the *gringos*. Throughout this *corrido* the railroad is pictured as a monster that bellows and threatens life in general.

The third and fourth stanzas show most clearly the popular feeling toward the intruder and its foreign associates. Young women are threatened by the railroad; "it would have been better had you brought along/the mothers that gave you birth." The singer chides the young men: "What, don't your faces burn with shame/to see that train/enter Guadalajara?" There is almost a pleading quality in the song—a plea to see the danger that the railroad brings with it.

The concluding stanza epitomizes the hatred, fear, and suspicion that characterize the Mexican folk attitude toward the coming of the rails. The train is denounced as a "monster/of the very worst kind" that "runs after money/and eats the cobs as well as the corn." Here, then, the train means nothing but evil for the people; it will do nothing but impoverish them and destroy everything that it touches. "Entrada del Ferrocarril a Guadalajara" symbolizes most completely and most effectively the feeling of Mexican folk ballads—a feeling which appears in all four *corridos* in varying degrees. Here these feelings are most explicitly and forcefully expressed.

The remaining two *corridos* both deal with disastrous train wrecks, which, of course, caused still more resentment toward the trains and the Americans who frequently operated them.

The first of these train-wreck ballads, "Del Descarrilamiento de Temamatla," has been cited by Vicente T. Mendoza as the archetype of the *corrido* that deals with disasters or accidents.[4] The ballad emphasizes the disaster and loss of life and suffering that occurred in the wreck. This *corrido* is typical of this class in its minute detail and a surprising quality of realism which these details provide.

The train wreck of Temamatla occurred on "Thursday, the twenty-eighth of February/in the year '95." The ten-car train left Ameca at eleven o'clock in the morning. The engineer was a foreigner, "the cause of so much grief." The passengers in the third-class coaches are pictured as happy and carefree, little suspecting the impending disaster. At Tenango the train derails and piles up into a mass of twisted wreckage. In the twisted remains of the third-class coaches are found heads, arms, and legs of the victims.

On learning of the wreck, the local government and the railroad act swiftly to send relief. Soldiers are dispatched to the scene also. The ballad devotes seven stanzas to the suffering of the injured and dying and the heroic efforts of the doctors and nurses to give comfort to those in pain. The statistics given in stanza 21 state that 405 were injured and seventy-two killed. For this terrible disaster, the stunned populace blames but one group—the management of the railroad.

The closing stanzas of the *corrido* emphasize the tragic aftermath of the wreck—homeless children thrown into orphanages, parents bereft of their children. The public response is forthcoming; charity benefits are held in many of the theaters of Mexico to raise funds for the protection of these homeless orphans. The ballad concludes with a prayer that God has forgiven all of those who perished in the wreck. The *corrido* then closes with the conventional *despedida*.

This *corrido* illustrates again the attitude found in the first two. The emphasis is upon the tragedy as caused by the train, a train owned and operated by outsiders. There is a clear implication that the foreign engineer was responsible for the wreck, and the blame for the whole tragedy is placed upon the owners. There is no sentimental feeling for the train here as in such pieces as "The Wreck of the Ol' 97."

The most impressive quality of "Del Descarrilamiento de Temamatla" is its realistic use of detail in the description of the scene following the wreck. The cries of anguish—"Christ! my arm, I die," and "I want to see my children,"—heighten the effect of confusion at the scene.

The other *corrido*, "Descarrilamiento del Ferrocarril Central de Zacatecas," is almost an exact parallel. It is somewhat longer and more detailed, with thirty-two stanzas as compared to twenty-six for the first. According to the ballad, this story is of a wreck which "has had no precedent/nor has had an equal." The wreck occurred on April 18 "del año que corre ya." The train was bound for Juárez and overturned on a curve. As in the first train-wreck *corrido*, the passengers are happy and unaware of the tragedy which lies ahead. The piling up of the locomotive, the tender, and the cars is described at length in stanzas 6-10.

Again a relief train is sent to the scene, and doctors and nurses are summoned from Zacatecas and Aguascalientes. The casualties of this wreck were not so numerous as at Tenango— seventy-five injured and ten dead. The *corrido* also states that the wreck involved about ten thousand pesos in property damage and destroyed equipment. The injured were carried to Zacatecas on stretchers; here more of them were to die. Another parallel to the Temamatla ballad is the use of charity benefits in the theaters to raise money for the families of the victims.

We know more about the train itself in this *corrido*. The engineer was named Lee and the conductor was a "Mister Moore." Both men were badly injured and were sure to die. The naming of the train crew shows again an association between foreigners and the reasons for the wreck. The investigation following the wreck revealed that Engineer Lee was partly responsible, since the train had been traveling too fast. The railroad received still more of the blame when it was discovered the train's brakes were not functioning properly.

Thus, in the mind of the folk singer, the whole responsibility for the disaster rested upon the foreign owners and operators of the railroads.

These four *corridos* dealing with the railroads in Mexico show clearly the difference in popular attitude of the Mexican balladeer and his counterpart in the United States. Instead of fondness and nostalgia, there is pronounced bitterness and even hatred. The Mexican looked upon the train as a symbol of foreign exploitation, a threat to his established way of life, and he was not very far from wrong in his view.

Perhaps with the passing of time, these feelings against the railroad will change. As the railroads of Mexico pass more and more into the hands of native laborers, there may yet emerge *corridos* which glorify the train and those who are associated with it. One indication in this direction is a *corrido* about a Mexican engineer, Jesús García, who in many ways is the Mexican version of Casey Jones. García discovers that his train, loaded with explosives, is on fire, and moves it out of town. In the explosion that follows, García is killed, but he has saved the whole population.[5]

CORRIDOS[6]

La Locomotora

Por aquí pasó la locomotora con conductores de reló y kepí;	This way passed the locomotive with conductors with watches and caps;
pero más me gustan ¡ay! los carretones	but, oh, I enjoy more the carts
del triste valle done yo nací.	from the sad valley where I was born.
Mil grupos miro de pintados pájaros	A thousand groups of painted birds I see
que andan por aquí y allí;	that fly here and there;
pero más me gustan ¡ay! las tristes tórtolas	but, oh, I enjoy more the turtle doves
del triste valle donde yo nací.	from the sad valley where I was born.

Entrada del Ferrocarril a Guadalajara

Por ahí vienen los gringos
con mucha satisfacción,
vienen echando medidas
pa' levantar su estación.

Here come the *gringos*
with much pleasure,
they come using measures
for use in building their station.

Oigan, oigan, oigan, oigan,
oigan al *ferro* bramar,
donde llevan a los hombres
al puerto de Mazatlán.

Hear, hear, hear, hear,
hear the train roar,
which carries the men
to the port of Mazatlán.

Muchachitas de Jalisco,
la máquina ya llego;
mas valía que hubieron *traido*

la madre que las parió.

Young girls of Jalisco,
the machine has already come;
it would have been better had you
    brought along
the mothers that gave you birth.

Muchachitos tapatíos,
qué ¿no les arde la cara?

de ver entrar ese tren
para ese Guadalajara.

Young men,
What, don't your faces burn with
    shame
to see that train
enter Guadalajara?

Pero cómo no se fijan
que ese nos viene a voltear,

ése nos viene a dejar
lo de atrás para adelante.

Why do they not realize
that the thing has come to change
    us,
that the train is going
to disrupt us completely?

Toda la gente corría
a la estación primorosa
a conocer ese tren
que nadie lo conocía.

All of the people ran
to the beautiful station
to see the train
that no one has seen.

El tren es un *tarasca*
pero de lo muy primero,
que corre en pos del dinero,
que hasta los *olotes* masca.

The train is a monster
of the very worst kind,
it runs after money
and eats the cobs as well as the
    corn.

Del Descarrilamiento de Temamatla

Escuchen, señores, esta triste
    historia
que traigo en el pensamiento,
de lo que hace poco pasó en
    Temamatla
con el descarrilamiento.

Listen, sirs, to this sad story

which I have in mind
about what happened not long ago
    in Temamatla
in the train wreck.

El corazón se entristece
tan sólo al considerar
que muchos quedan sin padres
en este mundo a llorar.

El jueves veintiocho del mes de
    febrero
del año noventa y cinco,
todos en Ameca para la estación
iban con gran regocijo.

Eran las once del día
y luego luego, al momento,
silbó la locomotora
y se puso en movimiento.

Diez coches jalaba la locomotora
número cincuenta y cuatro,
y su maquinista era un extranjero
causa de tanto quebranto.

En los coches de tercera
venían con mucho contento;

pues nadie podia advertir
que era el último momento.

Todos con placer venían admirando

aquel bello panorama,
sin comprender nadie que la hora
    fatal
estaba ya muy cercana.

Cuando a llegar a Tenango
kilómetro treinta y dos
el tren salió de la vía
causando un estruendo atroz.

Tres coches quedaron de los de
    tercera
toditos hechos pedazos,
y por dondequiera *nomás* se veían
cabezas, piernas y brazos.

A las tres supo el Gobierno
todo lo que aconteció,
luego a las demarcaciones
las órdenes pronto dió.

The heart is made sad
only to think
that many remain without parents
in this world to weep.

Thursday, the twenty-eighth of
    February
in the year '95,
everyone in Ameca to the station
went with great joy.

It was eleven in the morning
and promptly at the exact minute,
the locomotive whistled
and began to move.

The locomotive pulled ten cars,
its number was fifty-five,
and its engineer was a foreigner,
the cause of so much grief.

In the third class coaches
the passengers were riding with
    pleasure;
for no one could know
that it was the last moment.

Everyone was admiring with
    pleasure
that beautiful countryside,
and none knew that the fatal hour

was already very near.

On arriving at Tenango
mile post thirty-two
the train left the tracks
causing a terrific commotion.

Three third class coaches were

broken all in pieces
and everywhere nothing was seen
but heads, legs, and arms.

At three the Government knew
all that had happened,
then to all the stations
it immediately gave orders.

Luego que la empresa también se informó
de lo que allí había occurido
al punto ordenó partiera veloz
el tren llamado de auxilio.

Then the management learned

of what had happened there,
instantly it ordered to leave quickly
a relief train.

El ministro de la Guerra
también sus órdenes dió,
las que el cuerpo militar
con puntualidad cumplió.

The Minister of War
also gave his orders
to which the military
responded with swiftness.

Cerca de las nueve llegó el tren de heridos
andando con precaución,
pues todos lanzaban tan tristes gemidos
que partían el corazón.

Near nine the train with the wounded arrived
proceeding with caution,
everyone made such sad moans

that they broke the heart.

Los inspectores subieron
declaración a tomar
pero no lo consiguieron
porque todo era llorar.

The inspectors began
to take the statements,
but they could not continue
because all were weeping.

"¡Dios mío, pierna!" "¡Ay, ay, mi cabeza!"
"¡Jesus! mi brazo, me muero";
y los otros gritaban: "¿Donde están mis padres?"
"Yo ver a mis hijos quiero."

"My God, my leg!" "O, O, my head!"
"Christ! my arm, I die";
and others cried, "Where are my parents?"
"I want to see my children."

Pero todo era imposible,
se entristece el corazón,
pues de toditos los muertos
hecho estaba ya un montón.

But all was hopeless,
the heart is made sad,
for every one of the dead
were heaped up into a pile.

Cerca de las diez, cuarenta camillas
salieron de la estación;
el cuadro era triste, tan triste en verdad
que inspiraba compasión.

Near ten, forty stretchers
left the station;
the sight was sad, so sad in fact

that it invoked compassion.

Hombres, mujeres y niños
en un continuo penar,
en camillas los llevaban
al hospital militar.

Men, women, and children
in continuous suffering,
on stretchers they carry them
to the military hospital.

Todita la noche en el hospital

practicantes y soldados
alistaban camas para recibir
a todos los desdichados.

Y tan luego que llegaban
con muchísima atención
a todos les practicaban
la primera curación.

Cuatrocientos cinco eran los heridos

que allí fueron auxiliados,
y setenta y dos toditos los muertos,
que quedaraon destrozados.

La sociedad alarmada
asegura con firmeza
que de esta horrible hecatombe
tiene la culpa la empresa.

Familias enteras en triste orfandad

sin protección han quedado;

pero grandes sumas para
   protegerlas
en México se han juntado.

Funciones de beneficio
en los teatros se anunciaban
para auxiliar a las víctimas
que más los necesitaban.

En suma, señores, lo que aconteció
lo llevo ya relatado,
y sólo deseo que los murieron
Dios los haya perdonado.

Aquí se acaba cantando
la historia del sufrimiento
que en Temamatla causo
el gran descarrilamiento.

Through the entire night at the
   hospital
the nurses and soldiers
prepare the beds to receive
all of the wretched ones.

And as soon as they arrived
with extreme care
they gave to all
emergency treatment.

There were four hundred five of
   the wounded
who were aided there,
and seventy-two in all were dead
who were mangled.

The alarmed people
asserted with determination
that for this terrible hecatomb
the management is responsible.

Entire families in unhappy
   orphanage
without protection have been
   thrown;
but large sums to protect them

were collected in Mexico.

Charity benefits
were anounced in the theaters
to help the victims
who most needed aid.

Finally, sirs, what happened
I have already told you,
and I only wish that those who died
have received God's forgiveness.

Here is finished the song
the story of suffering
that the great train wreck
caused in Temamatla.

Descarrilamiento del Ferrocarril Central
de Zacatecas

El gran descarrilamiento
que vamos a relatar
precedente no ha tenido
no ha tenido nunca igual.

The great train wreck
which we are to tell about
has had no precedent
nor has had an equal.

El día diechiocho de abril
del año que corre ya,
aconteció la catastrofe
sin poderla remediar.

The eighteenth day of April
of this year
occurred the catastrophe
without anyone's being able to help.

Las doce y veinte minutos,
eran ya de la mañana
cuando el tren descarriló
con violencia inusitada.

It was twelve-twenty
already at noon
when the train derailed
with unusual violence.

Kilómetros setecientos (diez),
marcando estaba el trayecto;
pasaba por una curva
el ferrocarril ligero.

Seven hundred ten miles,
the distance is marked;
here the rapid train
passes along a curve.

Iba el tren a Ciudad Juárez
nadie sospechó el siniestro;
mas de repente sintióse
horrible sacudimiento.

The train was going to Juárez
no one suspected any trouble;
suddenly there was felt
a tremendous jolt.

La locomotora y ténder
se volcaron con violencia
aún corriendo por el suelo

The locomotive and tender
overturned with violence,
although still running along the
    ground

como espantosa culebra.

like a fearsome snake.

Siguieron luego los carros
de equipajes y de express,
invertidos desde luego
sin poderse contener.

Then followed the cars
filled with baggage and express,
turning over and over,
not being able to stop.

La tercera clase fué
a caer por un costado
cayendo sobre segunda
haciéndose mil pedazos.

The third class coach
fell on its side,
falling on the second class car,
crushing it in a thousand pieces.

Y acompañado todo esto
de un estrépito terrible,
y de intensa gritería
que describir no es posible.

And along with all this
a terrible deafening noise,
and anguished cries
which are impossible to describe.

¡Oh que atroz hacinamiento
de pedazos de los coches,
de locomotora y ténder
que se rompieron veloces!

Y allí mezclados se vieron
todos los muertos y heridos . . . ,
aquello estuvo horroroso,
como nunca se había visto.

Los coches segunda y tercio
hechos astillas quedaron,
y de la máquina solo

destrozos *nomás* se hallaron.

Se dió aviso oportuno
y el tren de auxilio llegó
a las siete de la noche
sin ninguna dilación.

¡Cuánto gemido y lamento
de heridos allí se oía!
¡Qué llorar y que aflicciones
de los deudos de las víctimas!

Heridos muy gravemente
se encuentran el conductor
y el maquinista tambíen
dando gritos de dolor.

De Zacatecas seis médicos
llegaron con ansiedad,
y el doctor de Aguascalientes,
director del hospital.

Con bastantes medicinas
y todas las provisiones
que en el caso se requieren,
se presentaron veloces.

Las primeras curaciones
desde luego les hicieron,
para después continuar
con el más cumplido esmero.

Se los llevaron a todos
camino de Zacatecas,
entre lloros y quejidos
que el alma partían de pena.

Oh, what an enormous pile
of broken coaches,
of the locomotive and tender
that were swiftly demolished!

And there were entangled
all the dead and wounded . . . ,
it was a terrifying sight
such as no one had ever seen.

The second and third class coaches
were left broken and splintered,
and nothing but pieces of the
    engine
could be found.

The news was given in time
and the relief train arrived
at seven that night
without any delay.

What moans and laments
of the injured were heard there!
What weeping and what pain
of the relatives of the victims!

Found injured very seriously
were the conductor
and the engineer also,
crying with shouts of pain.

From Zacatecas six doctors
arrived with anxiety
and the doctor of Aguascalientes,
the head of the hospital.

With sufficient medicine
and all the provisions
that the case required
they came quickly.

The emergency treatment
they then administered,
to continue later
with the most thorough care.

All were carried away
by the Zacatecas road;
among them were cries and moans
that tore the heart with pain.

Removiendo los escombros
en el lugar del siniestro,
cada día se encontraba
mayor cantidad de muertos.

Algunos de los heridos
se están curando en sus casas,
los más en el hospital,
víctimas de la desgracia.

La causa de este suceso,
según se pudo saber,
fué la violencia extremada
que le dieron a aquel tren.

Dicen además que fué
causante de aquel siniestro
el que los frenos tenía
la maquina descompuestos.

Las pérdidas se calculan
a más de las personales,
como en unos diez mil pesos,
con destrozo de equipajes.

Y los heridos contáronse
setenta y cinco cabales
y muertos han sido diez
en aquella gran catástrofe.

En muchos teatros de México
y de otras capitales
se preparan beneficios
para remediar los males.

Con los productos que salgan,

se atenderá a las familias
de aquellos muertos y heridos
que del tren quedaron víctimas.

En la actualidad algunos
de los heridos han muerto;
y otras agonizan ya
y morirán sin remedio.

Fué gran casualidad
que el maquinista, aunque grave,

no expirase desde luego
en la terrible catástrofe.

Removing the debris
every day they found
a larger number of dead.
from the scene of the disaster

Some of the injured
were recovering in their homes;
the greater number in the hospital,
victims of the tragedy.

The cause of this wreck
according to the investigation,
was the great speed
that the train was going.

In addition they say
the cause of that disaster
was the brakes of the train
which were out of order.

When the losses were calculated
aside from personal losses,
ten thousand pesos were lost
in the destruction of equipment.

And when the injured were counted
there were exactly seventy-five,
and there were ten dead
in that great catastrophe.

In many theaters of Mexico City
and in those of other capitals
benefits were held
for the aid of the victims.

With the goods which were
        salvaged
the families will be helped,
the families of the dead and injured
who were victims of the train.

In reality some
of the injured have died;
and others are still in pain
and will die without help.

It was a miracle
that the engineer, although badly
        injured,
did not immediately die
in the terrible catastrophe.

Aquel ingeniero Lee,	That engineer Lee
que resultó responsable	who turned out to be responsible
de aquel siniestro fatal,	for that fatal disaster,
difícil es que se salve.	it is difficult to save him.
El conductor míster Moore	The conductor Mr. Moore
también muy grave se encuentra	was also found dying
y no es fácil, según dicen,	and it is not easy, according to what they say,
que recobre la existencia.	to recover his life.
Y aquí termina el relato	Here ends the story
del espantoso siniestro;	of the dreadful disaster;
rueguen por todos las víctimas	pray for all the victims
del gran descarrilamiento.	of the great train wreck.

1. Henry Bamford Parkes, *A History of Mexico* (New York, 1950), p. 279.

2. *Ibid.*, p. 297.

3. *Ibid.*, p. 310.

4. Vicente T. Mendoza, *El Corrido Mexicano* (Mexico, 1954), p. xl.

5. This *corrido* is mentioned in Rubén M. Campos, *El Folklore Literario de México* (Mexico, 1929), p. 234. Since this article was written a text of "Jesús García" has been published by Terrence L. Hansen in "Corridos in Southern California," *Western Folklore*, XVIII (July, 1959), 228-29.

6. The text of "La Locomotora" is taken from Vicente T. Mendoza, *El Romance Español y el Corrido Mexicano* (Mexico, 1939). The texts of "Entrada del Ferrocarril a Guadalajara," "Del Descarrilamiento de Temamatla," and "Descarrilamiento del Ferrocarril Central de Zacatecas" are taken from Vicente T. Mendoza, *El Corrido Mexicano* (Mexico, 1954). The translations are the author's.

I Heard It on the Border

MEREDITH HALE

Robber's Revenge

DUSK IS THE BEST TIME for telling tales. The rosy glow of a setting sun and the occasional chirp of a lonely cricket can transform fact into fiction and exaggeration into truth. I was a part of such a twilight world several years ago in El Paso. Juanita, an old Mexican servant and an avid storyteller, sat with me on the front porch of our small house. Together we watched a neighbor sprinkling his lawn. On the sidewalk his two children played "matador" and "toro."

Juanita seemed to be dozing in her chair. I was in the mood for a story. "Nita," I asked, "will you tell me another story about your people?" To this day, I think my companion must have been lying in ambush for such a question. She opened her brown eyes, straightened her full skirt over her legs, and without further delay began to speak in a low, pleasing voice with a slight accent.

"When I was little, señorita, I lived with my father and my two brothers a few miles north of here. Papá did a little farming for a living. My brother Mario helped around the place until he got restless and wandered farther west. We never saw him again. He always was lazy. Rubén, my older brother, used to call him Señor Perezoso. We managed without him though. Rubén got a waiter's job in town, and I stayed home to help my father.

"One evening, Rubén came home all excited. A gringo had tried to rob the customers at the café and had been shot in the back while escaping. That night my brother was trembling all over, although he tried to hide the fact. He looked like a chicken that had just seen the shadow of a hawk."

Here, my curiosity aroused, I interrupted the story. I asked Juanita why Rubén should have been so frightened. He had seen a robbery and a killing, but that should not upset anyone so much, especially when the thief was a total stranger.

"Ah, one minute, *chica*," continued Juanita. "Let me finish." She paused a moment and then went on to complete her tale without more interruptions from me. "You see, my people believe that to shoot a man, any man, in the back is bad business. A murdered man will return to haunt his killer. A man shot in the back cannot see his murderer and will therefore leave his grave to punish the last person he looked upon in life, no matter who that poor soul may be.

"Well, señorita, the last person that robber saw was Rubén. My poor brother was standing near the door of the café when the *ladrón* turned to run out with his loot. Someone in the back of the room grabbed a hidden gun and began firing. All hell broke loose then. The robber was hit twice, I think, in the shoulder and once in the middle of the back. He dropped his sack of money and tried to crawl out into the night. He never reached the door. He slumped at the feet of my astonished brother and died. Everything would have been all right if he had not looked at Rubén for an instant with those staring eyes of his. Rubén told us that night that he would never forget those black eyes piercing his soul. That dead man would return; of that, Rubén and my father had no doubts.

"Soon my brother refused to return home at night from his work. He preferred to rent a room in town rather than to risk walking the two miles home in the darkness. He lived in terror week after week, month after month. Finally, I began persuading him to forget his silly ideas about that dead man. Dead people do not rise again to haunt anybody. I succeeded in getting Rubén at least to come home over the week ends. The

first two Saturdays, he wheedled his boss into letting him get
off an hour early. Those times, he was able to walk home before
the roads became too dark. But on the third week end he had to
work until the regular hour, around eight o'clock.

"Well, he did not want to go anywhere that night; but, as
it was our father's birthday, Rubén decided to forget his fears
and make the short trip home. He set out at a rapid pace and,
after covering half the distance, had begun to laugh at himself
for worrying. That glass of tequila he had drunk had given him
courage, perhaps. At any rate, he even began to hum a few notes
of 'La Cucaracha' and to smile a little at some of the interesting verses.

"Rubén first felt that something was wrong when he began
to smell a strange and repulsive odor. He glanced around
him but saw nothing except the shape of a hill in the shadowy
distance. The smell suddenly became stronger. Rubén's mind
began to whirl from the stench and, nauseated, he ran off
the road into the deserted countryside. A cactus thorn ripped
his leg, and he uttered a low cry of pain.

"The sound was answered by a scream, or a snarl, to his
rear. He whirled to see behind him the outline of a gigantic
black panther, the eyes of which were like tiny flames in the
night. Those eyes were almost upon him. Suddenly the horrible
smell of which he had long been aware seemed to envelop his
body, and he fell among the desert mesquite, senseless.

"A storekeeper from the town found Rubén lying unconscious near the road the next morning. He carried my brother
home and helped us get him into bed. For hours, Rubén lay
there without coming to his senses. He was as pale as a boll of
cotton, but we could find no injuries, with the exception of
the scabs covering the cactus thorn scratches. We were eating
lunch when he suddenly sat up in bed and began to shout some
gibberish about the eyes of a cat and the eyes of a corpse. We
calmed him down, and he slept. That night, he awoke in his
right mind, or so we thought. He told us the story of his night

journey. I did not believe him, of course. Papá did, but I suspected that my brother had been too drunk to know where he was walking and had simply collapsed near the road. It would not have been the first time that Rubén had let tequila get the best of him. Rubén insisted that his adventure was true and that that black devil had been the vengeful spirit of the dead thief. He said that he had seen eternity in those eyes; his face grew pale when he remembered the terrible odor, which he now recognized as the smell of decay and death.

"Well, señorita, that day passed, and I was still *muy dudosa* about Rubén's tale. The next morning, my brother awoke early, and we prepared to go to Mass. Rubén went outside to wash himself. I glanced through the window at him and almost screamed. He had stripped down to his pants and was standing with his back to me. In the middle of his broad back were great red gashes like the claw marks of some large animal. His shirt was not torn in any spot, and yet there lay those long gashes. My brother still bears the scars of those claw marks, señorita. Moreover, the *pobrecito* has never been completely in his right mind since that dreadful night."

More Panther Lore

I have heard several other tales concerning the panther from various inhabitants of the borderlands. Generally, as in Juanita's story, the puma is regarded by the people as a sign or symbol of evil. The animal, especially if he is of a dark color, has been branded with the mark of death. A Mexican laborer described the panther of any color as "un demonio" and related the following incident.

Years ago, a distant cousin of the laborer's named Felipe worked as a sheepherder for a wealthy rancher. Felipe was a rather indolent fellow and somehow usually managed to get paid for much more work than he actually ever completed. It was Felipe's custom to take his small herd of sheep up into the good grazing country several miles west of the hacienda proper. There he would search out the shade of some tree and sit down to doze for several hours. The animals, of course, wandered where they pleased. Some of them never returned. It is doubtful that Felipe ever missed them. His eyes were too blinded by sleep to see anything.

One night riders reported having seen the sleek figure of a panther cross the top of a brush-covered hill located near the edge of the ranch. The next day one of the hacienda's prize cows was found slain.

Felipe ignored the reports of a bloodthirsty killer in much the same manner as he ignored all else that did not directly concern his pay, his liquor, or his women. He continued to take his herd to graze. Now, he kept his eyes half open most of the time, for his boss had noticed that some sheep were missing and had warned Felipe that more lost lambs would cost the herder his job.

One evening, Felipe dozed longer than he intended. He was awakened by the sound of a lamb's frantic bleating, coming from a near-by patch of trees. He leaped to his feet and ran toward the grove. The lamb lay bleeding beside a thicket. Felipe caught a glimpse of a tawny form slinking away among the trees at the far side of the grove. "Panther!" The word sprang from his mouth.

Needless to say, the supper table and the bunkhouse teemed that night with talk of Felipe's experience and with "authentic" panther stories. Felipe was calm once again, and spoke very little. A friend of his chided him with these words: "Felipe, you have seen death when you have seen a panther within twenty yards." In reply, Felipe gulped another tequila, chuckled, and stalked out of the room. The young herder regarded as foolish the old idea that the sight of a puma within a certain distance meant sudden death to the unlucky viewer. Nevertheless, he put a buckeye in his pocket for luck, "just in case," he confided to his old dog.

Felipe left with his sheep early the following morning and

headed toward the west. The ranch cook, Jamón, watched him climb a rise and then disappear over the top. Jamón was the last person to see Felipe alive. Late in the evening, a vaquero found the herder's mangled body lying near a mesquite tree. On the corpse's face was frozen a look of terror.

Speak of the Devil

ARTELL DORMAN

SPEAK OF THE DEVIL to the border Mexican, and he can probably tell you several instances when the Archfiend has visited his home town. According to the stories told to me, the Devil even now will often assume various forms and walk among the sons of men. No, the storytellers haven't seen the Devil themselves, but they have talked to people who have talked to people who have talked to other people who have seen him. He usually appears, they agree, as a handsome stranger dressed in a black suit, and usually one of his feet is shaped like a rooster's claw. But, of course, he can take any form he chooses when he comes to punish people for disobedience, or pride, or some other sin.

The idea of punishment meted out by the Devil is not a remote superstition to many Mexicans. The following tales relate how the Devil came to punish disobedience. They were told to me by four Mexican students in Pyote High School in Pyote, Texas. The girls told their stories with considerable excitement and apparent belief. Whether their parents believe them is not clear. It seems that in the household such stories have a function similar to that of Anglo stories of the bogy man.

The Devil Under the Bed
Told by Trinidad Mendoza

ONCE THERE WAS this spoiled and selfish girl who lived with her parents and grandmother. The grandmother was very old and paralyzed and was always asking the girl to wait on her. But the girl was lazy and rude.

One day the grandmother said, "Please, child, bring me a glass of water."

"I'm tired of waiting on you," the girl cried angrily. "I wish the Devil would take you!"

"Dear child," the grandmother answered patiently, "that is a wicked thing for you to say. I hope you do not see the Devil yourself some day because of that."

But the girl only laughed and made fun of the old woman. "You're only trying to scare me," she said. "I'm not going to get you any water because I have to get ready to go to the dance tonight."

Late that night the girl came home from the dance and went to bed. Suddenly she woke up. She heard something moving under her bed and when she looked she saw that it was the Devil himself. She was so frightened she could not even scream, so she began to pray silently. When she prayed to the saints, the Devil went away.

"In the morning," she said to herself, "I will tell my grandmother I'm sorry for being so mean to her. I will tell her that I have seen the Devil and I know now that she was speaking the truth."

As soon as the light dawned and the girl was not so afraid, she got out of bed and went to her grandmother's room. The old woman was very still and the girl thought, "She is still asleep; I will wait until later."

But later, when she returned to the room, she finally saw that her grandmother was dead.

"Now I can never tell her how sorry I am," the girl cried. "Now the Devil can haunt me the rest of my life."

This girl never saw the Devil again because she had repented in her heart. But she was very sad for the rest of her life when she thought how she had treated her old grandmother.

The Disobedient Daughter

Told by Francis Lopez

MARIA LOPEZ was pretty, but very hateful and disobedient to her parents. One night they told her not to go to this dance, but after they were asleep, she slipped out of her room and went anyway.

Everybody was having a lot of fun dancing when, all of a sudden, a monkey came walking in the door and went straight to Maria. He touched her dress and then ran back out the door. At first, all the young people were excited. Then they decided it must be someone's pet and they forgot about it.

At midnight, a handsome young man wearing a black suit came in the door. He went directly to Maria and asked to dance with her.

Maria was afraid of this man, although she didn't know why. But the other girls said, "Oh, go ahead and dance with him. Look how handsome he is."

And when Maria saw the other girls were jealous of her, she gladly accepted his invitation. They danced around and around the room. When they passed the door for the third time, the stranger pulled Maria into the darkness outside. He was so quick that the people standing near the door could not stop him. But one of them noticed that he had the legs and feet of a monkey!

They all rushed outside and called for Maria, but no one answered. Although they looked for her all that night, neither Maria nor the stranger was ever seen again. At last the people understood that this was the Devil who had come for the disobedient Maria.

The Devil at the Dance

Told by Jesusita Natividad

IN BALMORHEA there is an old dance hall where all the young people used to meet every Saturday night and have a party. Now it's all nailed up and this is the reason why.

One night, during the dance, there were a lot of little children running around and playing on the dance floor. Nobody paid much attention to them except one man. He was a stranger in the town, a very handsome stranger who came to the dance in a new black suit. He cursed the children and chased them all outside.

All went out but one little boy who hid under a chair standing beside the wall. From there he watched the feet of the dancers. When the stranger in black danced by, the boy saw that one of his feet was shaped like a rooster's claw. Now even a little boy would know whose foot this was.

"It's the Devil!" the boy screamed.

The dancers stopped and stared at the stranger. But before they could escape, the Devil struck out with his rooster's foot and clawed them all to death. All but one. The musician was forming a cross with his fiddle and therefore the Devil couldn't harm him.

They closed the place that night, and nobody will go in it now, not even in the daytime.

The Devil Woman

Told by Flo Sais

MY MOTHER'S COUSIN, Manuel Natividad, once saw the Devil. This was in the old days when people lived far from town and rode horseback. Manuel went to town every Saturday night and went to a dance. He was to be married one Sunday, but that Saturday night he got ready to go to the dance as usual. His parents and his sweetheart told him it was bad luck to go to a dance on the night before his wedding, but he laughed at them and rode off to town.

As he was riding along in the dim moonlight, he saw a girl walking toward town. He stopped his horse and asked her where she was going.

"I'm going to the dance in town," she told him. "Why don't you let me ride behind you? It's a long way to walk."

"Well, I don't know," Manuel said. "I'm going to get married tomorrow and if my sweetheart hears about it, she might call off the wedding."

"Oh, it'll be all right," the girl told him. "I'll get off before we get there and nobody will know that I rode with you."

So Manuel pulled her up behind him. She looked like a very pretty girl. Under the shawl she wore over her head he could see that her hair was long and wavy. She had long polished fingernails.

When they were almost to town, the girl asked him for a cigarette and he gave her one.

"Well, light it for me, stupid," she said.

When he held the match to light her cigarette, he saw her face clearly for the first time. It was the hideous face of the Devil! He screamed and tried to jump off his horse, but she clawed at him with her long nails and tore the shirt from his back.

His friends found him the next day. He almost died from the terrible clawing. Everyone knew that the Devil had come for him because he hadn't listened to his old parents and his sweetheart. In fact, his sweetheart did call off the wedding and Manuel never married.

When he was an old man he would tell this story to his friends. "I know there is a Devil," he would say. "If anyone does not believe in these things, then let him look at the scars on my back."

The scars were clear and deep. My father saw them several times before Manuel died.

The Noell Madstone

MICHAEL J. AHEARN

"THERE IS no fountain of youth here but we have a madstone belonging to the Noell family." This quotation from the *Alto Herald* of August 30, 1901,[1] introduces us to one of the most fascinating and colorful facets of the history of early medicine in Texas.

Dr. J. M. Noell moved to the Alto area in 1820 from Virginia. The pioneer Texas physician had at this time, as family records show, a stone which displayed unusual powers of adhering to wounds inflicted by mad dogs. A newspaper account in 1900 states, "The stone has been in existence for several generations and is supposed to have come from India where the natives are exposed to the deadly bite of the cobra." The stone, still in the family's possession, is crystal clear, about one inch long and two inches in diameter. Oval in shape, the stone is flattened on one side; upon close examination under a powerful light the interior of the stone is revealed to be a finely divided maze of small fissures. In all outward appearances the Noell stone differs from the "bezoar madstone," which was widely believed to have drawing powers for poisons. An early notation by Dr. Noell states, "A John Minter came with a selection of madstones gathered about Texas on which he placed great reliance and which were proved to be useless. One stuck to the bare flesh uncut."

Treatment with the Noell stone followed a pattern widely used later by owners of the bezoar and porous lava stones. Dr.

147

Noell warmed the stone in milk and applied it to the wound.
The clear stone clung to the area and after considerable time
the minute fissures, which until this time were hardly visible,
began to turn green. It is reported that at the time when the
stone ceased to adhere, it was often so completely permeated
with the green substance that it resembled an emerald. A short
reheating in the milk removed this color and restored the stone
to its transparency. Dr. Noell's grandson reports that, in his
childhood, he can remember only one particular incident concerning the stone. When he was four his pet cat, Tom, drank
the milk that had been used to remove the poison from the
stone. The cat went into convulsions a few minutes later and
died. "To me, at that age," the grandson says, "the stone took
on some great significance, and in the future I made sure my
pets were kept well removed from the basin of milk during a
drawing episode."

It was usually recommended that treatment begin as soon
as possible after a bite, although in one case, that of Mrs. S. S.
Perkins of Lone Star, Dr. Noell's official ledger states, "This
lady was actually going into fits while the stone was drawing."
A newspaper article reporting the incident said, "In the case of
Mrs. Perkins, the stone was applied on the eighth day, after
unfavorable symptoms had developed, but which gave way
after the stone had been applied." A grateful letter later
attested to the fact that the "cure" was lasting.

In these early years, some six decades before the Pasteur
treatment was introduced, the madstone held the only hope for
anyone bitten by a mad animal. The Texas State Health Department reports now that 84 per cent of bitten and infected
individuals will still not contract the disease, but in those days
a bite was considered a warrant for death by a horrible malady.
An eyewitness account of the death of Horace G. Marshall
from hydrophobia appeared in the *Dallas News* for an
unidentified date in 1904:

When the News representative was summoned into the presence of

Horace Marshall Saturday last, just twenty-four hours before his death, it was to have placed in his keeping a message from the dead. The unfortunate man, who had already entered into the shadows of death, pulling the newspaperman closer, related his story.

"I want you as my friend to listen to me for the sake of humanity; I want all to know the way in which this comes upon one inch by inch. At first I dreaded that the dog might have been mad. I acknowledge that I was worried, but I convinced myself that the dog had just run fractious and for a period of several days I think I can say my mind was at rest as far as dread of going mad was concerned. The wound on my face healed rapidly and gave me little pain. On Monday or Tuesday last I had the most peculiar sensation in the wound. I can't tell you just how it felt. It was not a pain. As near as I can describe it, it produced a similar feeling to that one would have if they were walking along not noticing particularly what they were doing and someone should shout to them, 'Look out!' This was followed by a desire to look for something.

"Again the sensation was new to me. I wanted to do something, find something. I did not know what.—After a restless night I awoke with all the feelings one has of approaching grip. I wanted water, craved it, as I never had before, but as I crave it now in the face of the knowledge that I cannot swallow it. I tried to drink and then there came to my mind the conviction that I was going mad. My God! That my case may be the last one is my wish and for that reason I ask you to if the worst comes—no, I won't say worst because—because—."

The sob in his throat choked back his words and the haunted look in his eyes had given away to one of unspeakable appeal through tears.

The next day the *News* simply stated, "Horace Marshall died in convulsions of hydrophobia."

It is easy to see why, with a disease such as this, whoever was bitten would seek any aid available. The total number of those treated by Dr. Noell is unknown, but later his daughter, Miss Fannie, who carried on his work after his death, reported that it must have easily exceeded a thousand. A journal kept between the years 1900 and 1903 lists some eighty-one patients, with frequent references to those treated earlier: "Told of the madstone by Mr. Ollie Nix who was cured here in 1884.... Recommended by Dan Walker of Jacksonville, who was drawn here fifteen years ago (1887)." Even after the Pasteur treatment was introduced, the distance to St. Louis, then the nearest place to Texas where it was available, was far too great for many of the patients to travel. A few who made the long journey did so in vain, as they arrived too late. A clipping from the *Dallas News* in 1901 describes such a case:

> A little white coffin carried by two stalwart pallbearers was placed on a southbound train tonight and shipped to Caseta, Texas. The casket bore the body of Howard Thaggard, a boy of eight years, who three weeks ago was bitten by a stray dog, with which he was playing. Fearing hydrophobia, his parents immediately sent him to St. Louis for treatment. The disease developed despite the efforts of the physicians; the boy died today after terrible suffering from the convulsions of rabies.

Because of such cases, many people felt that a treatment near at hand was essential; for this reason knowledge of the Noell stone spread far and wide, mainly by word of mouth, although numerous references were made to it in various publications. Now and then East Texas newspapers would carry a story on the Noell madstone, as the following clippings show:

> Our readers will doubtless remember the account we gave of Mr. J. G. Perkins of Lone Star getting bitten by a mad dog a couple of weeks ago. Well, it seems that was only a beginning. Messrs. J. G. West and W. S. Owen, also of Lone Star, drove into town about half past three o'clock last Thursday aft. with four little boys ranging from six to nine years old, on their way to Alto to have the Noell stone applied. These boys were sons of Mrs. Roberts, a widow lady, Messrs. J. G. West, W. S. Owen, and Dr. Picket, all of Lone Star, and each had been bitten Monday August 19, by a dog which has since developed unquestionable symptoms of hydrophobia.—*Rusk Weekly Journal*

> R. W. Ivy, a prosperous landowner of this county was in town today en route to Alto in search of the madstone, he having been bitten last night near his home by what he considers a mad dog. — *Lufkin News*

> The chief event of the past week happened on last Thursday the 19th when Mr. W. M. Medford and son, Levi, of Lone Star came to Alto to have the madstone applied. Several other people came later on the passenger train. A little fice caused all the trouble, biting nine persons. The madstone stuck over four hours to Mr. Medford's wound. — All left Sunday morning for their homes. The visitors were Mr. Roberts, Mrs. Armine, Herndon Roberts, Mr. and Mrs. Guillion and son, Clinton. — *Alto Herald*

Information on this stone apparently was also available at the State Capitol, where Dr. Noell stated that he had registered it. A recent investigation did not disclose records of this and other madstones, but it is highly probably that these records were burned in the fire of 1881.

Many early physicians, realizing that they could offer their patients no hope, referred them to Alto to have the stone applied. Among these was Dr. E. E. Guinn of Jacksonville, Texas, who wrote, "Miss Fannie, this will introduce you to Mr. L. M. Lumm who has probably been bitten by a 'mad dog.'" Miss Noell, or Miss Fannie as she was better known, became so closely associated with the stone that people hardly ever mentioned one without including the other.

The "drawings" frequently required as long as eight to ten hours each. Those being treated, as well as their families and friends who usually accompanied them, "put up" at Miss Fannie's home. Besides overseeing the work of applying the stone, about which one newspaperman wrote, "As there was but one madstone and many anxious people, the work of drawing them had to go on day and night until completed," she would rush about trying to feed the visitors and make them at home. I say "visitors" because there was never any charge made for the treatment or for room and board for the retinue of the afflicted individuals. The only payment Miss Fannie received, or expected, from these frequent episodes was "Thank you" and "May God bless you." A few of the more ungrateful ones not only omitted thanks but, on leaving, might pick up any article in the home that caught their eye.

Notable among these "borrowing episodes," as Miss Fannie chose to call them, was the disappearance of the family silver. When questioned years later as to why she didn't bring charges against the guilty party, Miss Noell simply said that there had been seventeen or eighteen people "on the place," and not knowing which one took the silver she didn't want to embarrass the sixteen innocent individuals by questioning them. Such was her way. In later years Miss Fannie said, "The Noell stone is a thing of the past; I cannot refrain from thinking, however, that it must have helped." And we too cannot dismiss some evidence published in 1901, which concludes: "Just what virtue there is in the stone no one knows, unless it is that the poison is drawn from the system into the stone. Yet it is a fact that no one who has ever been bitten by a rabid dog ever died or had hydrophobia after having this stone applied."

NOTE. Dr. Noell kept a ledger or notebook (later continued by his daughter) on the madstone. In it were recorded the names of people on whom it was used, and dates of treatment, subsequent letters reporting cures, and newspaper clippings. My quotations are taken from this notebook, which is still in possession of the Noell family, of which I am a collateral member. As would be supposed, the exact source of the clippings is seldom given, so that I cannot make complete identification of many of them. For a general discussion of madstones, see J. Frank Dobie, "Madstones and Hydrophobia Skunks," in *Madstones and Twisters* ("Publications of the Texas Folklore Society," XXVIII [1958]), pp. 3-17.

Texas Singing Schools

EVERETT A. GILLIS

STILL SURVIVING to some extent in parts of rural Texas is a popular form of musical expression commonly known as a singing
school. The social phenomenon of a group gathered at a local
schoolhouse or church under the direction of a singing master
for a week or so of schooling in music goes far back in our
national cultural history. George Pullen Jackson notes its begin-
nings in New England as early as the 1770's, and in his study
White Spirituals in the Southern Uplands (1933) traces its
development as it moved westward with our expanding population, and especially its wide dissemination in the South. He
declares: "The beginning of all group singing is in the singing
school, the cradle of musical democracy in the South." And he
quotes the instructions given to would-be singing school teachers around the year 1900 by a certain P. M. Claunts. According
to Jackson, Claunts' list of the teacher's equipment included a
blackboard, a music chart (with graphic indications of diatonic
and chromatic steps in each key), plenty of heavy white paper,
blue drafting pencil, crayons, tacks and hammer, baton, pointer,
and music books. Above all he must have "a soul burning with
love for the work." He continues:

Then the work begins. The teacher explains the musical staff, symbols,
measures, note shapes and names (solmization), scales, etc.; and
impresses them by the question-and-answer method and by much choral
singing. And before the ten-day term is over, the group — a dozen to
many dozens, all ages but mainly young folk — will be do-ray-mee-ing

153

their different parts to the songs in one of the little manila-bound books which we have described above. When the school closes, another squad of singers has been prepared either to go on and deepen their elementary musical attainments at other singing schools later on, or to take part directly in church and revival choruses and to swell the singing throngs at the many big "singings" or conventions.

I made my first acquaintance with the Texas version of the southern singing school in 1937 while I was engaged in rural work in North Central Texas. I was invited to attend a "singing" that climaxed a ten-day singing school held near the rural community of Gordonville in Grayson County, just across Red River from Oklahoma. Fairly typical of Texas singing schools generally, this school was held in a local schoolhouse under the direction of a singing master from Dallas, who gave his class a thorough course in sight-reading, part-singing, and the necessary rudiments of musical theory. The end-of-school all-day singing consisted of numerous songs from the books the teacher had brought with him for his students to purchase. During the course of the day most of the members of the school were requested to lead the group in a song, "leading" consisting merely of standing before the group and singing out more loudly than ordinary, while the others followed. In addition, the master provided opportunities for special numbers consisting of solos, duets, quartets, and the like. The singing master, I learned, was connected with a Dallas music company that published the book he was using, and during the summer months he traveled extensively in the area, engaging in such schools as this at so much per pupil. He was boarded out among various families. The music used in the school and the singing was entirely religious; the fast and sprightly tunes were set to a strong beat, with frequent embellishments for the various voices, and a tendency toward syncopation. The class consisted mostly of younger members of the community, but there was a sprinkling of the older folk.

That the singing school has enjoyed considerable popularity

in Texas in the past is borne out by answers to a series of questionnaires sent out to people in various parts of the state who might have had opportunities to know about, or to have participated in, singing schools. Response came from informants in Hughes Springs, in Northeast Texas; Valley View and Cleburne, in North Central Texas; Gatesville and Valley Springs, in Central Texas; and Big Spring, Jones Community (near Littlefield), and Wheeler County, in West Texas. Especially helpful in suggesting informants were Mrs. Leita Reeder Davis of Hughes Springs and Mrs. Marjorie Morris of Odessa College.

One questionnaire was returned by a real old-time singing master, Claude C. O'Dell of Hughes Springs, who taught his first singing school in 1898, when he was twenty-two, and his most recent one in July, 1956, in the Bible Baptist Church in Hughes Springs. Out of his rich experience he provided the following information about his fifty years of teaching singing schools. "The usual length of time for a Singing School," he reports, "was 10 Days, 5 days a week for 2 weeks. I have taught all of the Singing Schools in this community except 2 in the past 50 years." Mr. O'Dell also taught numerous schools at other points in Cass County, his home county, and in bordering counties. These included Violet Hill, Harris Chapel, Friendship, Bivens, and Zion Hill in Cass County; Rock Springs and Jenkins, Morris County; Mims Chapel and Cedar Grove in Marion County; Karnack in Harrison County; and Liberty in Hopkins County. Most of Mr. O'Dell's schools were held in churches; he used only sacred music, as contained in such instruction books as *Showalter's Music Book* from Georgia and *Stamps Instruction Book* from Dallas; he ended his schools with an all-day singing and dinner on the grounds. Mr. O'Dell's remuneration varied. When he first started, he declares, he received one dollar per pupil for the entire school. Later, his pay ranged from $50.00 to $75.00; one year he received $100.00 for a twenty-day school. In most of his schools he was furnished room and board, sometimes visiting in a different home each night, sometimes remaining in one home, but eating dinner at a different place each day.

Professor Ernest Wallace of the Texas Technological College history department, who grew up near Hughes Springs where Mr. O'Dell lives and whose own father taught a few singing schools in the area, explains the function of the singing school as follows:

One of the major purposes of the singing school was to keep the community able to sing in church. The singing schools usually brought forth one or two people of the community, the lesser uninhibited, who afterwards would lead the singing at the religious services. If a number developed interest, then there would be local singings from time to time.

It might be a preliminary singing to ascertain if there was sufficient interest, but more often on the last day of the school, one of the music companies had representatives on hand. If it were V. O. Stamps or a group of his top performers (singers and musicians), the crowd would be enormous. Each recognized song leader on hand (and they were there from far and near) had an opportunity to lead a song or sing a special (quartet, trio, or solo). The quartet was the favorite. . . .

When a well-known singer was round-about, the odds would be that there would be a singing on Sunday afternoon or night at church or even possibly some night during the week at some home.

Professor Raymond Elliott of the Texas Technological College music department, who grew up near Cleburne in North Central Texas, informs me that the singing schools with which he is familiar normally lasted two weeks, from nine o'clock to four daily, and were usually "mastered" by outside teachers. "Having a local person conduct it," he declares, "would be like a pastor holding his own revival." The normal conclusion consisted of a "big sing," in which there was, he says, "mostly congregational singing with some duets and quartets. Most student leading was done during regular class sessions. The smart teachers used adults in the final program—influential leaders in the community who would promote the school for another year." In other words, good business! With regard to payment, he says: "The amount depended upon the teacher's reputation and crop prospects. Some teachers demanded a contract; community leaders underwrote the cost. These, for good teachers, would run around $100.00 per week."

A. L. Miles, of Gatesville, Texas, remembers several singing schools in Coryell County, in Central Texas, which were held during the first decade of the century. These followed the usual pattern, lasting from ten days to two weeks. They were conducted by persons outside the community, and were concluded by a special singing day at which students were given opportunities to perform. The singing school masters, as he recalls, were paid around $2.00 per session. Mr. Miles relates the story of an elderly itinerant singing master who attempted to set up an unsolicited singing school in the Levita community in Coryell County in the summer of 1910 or 1911. The old man drove up in a covered wagon followed by a little dog and set up camp near the schoolhouse. Having approached some of the community leaders with but little success, he turned to the younger set. Here prospects looked more promising. A number of boys between fifteen and eighteen years of age agreed to meet him at the schoolhouse on Saturday night and to register for his school at $1.00 for five lessons—one each night, Monday through Friday. Here is Mr. Miles' account of what happened:

According to promise about twenty or twenty-five boys assembled at the schoolhouse about dark. The old man lit up the coal-oil lamps hanging on the wall in front of their shiny tin reflectors. Everything looked promising. He gave the boys the best pep talk he could, emphasizing the advantage of knowing how to read music and sing by note. He asked for a show of hands of those who would pay their dollar and attend the school. It was unanimous. The registration was started by passing around a sheet of paper for the prospective pupils to sign. The boys told the old man they would register but could not pay the dollar until Monday night. The old man reluctantly agreed and every boy present signed a fictitious name ranging from Theodore Roosevelt to John D. Rockefeller. Needless to say this was the last time the old man saw this group of boys.

Mr. Miles never attended such singing schools himself, feeling, as he states it, "that singing was for the lace tonsiled crowd"; but he never missed the community singings, going, in his words, "strictly for the social feature." The "social feature" of singing schools and singings explains, in large part, the popularity of such institutions. As Mr. Miles points out, the singings provided a place for young people to go that had parental approval: "The Sunday evening singings were usually at someone's home. Boys would call for their girls in their Moon Brothers buggies drawn by a well groomed buggy pony and both would thoroughly enjoy the trip to and from the singing as well as the time at the singing."

The social value of the singing school institution is further reflected in a description of a West Texas school by Mrs. Una Dunagen of Big Spring, Texas. "The last day of singing school," she says, "was always a joyful one, and the girls took great pains in preparation for it. Much persuasion was used on the parents to get new ribbons for dress sashes and new hair bows to help create a special dressed-up look on that memorable day." At the singing, each boy would strive to sing a duet with his best girl, and dinner, picnic style, was served on long wooden tables placed under a brush arbor. One of the special features of this singing school was that it was taught by the local preacher, who opened and closed his sessions with prayer and used the regular church hymnal as a textbook rather than the special singing-school hymnals widely popular. In addition to hymns, he allowed his students to sing secular songs such as "Darling Nellie Gray" and "Aunt Dinah's Quilting Party."

In contrast to this locally-mastered West Texas singing school, a series of schools from 1930 to 1933 in the Jones community, fourteen miles west of Littlefield, Texas, employed a professional master who, according to Mrs. Martha Brown of Littlefield, taught *do, re, mi* by blackboard and out of "paper backed song books containing sacred, most of them fast or rapid time and 'choppy' or 'jazzy,' songs."

Professor John Q. Anderson of Texas Agricultural and Mechanical College gave me the following account of two other West Texas schools. These were held in communities in the Panhandle area, in Wheeler County, near the Oklahoma border.

> Music used was religious always and of the shaped-note [do-re-mi] variety, usually with emphasis on rhythms. . . . Classes began with description of the shaped notes and their place on the scale (staff), progressed through combinations (simple four-part harmony), key signatures with explanation of sharps and flats, measurements in rhythms, and rests. Each instruction period was followed by actual singing. The small class was divided into soprano, alto, tenor, and bass. Most of the students were young people, although a few oldsters who could already read the notes participated as well. . . .
>
> In the practice period following instruction, students were urged to "lead" songs and beat out the time. Usually, there was a special night at the end of the school at which many of the students would lead songs for the group to sing. "Graduates" of such schools often went to "singing conventions," all-day affairs on Sunday which featured such singing together with special numbers of quartets and duets.

What of the future of the Texas singing school, which as a group activity seems to exhibit many of the earmarks of a genuine folk institution? To my question, "Does your community still hold singing schools?" I got only one affirmative reply (Claude O'Dell's, from Hughes Springs). There was one other reply of "seldom"; all the remaining responses were negative. Most of the schools described here were held in the twenties or thirties, or earlier—though one informant, Miss Frances Smathers, a student at Texas Technological College, indicated that she knew of a singing school in Valley Springs, Llano County, as late as 1951 or 1952. Even in the bailiwick of our old singing master Mr. O'Dell, however, the program of a folk festival fostered by the Hughes Springs Woman's Club in the spring of 1957 included a singing school as part of a demonstration of *old-time customs!*

George Pullen Jackson suggests that shaped-note religious singing is gradually dying out in the South, and that singings and singing conventions (and of course the singing school which represents the means of providing the necessary training for such singing) are on the decline. The same is probably true of Texas also, as the result of the impact of the forces mentioned by Professor Jackson: the gradual urbanization of rural areas, the consolidation of small school districts into larger ones, the tremendously-shaping forces of radio, television, and universal education. Yet the tradition still persists: radio stations still broadcast programs in which quartets sing with gusto the exact type of music fostered by the old singing schools.

The singing school in Texas is perhaps gone forever; at least, it is rapidly declining. Yet for generations it played an important role in fulfilling the deeply felt folk need for song. This function is quaintly emphasized by a verse from a song collected by Professor Jackson:

> O tell me, young friends, while the morning's fair and cool,
> O where, tell me where shall I find your singing school.
> You'll find it in a large church beside the flowing spring,
> You'll find half a hundred and faw sol law they sing.

Negro Stories from the Colorado Valley

GIRLENE MARIE WILLIAMS

WHILE MAKING this collection I discovered that most Negro folk-lore of the Southwest is either amusing or mysterious. If the tales weren't funny or frightening they weren't remembered very long. This statement, however, does not apply to the songs and sermons of the Negro.

These tales were told to me by persons who were born and reared in the Colorado River Valley. "Buried Treasure Seeker" and "Cum Down Yere" were told by Mrs. J. M. Lofton of La Grange, Texas. "The Crowded Grave" and "One Mo' Ham" were related by Mrs. Callie Hornsby from Plum, Texas. "Jedge-ment Day" was told by Sherman Brown of Plum. The rest of the stories were told by my parents.

I had never heard most of the stories until I made this collection. I found two variants of tales in J. Mason Brewer's "Juneteenth." "Nassuh! 'We' Didn't" is a variant of "When 'We' Wasn't We," by Mr. Brewer. "Jedgement Day" is a variant of Mr. Brewer's "Voices in the Graveyard."

I Got Something for You

This story was told to my family many times by Mrs. Lydia Davis and her mother, Mrs. Parthenia Briscoe, who lived in Plum years ago. They said it was a true story which actually happened to them.

Up on Farris farm every "dark of the moon" a ghost dressed in white would come to Mrs. Davis when she was in bed asleep.

161

The ghost would shake her and say, "Wake up, Lydia, wake up. I got something for you. It'll do you good but you have to go with me by yourself."

Mrs. Davis said she was always too scared to say anything to the ghost and would always shake her husband and say, "Dave, wake up, here's that old woman again." By the time her husband awakened, the ghost would have vanished. Mrs. Davis told her mother about it and said she was afraid to go with the ghost. Mrs. Briscoe said she wasn't afraid. She went and slept in Lydia's bed until the ghost came again. Mrs. Briscoe was awake and watching for the ghost when it came. The ghost didn't say anything but it had a parasol and tried to jab Mrs. Briscoe in the face with it. Mrs. Briscoe dodged the parasol and jumped up. The ghost vanished and never came back again.

Mrs. Davis also said that after every big rain on this same farm they would find some coins. The coins would be out in the field in the same vicinity but they never investigated or told the owner of the farm.

Buried Treasure Seeker

Mrs. J. M. Lofton heard about this incident from Mrs. Mattie Jackson. It occurred on a farm near Plum.

A Bohemian man was digging for buried treasure at the edge of a field. A long, thick row of tall weeds grew just outside the field with a trail on the other side of the weeds. Mrs. Jackson was coming up the trail with a bundle of clothes on her head. When the man heard someone walking he was startled and looked up to see this bundle moving along over the top of the weeds. It frightened him so much he dropped his shovel, cried out, "Oh, Lordy!" and started to run.

Mrs. Jackson said, "Hey, don't run! It's me, Mattie."

He looked around and stopped. Trembling and perspiring he said, "I t'ought you was the de-vil." He stood staring at her and every now and then he would say, "Oh, Lordy!"

Cum Down Yere

This incident occurred right after La Grange got telephones. A Negro named Sam was working for a white man who had just had a telephone installed in his store. Mr. Smith and some other men in the store decided to have some fun out of Sam. Mr. Smith told Sam to call Mr. Lee and tell him to come down to the store at one o'clock. Sam said, "Yuh mean yuh wants me tuh call him on dat t'ere telifome?"

Mr. Smith said, "Why sure, Sam."

Sam picked up the telephone and shouted at the top of his voice, "Heh dar, Mistuh Lee, Mistuh Smif sey fuh yuh tuh cum down yere at one uh clock." The men were roaring with laughter by the time Sam replaced the receiver.

Nex' Week Sometime

My parents told me a boy sang this song at a school closing exercise in Plum over forty years ago. The boy and his family came from West, Texas, and apparently brought the song with them. No one had heard the song until he sang it.

> Muh fathah died w'en Ah wus sebben yers ole,
> An' he lef' me uh gre't big pot o' gole.
> De fun'est t'ing 'bout dat pot o' gole
> Was dat he bered it in uh gre't big hole.
> One night Ah wen' out fuh tuh dig dat gole.
> Som'in' stood ovah me jes' is white is sno',
> Sed, "Wait now, Bill, lemme he'p yuh dig dat gole."
> Ah tol' him, "Nex' week sometime but not now."
> Me an' dat ghos' run breast tuh breast
> An' da ghos' sed, "Nigger le's stop an' res'."
> An' Ah sed, "Nex' week sometime but not now."

Das Too Much fo' Us

Isaiah Jones and his wife Mandy had just moved to a new sharecropper farm. One Saturday Isaiah was looking at a big tree in the back yard and discovered there was a large hollow in it. He decided to climb up in the tree and look down in the hollow. On doing so he discovered a bucket of money in the hollow. He didn't know whether he should tell his wife or not. He finally decided to tell her. Mandy was in the house ironing when he called out, "Mandy, Mandy, come 'ere quick, honey."

"Now, Isaiah, yuh knows Ah's i'ning an' Ah ain' got no time fo' none o' yo' foolishment."

"Naw, Ah got som'in tuh sho' yuh. Chile, we's rich. We ain' got nuthin' tuh wur'y 'bout no mo'."

"Rich?"

"Yeh, Ah don' diskivvered uh bucket o' money up in da holler o' dat tree."

"Umm, umh, das too much fo' us," said Mandy as she went back in the house. She put on her apron and bonnet and out the door she went.

"Mandy, whar yuh gwin'?" asked Isaiah.

"Ah's gwin' tuh tell Mistuh Dan. We can't keep all dat much money wid'out telling dem white fo'ks."

No amount of reasoning would change Mandy's mind, and she waddled off to Mister Dan's at her fastest pace. When she got there she started hollering, "Mistuh Dan! Mistuh Dan!"

He came out and said, "What's the trouble, Mandy?"

"Come see whut Isaiah done foun' up in dat ole holler tree."

"You don't mean he found that money Grandpa hid?"

"Yassuh, yassuh, dat sho' am whut he did. Uh hole bucket full o' money. Ah jest cudn't keep hit tuh muhse'f. Ah jest had tuh come tell yuh."

Mister Dan really didn't know about any money being hidden in the tree—he just happened to ask the question. He told Mandy, "We didn't think anyone would ever find it so we just left it there." When he went and got the money he gave Mandy and Isaiah a reward of twenty-five cents each.

"Missi" Nothin'

Jim and his family left the Mississippi plantation of Master John and Mistress Mary and moved to Texas. They told Jim to be sure to let them know how well he was getting along.

The first time Jim wrote he said, "Dear Mr. John and Miss Mary, Ah'm doin' fine. Ah made uh good crop an' ah bought me uh house."

The next time Jim wrote he had made a larger crop and he said, "Dear John and Mary, Ah'm doin' fine. Ah made a big crop and Ah bought me uh car."

The next year Jim had done so well he decided to send a telegram. The message read, "Dear John and Mary, I'm doing fine. I made a big crop and I got some money in the bank." The telegrapher asked Jim if he wanted to send the telegram to Mississippi. Jim said, " 'Missi' nothin'—jes' 'Sippi'."

Slop fo' Muh Hogs

During Prohibition Roy Scott was running a still in Plum. The county sheriff was tipped off about it. When he went out and asked Roy about it he said, "Nassuh, Mistuh Tom, now yuh know Ah ain' makin' no whiskey. Yuh kin su'ch muh place if yuh wants tuh, but Ah sho' ain' makin' no whiskey."

The sheriff looked around until he found some barrels of sour corn mash. "What's this, Roy?" the sheriff asked.

"Aw, dat ain' nothin' but some slop fo' muh hogs."

"Now, Roy."

"Yassuh, das all, Ah'll sho' yuh." Roy poured some of the mash into the hogs' feeding trough. The hogs started eating it. After a while they got drunk and started staggering.

The sheriff said, "Okay, Roy, we'll call it slop this time but if I ever catch you with any more slop like this I'm going to put you in jail."

Whut Did Moses Sey?

One evening the preacher told a little boy to go over to Moses' house and tell Moses to send him a jug of whiskey. He cautioned the little boy not to tell anybody about it or what Moses said but himself.

When the little boy got back to church, services had begun. The preacher got up and started preaching. He said, "Whut did Moses sey?" The little boy squirmed in his seat. He didn't know what to do because the preacher had told him not to tell anyone but himself and now he was asking him to tell it in front of everybody. Again the preacher said, "Whut did Moses sey?" The little boy squirmed. The preacher said, "Ah sed, whut did Moses sey?"

The little boy spoke up from the back of the church, "He sey he ain' gon' sen' yuh no mo' whiskey tell yuh pay fo' dat yuh done already got."

Nassuh! "We" Didn't

A neighbor borrowed a slave named Jack from the Brown plantation to go hunting with him and carry the game. The first thing the neighbor killed was a jack rabbit. "We killed uh jack rabbit," said Jack.

"Now listen," said the neighbor, "you haven't killed anything. I shot that jack rabbit. I brought you along to carry the game and not to claim what I kill."

They went on a little farther and the neighbor shot a turkey. "Oh, we done killed uh turkey," said Jack.

"Nigger, I told you about that 'we,' " said the neighbor. They went on farther until the neighbor shot what he thought was a deer. It turned out to be a colt that belonged to Jack's master. The neighbor said, "Look, Jack, we killed a colt."

Jack said, "Nassuh! 'we' didn' kill dat colt. Yuh sed back yonduh yuh was doin' da shootin'. Ah'm gwin' tell Massa yuh done kilt his colt."

The neighbor said, "If you do I'll shoot you."

Jack said, "Massa sho' will be mad if yuh shoot his nigger."

He Sho' Gib Me uh Bad Time

Master George would always take his slave, Duke, with him when he went hunting. One day they were out hunting and saw a bear. Master George was going to shoot the bear but Duke begged him to save his "loads" and let him kill the bear with his hands. Master George finally consented and Duke went up and choked the bear to death.

The next day Master George's wife told him that every night when the ladies were on their way to church for prayer meeting they would hear a panther. Sometimes the panther would be so near they would get frightened and turn around and go back home. Master George told her that Duke could take care of the panther for her easily because he could kill a bear with his hands.

The mistress found Duke and told him if he would catch the panther they would give him a wife and set them free.

Duke said, "Yuh kin git her ready, Mist'ess, 'cause Ah's sho gwin' tuh kotch dat pant'er."

That evening Duke went down in the direction of the church. The panther caught Duke's scent and started screaming and closing in on him. Duke was scared and started backing up to the door of the church. The panther was coming closer and closer. Duke tried to open the door but it was stuck. When he got it open, before he could step in, the panther leaped for his head. Duke ducked and the panther landed in the church with such force he slid up to the altar. Duke slammed the door and tied it. He told the panther, "Yuh kin hab yo'self uh good time in dar preachin' tuhnight." Duke got some thorns and scratched himself all on the arms and hands. He tore his shirt and pants and then went back to the plantation. The next morning he said, "Massa, Ah kotched dat ole pant'er dat sker'd Mist'ess las' night. He sho' gib me uh bad time."

"Where is the panther, Duke?"

"He's down dar in da chu'ch house."

Master George sent word around to the neighboring plantations that Duke had caught the panther. Soon there was a whole line of people headed for the church. Duke got back on the end of the line. When they got to the church Master

George called for Duke and told him, "Well, Duke, do you want to go in and bring him out?"

Duke promptly answered, "Nassuh, das awright, Ah b'lieve Ah'm gon' let yuh shoot him 'case yuh kin see Ah had uh time puttin' him in dar."

Turn Me Loose!

A white man had been seeing something in the graveyard when he passed by at night. He was scared, so he told Peter, a Negro who worked for him, about it. The Negro said he wasn't scared of ghosts, but he really was. Mr. Moore, the white man, told Peter he would give him fifty dollars if he would go out in the graveyard that night and find out what he had seen. He told Peter he had to prove he had been in the graveyard by going to a certain grave and sticking a butcher knife in the middle of it.

That night the north wind was blowing and it was cold, so Peter had on his overcoat. He was scared and kept looking all around the graveyard. As he bent over to stick the knife in the grave, the wind blew the tail of his coat on the grave. He was looking back over his shoulder and without knowing it, stuck the knife through the tail of his coat. He started to raise up and the knife held on to his coat. He thought a ghost was pulling him down in the grave and collapsed, yelling "Turn me loose!" Mr. Moore was watching from the edge of the road and had to come and get him.

The Crowded Grave

A drunk man was going through a graveyard when he fell into a freshly dug grave. He tried and tried to get out but he couldn't quite make it so finally he lay still. Another man came along and fell in. He also tried and tried to get out. After a while the first man tapped the other on the shoulder and said, "Yuh can't git out o' here." With that, the second man leaped from the grave and ran as fast as he could.

Jedgement Day

Two slaves stole some chickens and killed them so they couldn't make any noise. They went down to the graveyard to divide them up. While they were getting through the gate they dropped two.

A boy passed by the graveyard and heard them saying, "One fo' me, an' one fo' yuh." He ran and told his master it was "Jedgement Day" and the Lord and the Devil were down in the graveyard dividing up souls. The master wanted to go and hear, so he and the boy went down to the graveyard. The slaves were almost through when they got there. The divider said, "Two fo' yuh—and dem two at da gate fo' me!" The master and the boy ran off as fast as they could

One Mo' Ham

A new preacher was disturbed because his congregation did not believe the Lord would give them whatever they asked for. He butchered a hog and one Sunday night he put it up on the roof of the church. He got a boy to go up on the roof and told him to drop down through the window any portion of meat he called for.

He got up and started preaching. He said, "Brothuhs an' sistuhs, de Lord will po'vide fo' yuh. All yuh has tuh do is as' fo' whut yuh wants. He'll sen' yuh any po'shun o' meat." One sister started shouting and said she wanted a ham. The preacher asked the Lord for a ham and one dropped in the window. Another sister asked for a side of bacon and some bacon dropped down. Someone asked for another ham and one came through the window. They kept calling for portions of meat until someone asked for another ham. The preacher said, "Oh, Lord, sen' dis brothuh one mo' ham.'

The boy stuck his head in the window and said, "Reverund, dat hog don' hab but two hams!"

Negro Folktale Heroes

FRED O. WELDON, JR.

ON READING THROUGH the large body of recorded Negro folk-tales, one is struck by the one-sided preference for trickster heroes, as compared to the well-developed traditions of quest and defender heroes found in abundance in the traditions of the Indians and whites living in close contact with the Negroes.

Negroes have borrowed freely from white cultural patterns; they quickly learned the language and were converted to Protestantism, and they readily adopted the economic and social patterns of the white man where it was possible for them to do so. But their folktales reveal an inability to adopt the American social values as symbolized by the quest hero. I am, of course, describing a condition that exists primarily in the southern United States, where the oral tales still thrive. In the North, where Negroes have gained greater social mobility, folktale activity has been noticeably weakened. In less segregated areas of the country Negroes still feel the sting of discrimination, but more direct forms of protest are open to them, especially in the cities where their political force has come to be felt.

Increased education and the consequent growth of critical thinking now available to Negroes in other parts of the country are also factors that break down folktale traditions. Richard Dorson gives an account of the difficulty he encountered in trying to gather folk stories among Negroes who had lived in an all-Negro Michigan community for a generation or more. He was able to find only a few scattered stories here and there until he was directed to residents of the community more recently from the South; here he struck a vein of Negro tales and superstitions rich enough to fill a fairly representative collection.[1]

The role of the hero or the American Negro hero may be clarified by reference to Orrin E. Klapp's classification, according to role, of world folk hero types.[2]

The *"Feat Hero,"* Klapp says, "is characterized by extraordinary power or deeds which exceed ordinary human capacities." Examples are Paul Bunyan, Hercules, Samson, and Moses. The *Contest Hero* is traditionally assigned a task or an ordeal which he must endure in order to attain a goal. Job, Christ, and the saints are examples of the type. Klapp makes a further distinction between the above types and the *Quest Hero*, who must meet a prolonged series of tests and contests, and perform feats of heroism.

Other types discussed by Klapp which seem logically to group together are the *Defender* or *Deliverer*, the *Benefactor*, and the *Martyr*. These three types are quest heroes who use their exceptional qualities for altruistic purposes. Examples of the deliverer are Achilles, Arthur, and Perseus. This class of heroes fulfill their roles by means of resolute action and outright The benefactor or *Culture Hero* includes some of the clever (trickster) heroes, especially in the North American Indian and African traditions. Robin Hood, Jesse James, Raven, Goolscap, Coyote, and Anansi (the Spider hero of Africa) represent a combination of the roles of the clever hero type with that of the culture or benevolent hero. On the other hand, many culture heroes fulfil their roles by means of resolute action and outright conquest of man's enemies. Examples of this type are Prometheus, Aeneas, and Moses.

Klapp's article discusses two more types that are usually underdog heroes. His terms for them are *Clever Hero* and *Unpromising Hero* or *Cinderella*. These are by no means similar in their activities, their methods, or their emotional appeal. They may nevertheless be classed together because they contrast with the above hero types in that neither employs direct action or conquers by strength. They each appeal to the sympathy for a weaker person competing with a stronger. The clever hero defeats his opponents by means of dissembling and trickery. Reynard the Fox, Rabbit, Coyote, Robin Hood, and Davy Crockett are Klapp's examples of this type. The tendency to consider the trickster as a rogue or villain is widespread. Often he is considered a villain in the legal sense only, while he is secretly admired by the people as a benefactor or representative of group wishes. Other tricksters, such as Anansi the Spider, are considered villainous even by the people of their own groups. The American Negroes' John (the slave hero) and Rabbit evoke both attitudes. The attitude of the people toward a clever hero may depend on the function he serves in the society. For example, the Spider is the object of all sorts of abuse in some African tribes; in others he is thought to be a semidivine being, even a savior, and in still others he is simply admired because of his ability to outsmart a stronger animal.

Whereas the clever hero is subject to differing degrees of admiration and contempt, the Cinderella seems to be invariably the object of sympathy. Sentimentality is behind the appeal of this hero. He is persecuted and deprived of the good things of life because of some deformity of nature, or because of his simplicity and goodness in a world of thieves; yet, because he is good or kind to animals, or because he is modest or pitiably weak, he is rewarded in accordance with a concept of natural or divine justice that compensates for a lack of power or wit. This concept—hence this hero type—seems to have developed all over the world.

In Negro folktales about Christ and the saints, the hero's character is reshaped to conform to the pattern of the trickster hero.

Christ tells his followers to pick up some stones and follow him. Peter selects a very small stone because he does not want to carry a heavy burden. They stop for a rest and Christ changes the stones into bread for dinner, but Peter goes hungry. When a second time Christ commands them to get some stones, Peter finds the biggest one around and carries it until they stop again. Christ declares that he is going to build a church and selects Peter's stone as the foundation because it is the largest, but Peter says, "No, you won't, Lord. You're going to turn this rock into bread—I'm hungry."[3]

The Negroes in America were late in developing the close group identification necessary to identify heroism with the group. American Negroes have tended to try to escape the group and improve their status in American life as individuals.

Individual Negroes do, of course, empathize with their heroes—otherwise they would not have them—but their empathy seems to be more personal than group-related. I have read very few Negro tales in which the narrator compares the situation or the characters to social situations involving the Negro and the white man. The parallels between story and real life seem for the most part to be due to unconscious habit. Slavery and prolonged abuse would seem to have given the Negroes sufficient reason to unite around a deliverer hero, or some symbol of their group in conflict with the whites, but the nature of the social environment has undermined any possibility of such unity.

The one contest hero of the Negroes is John Henry. He is one of the best-known folk heroes on the American scene, among whites and Negroes alike, but his role is never that of the deliverer or representative of the group in conflict with whites. He is the only hero I know in Negro folklore who is not a passive, self-effacing trickster. He has been interpreted as representing a challenge to the encroachment of the machine (as symbolic of the white man) in the one area of American life where the Negroes held a monopoly, that of unskilled day labor. But there is nothing in the songs about John Henry to suggest protest or anti-white feeling. Negroes seem to understand his heroism in defeating the steam drill, but have consistently failed to connect this victory with their group as a whole. Guy B. Johnson's study of this ballad discusses the historical incident that might have been the origin of this tale. He reports alleged eyewitnesses to John Henry's contest with the machine as saying that it was an ineffective tool and no match for even an average man.[4] The machine's inefficiency, however, might not have been generally known and it could conceivably have struck fear into the Negroes whose economic security it seemed to threaten.

The popularity of the song seems to indicate that its appeal lay not in any actual heroism, but in the sheer tragic romance of a man's working himself to death in a race against a machine. As the only widely known dramatic personality in the Negro folk hero tradition, John Henry must be regarded as unique.

The American Indian quest and culture heroes conveniently illustrate the motifs of the hero type which the Negroes did not develop. Stith Thompson gives a concise discussion of the Indian myths and legends.[5] He divides the heroes into mythic (or culture) heroes, test heroes, and trickster heroes. The myths explain creation and post-creation ordering of a world imperfectly created by the wedding of a Sky Father and Earth Mother. The mythic heroes have either animal or human shape. Coyote is the central character in the myths of the California tribes; Goolscap is the culture hero of the northeastern tribes; and twin heroes are important in the mythology of the Iroquois. The culture hero regulates the seasons to benefit mankind. In the northeastern tribes windstorms were thought of as caused by a giant bird flapping its wings; by overcoming the bird and breaking its wings, Goolscap caused a calm which lasted until the wings, now smaller, healed. There are legends of the theft of fire, light, and water from a monster.

It is possible to show that some cultural borrowing and racial mixture did take place between the Indians and the Negroes where they came into contact; hence a comparison of their separate traditions before and after the Negroes' arrival in America might show a pattern of motif selection and rejection. The best opportunities for borrowing would have been in the Southeast, where the Cherokees, Creeks, and Seminoles lived. According to Thompson, the quest hero is relatively well developed in the North Pacific, Plains, and Great Lakes regions and shows least development in the southeastern tribes.[6] It may be that these quest heroes originated in the areas of strongest concentration and spread to the other areas but failed to gain prominence over the indigenous tricksters. One reason for this might be that the Southeast is precisely the region where the Indians came into closest contact with the Negroes, who brought up with them and kept a tradition predominantly made up of trickster motifs, and that the Negro influence on Indian folklore was greater than was the influence of other tribes.

If the quest hero and quest motifs existed well within reach of the Negroes in both Indian and white cultures, they consistently refused to borrow them. On the other hand, there is a great deal of similarity between the Negro and Indian trickster patterns, but this does not necessarily indicate borrowing by either Indian or Negro. Much of the similarity probably existed at the time of the Negro's arrival from Africa. The character of the trickster and the kind of tricks he plays are pretty much the same the world over.

Elsie Clews Parsons reports several of the most popular Negro motifs from a Cherokee family in North Carolina.[7] "Playing God-Father," "Rabbit Makes Wolf His Riding Horse," "Above Ground and Under the Ground," "Tarbaby," "Dog and Dog-Head," and "The Devil Bridegroom" were all familiar to them. Anne Virginia Culbertson has made an entire collection of animal stories designed to illustrate similarities between Negro and Cherokee animal tales.[8] In this collection it is difficult to distinguish which is told by an Indian and which by a Negro.

Folktales and ballads are art forms. In American society

where the Negro folk are subject to an oppressive authority, the artist enjoys a freedom of expression that others do not have, for in his art he can generalize and abstract the statement of protest so that the tyrannizing authority either does not recognize it as insubordination or considers it harmless, even enjoyable. The song "Blue-Tail Fly" subtly reveals a slave's hatred for his dead master, but it has become as popular among whites as among Negroes. So it is with the folktales: they serve to disguise—perhaps from the Negro himself—the desire to curse, or do violence to, the white master. Rabbit is in a sense the Negro in his battle with the symbolic stronger animal. The "Tarbaby" is only one incident from a whole cycle of Rabbit tales, and what white child in the South has not heard of and been delighted with the Rabbit's victory over the other animals? Several of the stories are so contrived as to prepare for an ending either of "cussing the master" with impunity or doing harm to his body or to his pride.

In choosing his relationship between characters, the storyteller selects motifs that amuse him or move him to pity or admiration. These tastes are unconscious habits, for the most part determined by cultural conditioning. There has been a long period of conditioning the Negro to his inferior status in American society. He has not only had to accept a theory of his inferiority, but a rigid implementation of that theory backed up by an ever-present threat of an outcropping of white violence.

By belief and in practice the Negro has been rendered completely subordinate, and hence socially inferior, to the white majority that he depends on. The philosophical and scientific arguments of the racist dogma promulgated in the nineteenth century were developed by whites with prestige and education. Negroes, uneducated and not free to dispute the doctrine, were unable to defend themselves intellectually. If the doctrine had any effect on the Negroes at all, it probably became accepted as truth. But even if the Negroes were not affected by the abstractions of scientific, legal, and philosophical debates among whites, they were in a practical situation from which only one conclusion could be drawn: that Negroes had better be inferior for their own good, at least as long as they were in the South. This practical day-to-day relationship with the whites was itself enough to convince Negroes of their own weakness, which by available standards meant inferiority.

Where, as in the South, arbitrary taboos are placed on a group of people for any reason it is likely that a good deal of folklore of one kind or another will arise around the tabooed acts. But in the case of southern Negroes desire for revolt or familiarity with whites has not gone beyond the stage of folklore.

Social isolation of the Negroes has had another apparent effect on the characters of the individuals in the group, whether they be storyteller or listener. Negroes are in a position where the slightest mistake (failure to speak with proper respect to whites or merely looking at a white woman) may be dangerous to life and limb. The southern Negro defends himself by adopting the habit of accommodative behavior and an uncomfortable watchfulness and deferential evasion when around whites.

The brutal manhunts and lynchings have probably seemed to the Negroes enough like white man's sport to suggest the hunt. Being chased or hunted for breaches of discipline or for escape was probably not uncommon to the slaves. One of John Dollard's informants went into great detail in telling about the evasive tactics used by the raccoon to escape the hunter's dogs.[9] Whether his hunting lore was accurate or not makes no difference. What is important is that the Negro had studied the evasion so closely and—though it may have been his dog chasing the coon—seemed to admire the intelligence of the hunted animal.

The Negro's interest in hunting lore may be partly determined by the necessity to supplement his food supply with wild game—and knowledge of the hunted animal's tricks would

make him a better provider—but in the light of his preference
for the small, often-hunted animal folk hero, it seems that the
interest is deeper than mere proficiency in hunting.[10]

There are two main folktale cycles in Negro folklore: the
tales told about Rabbit and those told about John, the slave
trickster. There are differences of characterization of the two
heroes, apparently determined by the fact that the Rabbit is—
because he is an animal—recognized by narrator and listener
alike as pure fantasy. John is not only a man acting in a real
world, but a historical and, to some extent, contemporaneous
fact. The Negro's identification with the Rabbit is unconscious;
he can sympathize with Rabbit's problems and triumphs with
the same impersonal amusement that Dollard's informant got
from relating his coon lore. Furthermore, the storyteller is
more free in his choice of motifs; unlimited by reality, he is
dealing with a world in which animals speak and behave as
humans. John is the Negro; the reality of his personal identification permits only just so much freedom of action (hence
motifs), and aggression against the white man is not part of
that freedom. This basic separation of the cycles gives the
John tales slightly different shapes from those in which the
animal tales are cast.

When read as a group, both cycles give one a feeling of
never-ending strife between Rabbit and Wolf or John and Old
Master. Sometimes the struggle is conceived of as good-
natured, even playful, but more often there is an element of
grimness—a cruel, motiveless trick, or punishment for mistakes
as a constant threat. In some of the stories Wolf or Old Master
is victorious; in others the hero wins out. It is unimportant
whether the Negroes let one or another of the opponents win;
it is only significant that they think of their heroes as being
in defensive conflict with the symbols of power and authority.
If characteristics of the heroes do in any way represent a symbolic identification with real experience, then it is useful to
understand the natures of the heroes and adversaries in order

to gain some insight into how the Negro views himself in relation to this society.

Where Rabbit is free to take active steps to plot and execute his treachery, John is more passive; his revenge is usually no more than getting the satisfaction of having the last word on Old Master or in seeing him made uncomfortable through his own overbearing actions.

A generalized plot around which the tales are usually built can be summarized briefly in this way: (1) The hero is lazy and shirks his duties, he steals, lies, or otherwise breaks taboos; (2) he is caught in the act by the master or stronger animal; and (3) he attempts to save himself from punishment by the use of trickery or—in the case of John—humorous language. John does not employ aggressive trickery against the white man, but saves it to get himself out of the scrapes his lazy or thieving nature has got him into. Very often the attempt to escape is nothing more than another incredible lie:

John was forbidden to catch catfish from the creek on the plantation, but the master allowed him to catch all the perch he wanted. One day John caught a big catfish and had strung and tied it separate from the perch he had caught. When the master came by and saw the catfish, John began to unstring it, explaining that the fish had been robbing his hook and that he had just caught him and tied him to the bank until he had finished fishing. Since he was through fishing he would let the catfish go.[11]

Many of the most popular animal stories vary from this idealized plot a great deal. In the story "Fatal Imitation" the interest lies in the moral lesson—if one is intended—of Rabbit's foolishness in believing and imitating the Rooster:

Once there was Ber Rabbit an' the rooyster. Every night when Ber Rabbit goin' home from work, he would see how de rooyster had only one leg an' no head at all. An' in de mornin' he would have his head and two legs. So Ber Rabbit asked Ber Rooyster why he cut his head an' leg off at night, an' put it back in the mornin'. So Ber Rooyster tol' Ber Rabbit he rested dat way. So he wen' home an' tol' his wife to cut off three of his leg an' his head, so that he can rest. So, when Ber Rabbit wife cut Ber Rabbit head off, Ber Rabbit began to jump. So Ber Rooyster hold up his leg an' took his head from under his wing, an' clap his wings, an' said "I have my head!"[12]

In the story "Rabbit Shows Bear What Trouble Is" Bear claims he has never experienced "trouble." So Rabbit promises to show him what it is. He leads Bear to a patch of weeds and directs him to lie down and go to sleep. Then he sets fire to the weeds and traps the Bear in a circle of fire and taunts him.[13] Rabbit's deception here seems especially cruel because there is no apparent reason for the act except his maliciousness; taunting the burning bear only heightens the cruelty of the act.

The difference between this tale and the usual pattern is that the trickster starts the action of the story by taking definite steps to bring harm or discomfort to his opponent. John is the hero and usually responsible for the action in his stories, but it is not his deeds, but the master's, that initiate the conflict. John arouses the disfavor of the master, who threatens to punish him. Interest then centers around John's humorous lie or comment on the predicament as in the story "Baby in the Crib."

John stole a pig from Old Master, but the master saw him. After John got home with the pig he saw the master coming down to his hut, so he put the pig in the cradle and covered him up like a baby. When the master came in John was rocking the crib. Master asked him what was wrong with the baby and John told him it was the measles, but the master insisted on seeing him. John told the master that the doctor had said the measles would "go back on him" and kill him if he was uncovered, but the master insisted again and reached down to uncover the pig. John said, "If that baby is turned to a pig now, don't blame me."[14]

In the series of stories about Old Master and John at the praying tree the white man is sometimes given the role of trickster and John serves as the butt of his joke. The point of the story is, again, John's absurd comment on his own discomfort. Effan started praying for the Lord to kill all white folks and spare all the Negroes. The master overheard him and decided to play a trick. He put a sheet around himself and went to the slave hut where the Negro and his wife were praying. He hit the Negro in the head with an ax handle, and the Negro fell over on his back and looked up at the master and said, "Oh, Lord, don't you know a white man from a nigger?"[15]

The sparseness of detail in all Negro storytelling makes it difficult to tell whether the Rabbit had plotted his trickery beforehand with some revenge motive in mind, or merely thought of it on the spur of the moment. In either case it is rare for the stories to suggest motivation for the acts. Moral justification of villainy is not necessary for the Negro listener, who knows the feel of the stronger animal's abuse and can supply his own motives for revenge. And conversely, when Rabbit and John are beaten at their own game, it need not be stated that they deserved it. Although the stories are often made up of but a single motif, the listeners have an intimate knowledge of the entire cycle; they know Rabbit's character and his motives because these are abstractions of their own. These people have a clear sense of justice and guilt; Rabbit and John are capable of vengeance, greed, gluttony, laziness, and all human failings, but they must pay for their sins by occasionally being punished in the tales. Rabbit—as does John to a lesser extent—serves the purpose of wish fulfilment insofar as the Negro is able to execute his cruel tricks on the symbol of his persecutor, but the heroes also serve the conscience when they are severely punished for their malice.

To the narrator the art of telling a good story is as important as what happens in the story, and more important than any possible symbolic meaning it might carry. In the John tales there is actually very little action; it is in these stories that the teller must depend on his ability with the language and subtle dramatization of fear or dismay. In this sense the John stories seem to be more nearly "pure art" than the rabbit stories, which are told more for their narrative interest and depend more on elaborate motifs and less on humorous twists of language and sounds.

Another device for humor used in the following story is profanity or a subtle dramatization of how frightened the Negro or master was.

There was a cripple who had his sons take him down to the tree when they treed a possum. The boys had begun cutting the tree down when something came running down out of the tree and frightened them all. The boys ran home as fast as they could and their mother asked what had happened and they said, "Lord, Mammy, something come runnin' out o' that tree. It got all our lights an' whipped the dogs an' then we left." Then they all started worrying about the old man, but they looked in another room and found him. They were surprised and asked him when and how he got in. The old man said, "Lord, chile, I come in wid de dogs."[16]

Two stories suggest the Negro's desire to violate the most sacred taboo of the southern caste system, that of familiarity with white women. In "The Fight" John slaps the master's wife and gets away with it.[17] In another story John brags to his friend that he has put his hand under the master's wife's dress. The other slave tries it and is severely whipped. The violation is only of secondary interest since the story is told as a joke on the other slave: John had tricked him by not telling him that at the time he had put his hand under the woman's dress, she was not wearing it.

Folktale explanations of why the Negro has to work, why he is black, or why he has kinky hair include the Negro's disobedience to God, his laziness, or his greed in trying to get the biggest bag for himself.[18] Attributing the curse of blackness and misfortune to some original sin no doubt reflects the influence of the Christian ideas of sin and atonement.

These origin tales are anecdotes like the other popular

stories, and there is no evidence that they are believed any more than the Rabbit or John stories. They are a popular unofficial handling of mythological motifs. Again the Negro takes a look at himself, and in his healthy way laughs at what he sees. But the important fact here is that the Negro has accepted his inferiority so completely that even in jest he must give supernatural explanations for the condition.

Negroes are accused of glorifying less socially acceptable qualities such as "hell raising," sexual freedom, thieving, lying, irresponsibility, and laziness. Very likely the accusation is often true of lower-class Negroes. Apparently the ego has been so undermined in Negroes that they are willing not only to accept the truth of their status as society's clowns, but to act out the role, and at the same time take full advantage of all the pleasures that the position gives them freedom to enjoy— freedom that, indeed, most white men do not enjoy. It is little enough compensation.

All the animals in the forest were holding a meeting. God was going to bless 'em all. At two meetings they'd had, the rabbit and the deer were always there first getting their little blessing. Every time the dog would get there, they'd done give away all the blessings. This one was set for Sunday at two o'clock and all of them was supposed to be there, and the fowls too. So the old hound dog taken out that Sunday, going with the crowd, and along the road he found a bone. He stopped, picked up the bone, and taken it on to the meeting. God blessed the deer to run fast, and the rabbit too. Then he looked over where the dog was just chewing on the bone, making a lot of noise. "For your disobedience I should name you a dog. And you should chew bones for the rest of your days."

This time the dog said to God: "You been giving out blessings all the time and I ain't got nothing. I don't give a damn about what you had in store for me. I'm going to eat this bone, and damn the rest."[19]

The methods of "folklore science" with its endless comparisons of versions and variants and its historical and geographical emphasis frequently seem to lead its students away from the emotional values expressed in folktales. Like plays and novels, folktales are told for the pleasure of communicating feelings arising from the common experiences of the ethnic or cultural group. In Negro folk art the feeling of frustrated protest affects the very form the stories take.

A comparison of versions of a tale becomes meaningful when its social function is considered. For example, the story "Big Claw and Little Claw" is clearly a borrowing from European folklore. It keeps its European features; even the names "Big-Thumb" and "Lee-Thumb" show an etymological connection with Hans Christian Andersen's "Big Claus and Little Claus."[20] Zora Hurston's version of this tale gives John and a white man the roles, and the story becomes a vehicle for unusual freedom of action and revenge on the part of the Negro.[21] The story is brought closer to the Negro, calls forth full play of all the emotions surrounding the slave system, and is revitalized with new emotional meaning.

Both Hurston's and Dorson's informants refer to their storytelling as "lying." The lying is done in the spirit of competition when several Negroes are brought together either in a social gathering or at work in the fields. Anyone who has ever been within shouting distance of a cotton field where there were Negro pickers or near a railroad gang has probably heard the frequent laughter from the stooped figures. It is under these circumstances that there are the time and the stimulation to talk and tell stories. If the stories are told at a social gathering in the evening the same conviviality pervades the air, with women and children joining in.

Negroes are caught between two different systems of mores, their own (which whites force them into against their will) and the white man's. Negroes do not necessarily aspire to live by the white man's mores, but in some cases they want the benefits of white social acceptance enough to go to the extremes of white standards. Upper middle-class Negroes are sometimes referred to as "black puritans" because of their strict observance of middle-class standards.[22]

If the Freudian concepts are accepted—i.e., that inner conflicts are a function of the very physical organization of the family and that resolving these conflicts is itself the first manifestation of social adjustment—the abnormalities of the personality developing in the Negro family are readily apparent. The typical Negro child's natural father is either not dominant in the family, or he is not present. The child does not have an immediate rival or hero to whom he must adjust. The masculine authority that the social order does offer is the white man, who is probably not the child's sexual rival. In any case, prevailing thought among the Negroes has always considered, and still considers, open defiance against the whites as foolhardy rather than heroic.

Bronislaw Malinowski studied the workings of the Oedipus complex in the matrilineal culture of the Trobriand Islanders.[23] He concluded that this institution has had the effect of lessening the father-son rivalry. Among these islanders the authority figure is not the child's real father, but his maternal uncle, usually living in another village. The father is subordinated to the mother and children. His function is that of playmate and part-time nurse. If this proposition can be generalized to other maternally oriented families, such as the Negroes', in the early formation of his personality the child does not have as intense an urge to revolt against the father as the white child does, and so does not reach maturity with as strong a propensity to admire heroes of revolt.

In the light of the white patriarchal system, it is significant that the Negroes are often described as "like children" by southerners. They give as evidence (and this is one of the white man's blanket excuses for refusing the Negroes equal social status, usually with the statement that "they are not ready") the Negro's total economic irresponsibility and his disregard for middle-class white standards. Evidently southern whites have extended their concept of the patriarchy to include the relation of the white race to the Negro race. It is a convenient rationale since it serves as both means and justification for keeping the Negroes in a state of perpetual childhood, "unready" for social integration.

The effect of this pathological social form operating within the culture has been to weaken the stability of the family in its normal function and hence to weaken the confidence of the individual members of the family in their dealings with the society as a whole. The economic and moral value of the American white family, based as it is on the male role of provider, demands masculine leadership. The pioneer family type responsible for the conquest of the West embodies the American ideal of independence, rooted in the relatively self-sufficient family united under the masculine head. In white society the father, as provider and leader, has traditionally been in position to gain the admiration of his sons and perpetuate his ideas of courage and independence, but the Negro family has not been permitted to develop the American type of family unity. The father's position is usurped by the white (both economically and morally), but the white "father" does not pass on to the Negro the same ideals that he gives his own sons. Rather he keeps the Negroes dependent.

Isolation has defined the Negroes as a less privileged and despised group. It has destroyed their self-respect on several levels to the extent that their inferiority is no longer merely an abstract moral justification, but a social fact. The special forms that the isolation has taken have forced the Negroes to develop habits of thought and action that constantly feed back into their psyches and further undermine confidence. They have been made economically and socially dependent on the white majority, and in order to survive are forced constantly to yield to the white man's whims, but at the same time are drawn inexorably toward the fruits of American society. These sustained cross pressures have had the effect of creating abnormal social patterns in the group which have in turn damaged the Negro's character and made him despised in his own eyes.

Heroes are ultimately the products of experience. They

are believed to have once lived, or they originate as fantasies or wishes of individuals and groups. The wish may be revolt or it may be conquest and aggression; in the individual it fulfils the emotional demands of the ego. The Negroes have both a feeling of competition with the whites and a desire to improve themselves, but group identification has been so weakened that these feelings cannot manifest themselves in the form of group heroes. The heroes that do emerge are ineffectual dissembling tricksters who, all too often, get only private revenge, not even perceived by the white man.

If Negroes ever should come to see clearly that their wants might be gained through identification with the group, then Negro defenders and quest heroes (real or legendary) might emerge as rallying points for anti-white protest. Martin Luther King might well become such a hero. On the other hand, geographical dispersion and other broad social trends now operating may eventually permit a greater degree of absorption of Negroes by American society. The result of this would inevitably be a weakening of the trickster tradition as it now exists.

1. Richard M. Dorson, *Negro Folktales in Michigan* (Cambridge, Mass., 1956), pp. 3-7.
2. Orrin E. Klapp, "The Folk Hero," *Journal of American Folklore*, LXII (1949), 17-25.
3. Dorson, p. 158.
4. Guy B. Johnson, *John Henry* (Chapel Hill, N.C., 1929), p. 41.
5. Stith Thompson, *The Folktale* (New York, 1951), pp. 303-44.
6. *Ibid.*, p. 344.
7. Elsie Clews Parsons, "Folklore of the Cherokee of Robeson County, North Carolina," *JAF*, XXXII (1919), 384-93.
8. Anne Virginia Culbertson, *At the Big House* (Indianapolis, 1904).
9. John Dollard, *Caste and Class in a Southern Town* (Garden City, 1957), pp. 412-13.
10. I might also remind the reader of the expression "coon," which formerly was used by whites for Negroes.
11. J. Mason Brewer, "John Tales," *Mexican Border Ballads* ("Publications of the Texas Folklore Society," XXI [1946]), p. 87.

12. E. C. Parsons, *Folktales from the Sea Islands, South Carolina* ("Memoirs of the American Folklore Society," XVI [1923]), p. 33. Other versions may be found in Parsons' collections from Maryland and Pennsylvania and North Carolina, *JAF*, XXX (1917), 190, 226; Parsons, "Folktales from Aiken, South Carolina," *JAF*, XXXIV (1921), 7; in Bacon and Parsons, "Folklore from Elizabeth-City County, Virginia," *JAF*, XXXV (1922), 278; in Arthur Huff Fauset, "Negro Folk Tales from the South," *JAF*, XL (1927), 218; and in Alcee Fortier, *Louisiana Folktales* (*MAF*, II [1895]), p. 25. These collections represent six states. The story is remarkably stable; the only variation I have found is in the choice of the fowl. The motifs are J2413.4.1 and J2413.4.2 in Stith Thompson's *Motif-Index of Folk Literature*.

13. Dorson, p. 35. Other versions may be found in Parsons, *Sea Islands*, p. 59; Parsons, "Guilford County," *JAF*, XXX (1917), 179; Bacon and Parsons, p. 272; Charles C. Jones, *Negro Myths from the Georgia Coast* (Boston, 1888), p. 1. Dorson gives references to other white and Negro versions. I have not found any references to African prototypes. There is, however, a version in the Anansi Cycle of Jamaica. See Martha Warren Beckwith, *Jamaica Anansi Stories* (*MAF*, XVII [1924], p. 15. The motif is nearest to the one numbered K1055, "Dupe persuaded to get into grass in order to learn new dance."

14. Dorson, p. 56. There is another version in Brewer, "Juneteenth," *Tone the Bell Easy* ("Publications of the Texas Folklore Society," X [1932]), p. 11. Dorson gives extensive notes on this tale, including references to the variant in the "Second Shepherd's Play" of the English Townley Cycle. He also mentions a large number of versions, both white and Negro, but no African versions. The motif is K406.2.

15. Dorson, p. 65. The incident of the trickster's overhearing the prayers of the dupe is a very popular one in the John Cycle, and there are many variations: Dorson, p. 61; Brewer, "Juneteenth," p. 26; Zora N. Hurston, *Mules and Men* (Philadelphia, 1935), p. 121; Bacon and Parsons, pp. 294-95; and Fauset, p. 262. Frequently Old Master is given the trickster's role and the Negro slave, that of the dupe. See motif J217.0.1.1.

16. Fauset, p. 271. Other versions are in Bacon and Parsons, p. 297; and Brewer, "Juneteenth," p. 38.

17. Dorson, p. 55.

18. Hurston, p. 102. Other versions are in Fauset, p. 275; and Dorson, p. 76. The motif Index lists this as motif A1671.1, "Why the Negro Works."

19. Dorson, p. 162.

20. Presumably the Negroes first corrupted the word "Claus" to "Claw." "Claw" was apparently misinterpreted to mean "hand" or "forepaw," of which the thumb is a part. There is one version of this

tale that relates the story to the crab, which has one large and one small pincer.

21. Parsons, *Sea Islands*, p. 69. Two other versions are in Fauset, p. 253; and Hurston, p. 64. This is tale type 1535; the motifs employed are K114 (deception through sale of horsehide), K944 (enemy induced to kill all his horses), K500 (escape by deception), K842 (dupe induced to replace trickster in a bag on the promise of going to heaven), and K1051 (deception into self injury).

22. For a complete discussion of this point see Dollard, pp. 61-96.

23. Bronislaw Malinowski, *Sex and Repression in Savage Society* (New York, 1955), pp. 32-33. Published first in 1927.

Why the White Man Will Never Reach the Sun

RICHARD LANCASTER

THIS STORY was told to me by James White Calf, Chief of the Piegan or Southern Blackfoot Indian Reservation of northern Montana. Chief White Calf, then 101 years old, has been Chief of the Piegans since 1897. He is the last of the great Piegan war chiefs, the most famous of all the Blackfoot orators, and the most renowned living expert on the sign language of the Plains Indians.

I met Chief White Calf during the summer of 1958, and it was no chance meeting. I was making a camp-out tour of the western states, searching for authentic stories and historical data about the Plains Indians, and my quest led me eventually to the little ranch, about twenty miles outside of Browning, Montana, where the Chief lives with his son, Jimmy Eagle Plume.

I arrived at the Chief's ranch at dusk, and was immediately invited to supper. And by the time the last venison rib had been gnawed clean, I knew that I had really found the right place. From braided steel-gray hair to moccasined feet, here, in truth, was a man. A big man, large-boned and barrel-chested, with a hand that swallowed my own in a firm handshake, and yet a man whose eyes twinkled with genuine warmth and good humor (those same eyes that had once seen the buffalo herds blacken these deep-grassed Montana plains from horizon to horizon). This was Chief White Calf, Chief of the Piegans.

The Chief invited me to pitch my camp anywhere on the

well-watered ranch that might suit my fancy, and I gratefully did so. I spent the next several weeks in getting to know the Blackfoot Indians, their language and their customs. In the evening, the Chief, Jimmy, and I would retire to the stove-heated living room of the ranch house, where the Chief would tell stories of the old days. And he had much to relate, for Chief White Calf personally experienced the days of the great buffalo hunts; a participant in numerous battles with such enemy tribes as the Crow, the Cree, the Assiniboine, and the Sioux, he suffered wounds in some battles and took enemy scalps in others (a Cree scalp decorates the handle of his brief case).

Although Chief White Calf understands English, he speaks only Blackfoot (with the exception of "O.K."), and since I did not have a tape recorder, the storytelling procedure went this way: the Chief would recite a sentence in Blackfoot, Jimmy would translate it into English, I would write the sentence down, and then I would read it back to Jimmy, who translated it back into Blackfoot for the Chief's approval (he was very insistent that the stories be transcribed with complete accuracy). This procedure was, of course, laborious and slow, but it assured the absolute authenticity of the translation.

Although I immediately felt a great respect for the Chief (which was apparently returned, for he eventually adopted me as his son), my attitude at first was shamefully typical of the white man's attitude toward the Indian. Here was a fascinating person surely, but he was, after all, an uneducated Indian —and more than one hundred years old at that. But I got my come-uppance in short order. After he had beaten me in four straight games of 500 rummy, it was quite obvious that the Chief's intellectual faculties were entirely unimpaired by age, and eventually it became apparent that Chief James White Calf is a brilliantly perspicacious person by any standard. Indeed, the Chief's awareness of the world around him—not only in the national but in the international sphere—puts to shame that of many persons of lesser age and greater formal education.

Since he cannot read, the Chief's main contact with the world at large is through his radio. He keeps a sharp ear tuned to political developments at all levels, and one evening, after becoming informed that men were attempting to direct a rocket to the moon, he motioned for me to fetch my writing pad and for Jimmy to draw his chair closer. Then, after a long, pensive silence, Chief James White Calf grunted a thunderous "O.K." and began another story.

But it was not merely another story. It was the traditional Blackfoot story of creation, the most significantly religious and formally detailed of all Blackfoot legends—a story that the Chief tells only to his sons. It became apparent as the story unfolded that much of the traditional Christian belief, as related by the early missionaries, had been incorporated into the Blackfoot tradition. And it became apparent, too, that here was not merely a classic of American Indian legendry; here was a classic of philosophical tolerance from which our modern, overly sophisticated world might well derive a meaningful lesson.

This is that story, exactly as Chief James White Calf told it to me.

I AM RUNNING WOLF, the same who is Chief White Calf, Chief of the Piegan Blackfeet, given to be chief in the year 1897 by my father, Last Gun, who was Chief White Calf of the Blackfoot Nation before me, and who gave me to be chief because he was getting pretty old. I tell you who I am so you will know that what is spoken here is spoken by me, and you know that I am Chief White Calf of the Piegans and I speak with one tongue. What I say here is the truth, and if anybody says to you that it is not the truth then you ask them how they know, for they were not there at the beginning.

Hear me, I am Chief White Calf of the Blackfeet, and you are my son, Last Gun, for I have given to you the name of my father who was Chief White Calf before me and who was called among the Piegans as Last Gun. I have given you the beaded gloves to show that I am glad to have you for my son and I love you as my son, and your brother, Jimmy Eagle Plume, has given you the beaded moccasins to show he is glad to have you for a brother and he loves you for his brother, and now I give you this story, for this is the way it was in the beginning.

I am Chief White Calf of the Blackfeet, and I am one hundred and one years old, and I give you this story that I got from my father, Last Gun, who got it from the old men of the tribe. I am one hundred and one years but I am not old, for when I was a young man and hunted the buffalo and made war on the Crees and Assiniboines and Crows and counted coup on them and stole their horses I was never afraid because Nah-tóh-seh came to me in a dream and told me that I would live a long time but I would never be old. But he gave me just so long to live and I don't know when I will die, so I give you this story so it will not be lost. No other of the Blackfeet know this story because I have not told them, because it is the true story of how things were in the beginning and it is given by the Chief to his son so it will not be forgotten. You are my son, and I am White Calf, Chief of the Piegan Blackfeet and I give it to you.

Only once before I tried to give this story. There was a missionary and I called him son and gave him a name and tried to give him this story but he would not take it because he said that this is not the way things were in the beginning. But I was not proud to have him for my son because he says there is only one path through the forest and he knows the right path, but I say there are many paths and how can you know the best path unless you have walked them all. He walked too long on one path and he does not know there are other paths. And I am one hundred and one, and I know that sometimes many paths go to the same place.

Hear me, you are my son, Last Gun, and I know you will tell this story the way I tell it to you and not change it the way white men do, and so I give this story to be yours, for this is the way it was in the beginning.

O.K. In the beginning there were just two of them, a Man and a Woman, and they made the whole world. There were no oceans at the beginning of the world, and there were no mountains and no trees and no rivers that flow into the oceans.

So before they began to build the world, the Woman said to the Man, "We have a lot of work to do to build the world, so let us have two children right away so they can help us with the work."

And the Man answered her: "No, we are not ready for children yet. We will have them later on."

But the Woman said that they should have children right away and the Man said no, they were not ready yet. Three times the Woman asked to have children to help build the world, and three times the Man said no, they were not ready for children yet. But the fourth time the Woman said they should have children, the Man finally said all right and he asked her if she wanted boys.

And the Woman said, "I want two boy children, so they can help us build the world, for girls could not help us as well as boys could."

So two boys were born, and they grew to be eight years old. One of the boys was very wise and clever and he has no Indian name but is known as Mu-ká-kí, which means *very smart* in the Blackfoot tongue. But the other boy, whose name is Náh-pi, was pretty stupid and the Blackfeet call him Mut-tsáhp-tsi, which means *crazy* or *old man*.

Then one day Mu-ká-kí, who was the wise boy, found that his mother was running around with another man. So he told his brother, Náh-pi, who was not so smart, and Náh-pi asked him what they should do about it. And Mu-ká-kí said, "We will tell our father that our mother is running around with another man." And so they told him.

"When our mother goes out to build the world," they said,

"she works for only a little while and then she goes down by the big tree and plays with another man."

But the Father said, "This cannot be, for there are only the four of us in the world. We are not yet ready for other people until we finish building the world."

So Mu-ká-kí, who was the smart boy, said to his brother that they would go down and hide by the big tree and spy on their mother. So they hid down there, and pretty soon the Mother came down and began to hit all around the tree. The tree was really just a big stump, and after the Mother had beat all around the big stump for a while, a big snake with a horn on his head came out of the top of the stump and started to crawl down. And when he was halfway down the stump, he jumped, and when he landed on the ground he was a handsome white man. And the white man and the woman began playing together by the big stump. And the boys ran back and told their father that the Mother was playing with the white man down by the big stump, but the Father would not believe them. "There are only the four of us," he said. "We are not ready for other people yet until we finish building the world."

So two more times the boys hid down by the stump and watched the Mother playing with the white man, and each time they ran back and told the Father that when the Mother went out to make the world she would work for just a little while and then go down by the big stump and play with the white man. But the Father would not believe them.

So for the fourth time the boys went down to watch their mother, and this time when they came back to tell their father he believed them. So the Father sent his wife out to work again but pretty soon she came back, and he said to her, "You should keep working. We have a lot of work to do to build this world."

So the Woman went back to work, and while she was busy working, the Man put on a woman's dress and combed his hair like a woman and went down to the big stump and beat on it like a woman. And pretty soon a big snake with a horn on his

head came out of the stump and started to crawl down, and
when he was halfway down he jumped and when he landed on
the ground he turned into a white man. So then they fought,
and pretty soon Man killed the big snake.

And then Mu-ká-kí, who was the smart boy, said to his
father, "Our mother will be after us now for sure, because we
have killed the white man she was playing around with. She will
try to kill you, Father, but you should try to kill her first. We are
your sons, and we will help you fight."

And sure enough, the Woman chased after her husband and
caught him and then they fought for a long time. Finally the
Woman got her husband down and was going to kill him, but
the boys helped their father fight and together they killed the
Mother and cut off her head.

But pretty soon the Mother's head began to chase after
them and the Father said, "Boys, we are going to leave here
and go some other place."

So they started to travel, and the Mother's head chased after
them, so the Father started to build up the timber behind him
and the boys so the head could not get through. But the head
got through anyway.

So after he built the timber, the Father built up the mountains so the Mother's head could not follow. But the Mother's
head followed anyway.

So then Mu-ká-kí, who was a pretty smart boy, said to his
father, "Father, Mother's head must be back together again
with the body, otherwise she couldn't follow us so fast. Now
that the timber and the mountains are finished, we have no
place to go. How are we going to get away from our mother?"

But the Father said, "Boys, we have one more thing to do to
get away from your mother." So then he made the oceans all
around the place where he was so the Mother couldn't follow,
and he stayed on the islands where he was and that was the
Indian country. Nowadays they call it United States.

So then the Father started to make the rivers and the

streams, and his son Mu-ká-kí, who was pretty smart, said, "Father, you keep this up and pretty soon you'll have this land all covered with water."

But the Father, who was pretty smart too, said, "No, this land will never be covered with water, because I make the streams to run into the rivers and the rivers to run into the ocean."

You can see this is the true story, because even today the rivers all run into the ocean and the land is not covered with water.

O.K. But then when the streams and rivers were finished, Mu-ká-kí, the wise son, went to his father and said, "Father, Mother is here. She came across the ocean."

So the Father said, "Now I don't have any more place on this world to go, so now I'm going to another world. But first I'm going to send your mother to another place so she won't see me go. She will disappear for thirty days, and four days after the thirty days she will be back, but I will be gone. When your mother leaves it will be dark, so she can't see, but when I leave it will be bright daylight so you will all be able to see. No matter how hard they try, nobody will ever be able to get to the world where I am going."

So Woman went up to the moon in the dark of night, and Man went up to the sun in bright daylight, and even today there is a woman in the moon and a man in the sun.

But before he left for his new world, Man spoke to his two sons: "Boys, I've got to leave for my new world, but my work here is not finished because I haven't made the people yet. So you two boys will have to finish my work for me. Mu-ká-kí, who is the cleverest one, will go back across the ocean and make the people there, and Náh-pi, who is not so clever and who will be called Mut-tsáhp-tsi, will stay here and make the people here. Mu-ká-kí, who is clever, will go back across the ocean and make people, and for them he will make machines and big weapons. He will do this because he is clever. But

Náh-pi is pretty stupid, so he will stay here and just make the people.

"The people of Mu-ká-kí will have white skins, and in the beginning they will all speak the same tongue. The people of Náh-pi will have red skins and in the beginning they will have their own language that they will all speak. The people of Mu-ká-kí will be clever and have many tools, and one day they will try to build a big tower and reach the new world of Man, but one day when the tower is only just so high, one of the men will say to another, 'Hand me that tool there,' and at that time the man will not understand him because the language will change and everybody will speak a different tongue. And from then they will be enemies and fight amongst themselves because they cannot understand one another, and they will be so busy fighting that they will forget all about the tower.

"And at the same time that the languages change amongst the whites, they will change among the red men, and each tribe will speak a different tongue and they will fight amongst themselves because they do not understand one another."

And all that Man said came to pass. Even then there were dogs and they spoke like men, so when the Woman in the Moon played around with other men, the dogs could spy on her and tell Man in the Sun. But at the same time as the language changed, Woman in the Moon put filth in the mouth of Dog and said, "From this time on, no dog can talk to any man; dogs will understand what men say, but when Dog tries to tell Man about Woman, Man will not understand." And so now when it is four days past the thirtieth day, Dog howls at Woman in the Moon to come and give him his voice back. So when you hear the dog howl at the moon, you know that this is the true story of how it was long ago in the beginning.

I do not know how Mut-tsáhp-tsi worked when he made the people over the ocean, for I do not understand the ways of the white men. But the Indian people were made by Náh-pi, and he made them like little dolls from clay. When he had finished he put them into little groups, so that each one knew what group he belonged in, and then after four days they began to walk around.

Pretty soon Náh-pi married one of his people and then pretty soon they had a boy child. Then Náh-pi said to his wife, "When we die we will die for four days, and then we will come back."

But his wife said, "No, that way there will soon be too many people. Why don't we die for good!" And pretty soon Náh-pi said O.K.

But then their little boy who was their only child died, and Náh-pi's wife said to him, "Why don't you say it again—to die for four days and come back!" But Náh-pi said, "No! It's too late now. We die for good!"

And then Jesus was born across the ocean. When he was born, the Jews tried to find him and kill him as a baby because they were afraid he would become chief of all the tribes. But then he grew up, and finally they found him and crucified him on a cross. He stayed on the cross four days and then came back to the village and said, "Good-bye, I'm going to the other world."

So the Catholics knew there would be a big flood at that time and they built a big boat and almost everybody got on it. And while they were on the boat a pigeon brought a leaf to them, and then the Priest made magic and all the water turned to land again. So that is why you find the bones of the buffalo in the banks alongside the streams.

So over there they call him Jesus whom they saw going up. So over there they believe in him as God. But here they believe in the Sun and the Moon, and they pray to Sun, the Man, and Moon, the Woman. For Náh-pi said to his people to pray in the nighttime to Mother Moon, and in the daytime to pray to Father Sun. And that is the true story of how things were in the beginning, and you know that it is I who tell you this and that what I tell you is true, for I am Running Wolf, Warrior of the Crazy Dog Clan of the Piegans, known as Chief White Calf, Chief of the Blackfoot Nation.

And now I hear that white men are trying once again to reach the New World, Sun, home of Man. But they will never get there. Their towers will get just so high and no higher, but they will never reach the New World, Sun, where Man and Jesus went up, because their tongues are different and they do not understand one another, and they fight amongst themselves and do not work together.

And the same is true for the Indians. Their tongues are different and they do not understand one another and they fight amongst themselves. So they can never reach the New World.

Only when all men are of one tongue and one heart and work together and stop fighting amongst themselves will Man and Jesus return. In the meantime the only way to get to the New World where Man and Jesus live is to be dead for good.

Hear me, I am Chief White Calf, Chief of the Piegans and all the Blackfeet, and I have spoken.

Vigilante Justice in Springtown

G. A. REYNOLDS

THERE WAS very little law in and around the village of Springtown, in northern Parker County, Texas, before 1880; and strong feelings were more often exhibited than suppressed. This was no longer a part of the frontier, but the ways of living and dying were still much the same. The rugged individualism so necessary on the frontier was little less than necessary here, where horse thieves and Indians abounded. Nothing, incidentally, was considered lower than a horse thief. The horse was indispensable, and his loss usually meant real hardship for someone. There was always some law and order in theory but not always in practice. Tales of those days are still told in Springtown.

There was one family living near Springtown who were said to have absolutely no respect for either the theory or the practice of law and order; this was the family of a man called Al whose log cabin was about a mile southwest of the village. There was a creek about twenty feet from the back of the house. Making the most of the situation, the enterprising Al dug a tunnel from the house to the creek and rigged a trap door through which the tunnel could be entered from the house, which soon became known as a refuge for horse thieves and others who had reason to be on the run. Several times law officers approached the house after seeing fugitives disappear in that direction, but a search of the building was always fruitless. It was a simple matter for a fugitive to slip through

the trap door and run through the tunnel to the creek, where
he could find a place to hide.

One man who used the tunnel in this manner had been on a
cattle buying trip with his partner, who was carrying six
thousand dollars in cash. The temptation was too great; he
killed his partner and took the money. The killer had heard of
Al's friendliness toward such as he, and he quickly made his
way to his house to hide. He had been there only a few days
when a posse flushed him and forced him to use the tunnel in a
hurry. Folklore says that he buried the six thousand dollars
somewhere near the house and was never able to return for it.
True or not, this story has caused treasure seekers to sift the
earth in the vicinity ever since.

Al and his wife had six daughters and two sons. They
owned 160 acres of good land, but they were not farmers;
they found that it was much easier to profit from the labors of
others. They were so vicious that grown men feared even the
women. Al was said to be as mean as a lonesome stallion; and
one man said that he was "as scared of the oldest daughter as
of an Indian."[1] Another man, investigating the sound of a shot,
found this same girl wrestling with one of his hogs. Her shot
had only stunned the animal, which had revived; and she, yelling and enjoying the fun, was finishing the job with a knife. The
man, preferring his private dishonor to an encounter with the
girl, quietly crept away.

This girl had many claims to fame. She must have been as
strong as a bull, and about as brutal; it was said that, in a fight,
she and any good man were equal to three. One story is that
once she was riding along on her horse when she began to feel
labor pains. She stopped, tied her horse to a tree, and promptly
gave birth to a baby. Then she crushed the infant's skull with a
rock and threw the little body into a brush pile. After a few
minutes' rest she remounted her horse and resumed her
interrupted trip.

The members of this family had a remarkable sense of

humor; they got a great deal of enjoyment out of riding around the square in Springtown and "shooting up" the town. It was great fun to watch the stampede as people sought shelter. On one occasion, however, a man failed to run; he was lying asleep on his cellar door. When Al saw him he decided to shoot the luckless fellow "just to see him kick."[2] The man died and the honest people of the town chalked up another black mark beside Al's name. By this time there were quite a few marks. How much more could the people stand?

One day a man who did not know just how tough Al's women were rode by their house. Seeing two of the women in the yard, he followed the custom of the day by tipping his hat and speaking a word of neighborly greeting to them. He was then startled and a little frightened to hear them curse like angry mule skinners and threaten to kill him for trying to flirt with them! On the return trip he was careful as he passed the house. The same two women were in the yard, but he kept his eyes on the road and his mouth shut. Imagine his consternation when they cursed him and threatened to kill him for *not* speaking to them! From that time on, this man avoided the house completely, even if it meant taking to the woods.

The law officer at Springtown, Constable Hemphill, began to give Al's family more trouble than they thought proper; therefore, they reasoned, the logical thing was to shoot him. They worked out a foolproof—or nearly foolproof—plan; one night when the constable was attending church at Veal's Station, about three miles south of Springtown, they prepared an ambush on the road which they knew he would take on the return trip. Everything worked perfectly, except that they shot the wrong man when they became confused in the darkness. Then they blamed the whole thing on some Indians who had a camp near by. Most people were ready to believe anything bad about the Indians, who were inveterate thieves; and the truth did not come out until years later. Constable Hemphill, with his charmed life, continued to plague Al and his folks; but he was afraid to go too far. This family was simply too much for the law of that time.

They dealt with horse thieves in an interesting manner. Since their reputation had spread far and wide among the lawless element, any man bent on a little thievery usually looked them up soon after he hit town. Having scouted the countryside and learned the locations of the best stock, Al and his family were in a position to tell the stranger just where he could expect to find good horses and just where to watch out for law officers. That night the stranger could sleep with his choice of the daughters. Early the next morning he could collect the horses and be on his way to parts unknown. This system provided recreation and extra income for the family in a country where there was little to do with spare time.

The people of Springtown put up with the family for several years; but finally, in the winter of 1863, the citizens decided they had had enough. Something had to be done, but obviously the law could not handle the job. Eventually, ten men met secretly and pledged themselves to the task of ridding the country of the trouble. Folklore says they all rode white or light-gray horses.[3]

The first chance for this vigilance committee to act came one day when one of the group found Al alone several miles from his home. This member quickly rounded up the others. Then the whole committee rode up to Al and surrounded him, telling him he was under arrest. Everyone knew he was as crooked as a dog's hind leg, but there was little chance of punishing him legally; therefore, the leader of the group told him that he was free to go but that he had better run for his life. As he ran, ten rifles spouted death and he fell. They left him where he lay, in thick woods.

Al's wife wondered for about a year what had happened to her husband; there was no word or sign of him. She wondered if he had deserted her. Then one day she happened to stumble upon his body, now nothing but bones. She was able to identify the remains by the wallet and shoes. Carefully she gathered every fragment to take home for burial. Somehow she stuck a sharp splinter of bone into one of her fingers, which later became infected and had to be removed. She never knew how her husband died.

After the killing of Al, the members of the vigilance committee thought that the women would either behave or leave the community; and years went by without any sensational occurrences. In 1870, however, the older of the two sons was killed "in a difficulty with another man in Palo Pinto County, Texas."[4] Now the mother, the six daughters, and one small son were left.

The activities of the remainder of the family became more and more violent. The oldest girl was the worst of the lot. Neither she nor any of her sisters pretended to be "ladies." In a day when all ladies were supposed to ride their horses side-saddle, these women threw their legs over the animals with as much abandon as did men. Once more the vigilance committee came into being — to deal with the oldest girl. The committee assembled one day in 1872 and started for the house to get her; but somehow she got wind of their intentions and fled northward, seeming to know that at last the day of reckoning had come. No longer was she anything to be feared; she was now a frightened doe running ahead of the relentless hounds. The hounds caught up with their quarry, bringing her to bay "near the line of Wichita and Clay Counties, Texas."[5] Here, in desperation, she changed back from a doe to a tigress. She was probably at least the equal of any man there, but she had no chance against ten. She was hanged from the nearest tree.

Men have always been reluctant to kill women in the American West, under any circumstances; but now the reluctance was overcome. The members of the posse returned to Springtown, and then in a meeting a few days later they decided to carry their brand of justice still farther. Going to the home, they found there only two of the daughters, who

were taken into custody. According to some they were given a
fair if speedy trial, a well-known lawyer being brought to the
gathering in the woods to defend the women. Other versions of
the story say there was no trial; but all agree on the outcome
of the affair. The men found a tree, about fourteen inches in
diameter, growing on the south bank of a creek and leaning
so that it overhung the north bank. They tied ropes around the
necks of the two women, led their horses under the tree on the
north bank, and threw the ropes over the trunk. The ends of the
ropes were tied to another tree, and the stage was set. The
women were given a chance to say a few last words, but
they were defiant to the end. They never broke down, and
they never asked for mercy. The only emotion they showed was
contempt. The horses were slapped sharply, and they bolted
for home. The men separated and went to their own homes.

Again the men gathered to discuss justice and punishment.
After a short conference they rode once more. Al's widow and
her four remaining children were at home, but they saw the
men coming and fled. When the men reached the house and
found it empty, they delayed only long enough to set it afire;
then they took off in pursuit of the fugitives, who reached a
point about eight miles west of Springtown before they were
overtaken and captured. The boy and one girl, being small, were
sent away. Al's widow and her last two daughters were taken
to a clearing and shot to death.

The common people of Springtown knew about the shooting, but they had no idea what had happened to the two girls
who were hanged. They considered the disappearance good rid-
dance and did not ask questions. One day, however, two men
went out to hunt some strayed sheep. These men chanced to
cross the creek about a mile downstream from the tree on
which the two women were hanged, and in a pile of driftwood
they saw a human skull. They followed the creek upstream,
finding more members of bodies on the way, until they reached
the scene of the hanging. On the trunk of a tree were carved the

letters "HT," which probably stood for "Hanging Tree."[6] They examined the scene and then went on their way, telling others about it later.

Many people thought that the remains should have a decent burial, but no one had the nerve to do anything about it except a man named Al Thompson. Al was one of the roughest acting, hardest drinking, loudest cursing reprobates of the community; but he made the "decent" people ashamed of themselves because he was the only one with courage enough to bury the bodies. He expected trouble; therefore, he buckled on his gun before he set out. Then he dared anyone to start anything. He drove a sled pulled by two mules to the spot where the hanging had taken place, gathered up all the bones that he could find, and took them to the Springtown cemetery, where he buried them. More than a few people did not want their cemetery "defiled" in this way; but none was going to buck Al Thompson.

The two small children were given to a kind family and raised by this family to maturity. The boy, it is said, displayed his "bad blood" by getting into trouble frequently and was eventually killed in a gunfight.[7] The only survivor of the family was the smallest girl. She is said to be living now near a small Texas town—with her past effectively hidden. The few people who could tell the truth about this facet of the case are either dead or respectfully silent.[8]

An element of mystery entered the case a few years ago. Al was known to have buried twelve hundred dollars near his home in an old iron pot. Then, many decades later, someone found the buried treasure by cutting six inches deep into the trunks of several trees to find nails which Al had driven into them to serve as some sort of code to give directions.[9] How did the finder know which trees had the nails driven into them? How did he know what the nails meant? How did he know just where to cut each tree? These questions are apparently destined to remain unanswered, but obviously the money was found. An empty hole with the old iron pot beside it gave mute testimony to this effect.

Most of the peole of Springtown were ashamed of the story of Al and his family, but most of them also felt that what happened was necessary. They said that the vigilantes probably were not motivated by vengeance entirely; they were establishing law and order in the only way that they knew. What they did was probably wrong, but it was a means to a necessary end. This was one of the "growing pains" which our country suffered during its youth. It is nothing of which to be proud, but the story has always found attentive ears as it has been passed down from each generation to the next. "Hangman's Hollow" is only a small ravine today, but it is still famous in Parker County folklore. Almost any citizen of Springtown will point out some likely-looking place to the visitor if given a chance, and will call it "Hangman's Hollow" and tell the story of the women who should have been men and should have lived on the early frontier.

1. William T. Hutcheson, interview in Springtown, April 4, 1958.
2. Aldon C. Huddleston, interview in Springtown, February 8, 1958.
3. E. A. Williams, interview at Springtown, March 6, 1958.
4. John W. Nix, A Tale of Two Schools (Fort Worth, 1945), p. 26.
5. Ibid.
6. W. P. Lynch, interview in Springtown, April 4, 1958.
7. William T. Hutcheson, interview in Springtown, April 4, 1958.
8. E. A. Williams, interview in Springtown, March 20, 1958.
9. William T. Hutcheson, interview in Springtown, April 4, 1958.

The Sinking Treasure of Bowie Creek

J. R. JAMISON

IN THE SPRING OF 1956 a party of five men pooled their resources and entered into an agreement with W. T. Jamison to hunt gold on his land in Liberty County, Texas. Being a son of the land-owner, I became extremely interested in what they based their theories on and how they planned to carry out this operation.

It seems that the one with all the information was willing to talk freely with me about his knowledge of the treasure, and I would certainly be the last to discourage him, no matter how remote from fact I really thought his story was. His name is Sambo Reeves and he is from the Trinity River bottom land somewhere near Moss Hill, Texas.

Mr. Reeves looks the part, to say the least. He is an elderly person with soft gray hair, usually wears a quarter-inch beard of a like texture, and has a pot belly that amply fills his blue overalls. He has no teeth; he enjoys a healthy dip of Garrett snuff, some of which occasionally finds its way down the apex of his oval chin. I learned to like this old man. He's the type of person you might visualize as one to tell of mysterious legends of hidden treasure, spirits of the swamps, and "true" experiences with the supernatural. For a person who was as sure as he that there was so much gold in the locality, he remained unchangingly calm and collected. Even during the actual digging when items were uncovered which would quite startlingly verify his story, he would consider them with no surprise at all. In fact, his nonchalance would reveal only a

209

hint of bewilderment because we made such a fuss when his story would check out correctly. His pale blue eyes had an eternal gaze of complacency and his speech was soft as he consistently assured us that one of the largest shipments of Spanish gold ever to cross Texas was buried in the area known as Bowie Creek.

Many years ago, according to Mr. Reeves, Spanish soldiers were escorting a mule train with the payroll for troops located in Louisiana or somewhere in East Texas along the Old Spanish Trail, which crossed Bowie Creek Swamp approximately a mile and a half north of the present United States Highway 90 (the creek runs north and south between the towns of Liberty and Dayton). The soldiers were attacked by a band of Indians, and a terrific battle took place in an open field near the wooded swamp land of Bowie Creek. After the encounter there remained alive only a handful of Spaniards and no Indians at all. Since there were too few to risk carrying the gold farther, the survivors sought to hide it in a high spot near the edge of the creek and on the northeast side of the field. They dug a hole and placed in it a copper box containing twelve jackloads of gold, each jackload weighing not less than three hundred pounds. Then they dug a trench eight feet deep due west from the gold. There they buried their deceased comrades, mules, Indians, and all.

As was customary for all buried treasures, they left a clue to mark the place. Mr. Reeves claims to have known when he was younger a lumberman who, on felling a large hardwood tree in the Bowie Creek area, noted carvings of signs and numbers on the tree. It was concluded that these markings had some significance as a waybill, but it is very possible that they were the vital clue to the whereabouts of hundreds of thousands of dollars in gold. However, the discovery of this probable clue did not begin to dovetail with the legendary story of the Indian battle and the buried gold until several years after the tree had been destroyed. Although Mr. Reeves says he has heard all of his life that there was some buried gold somewhere in that locality, it wasn't until near the turn of the century that a Mexican showed up in the area with a waybill supposedly of the ill-fated mule train. The Mexican dug in the area several weeks but finally became discouraged and disappeared.

About a decade later a family of Negroes (none of whom are available or even known now) moved to the area and built a house. Whether or not the colored people had heard there was gold in the vicinity isn't certain, but they learned of it, according to Mr. Reeves, by hearing the movements and voices of the Spanish soldiers' spirits, or by seeing the light coming from the gold through the surface of the ground, visible only at certain times on particular nights.

At any rate, the Negroes were sure enough that there was gold in a certain spot to begin digging in the rich sandy land. The sand began caving in on them as they dug deeper, and they were forced to board up the sides of the hole, which became a rectangular shaft. As they dug almost to the water sand, which was about ten feet deep, they hit the chest, breaking a small opening in it. Then and there they feasted their astounded eyes on the fabulous treasure for the first and last time. Hoping to exhume the entire chest, they sharpened two posts to pry it from the damp mud. First they pried with one post and then the other until one of the posts snapped. Trying desperately to hold the heavy chest, they finally realized they must let go, and they watched thirty-six hundred pounds of gold slowly sink back beneath the oozing quicksand.

Mr. Reeves says the reports he has heard vary on only one point. Some say there was sitting on top of the chest a small box or basket of jewels which the Negroes salvaged, so that it was possible for them to move near Chicago where relatives lived. Others say they took the jewels and moved to the city for reasons of safety, and still others say no jewels were found on the chest. "Whether the jewels were found or not," says Mr. Reeves, "has little to do with the fact that the discovery of

the chest authenticates every story I've heard about the gold
being buried there."

With all these tales Mr. Reeves went to several men who had
the money and equipment for an expedition. Of course they
felt just like you or me: the thing is fantastic—who ever heard
of buried gold in Liberty County? Just for the fun of it they
decided to go to the place with Mr. Reeves to take a quick
look and then forget it. Well, Mr. Reeves took them to Bowie
Creek to look over the lay of the land. Actually they found a
place resembling the area Mr. Reeves described, and then they
found a bluff-type embankment at the edge of a swamp. Mr.
Reeves insisted that was the place, since it was in the corner
of the field and at the edge of the creek. He told them all they
needed to do was to take a bulldozer and begin digging off the
bluff so that they might discover the remains of the old shaft
dug by the Negroes. There was no evidence on the surface of
the ground of any such digging, but they decided that, since
it would take very little time to blade off such a small area, it
might be worth trying.

At this point the men all signed an agreement with my
father, the landowner, that in the event any gold or other
treasure was located in the area by this group, the said gold
would be divided equally. Then, with permission to enter the
property, the bulldozer was moved in. Several large scrapes
were made on the surface of the ground and almost immediately
fragments of bones, pottery, and a few arrowheads were
turned up. Everybody but Mr. Reeves was astounded when
several pieces of badly decayed wooden planks showed up in
the sand scraped from the crest of the embankment. After several more feet of dirt had been moved away it was obvious that
a shaft had been built there many years ago. Since the bulldozer
was limited as to the depth it could go, the men brought in a
dragline and began digging where the shaft was located. After
a considerable amount of dirt was removed, the area of the
hole began getting bigger and bigger with the caving-in of

sand. Work was halted momentarily upon the discovery that what looked like pieces of root deep in the ground proved to be, when extracted from the hole, two fence posts. Strange, isn't it? What is even more strange to me is that one of the posts was cracked in about a 20° angle, as if it had been used to pry something heavy. Mr. Reeves remained calm as he casually inspected the posts, and assured the diggers that they should go a little deeper to find the gold.

As the digging progressed, a sudden halt was again called for a close examination of some traces of green substance in the sand which looked strikingly as if it had been caused by a chemical reaction or oxidation such as corrosion of a coppery metal. The phenomenal evidence of a copper chest lying in this spot for many years was visible, and the story of the shifting quicksand's taking away the chest of gold on the brink of its removal by the Negroes was pounding in the thoughts of the silent group of men.

The following weeks were spent in desperate efforts to dig deeper through the quicksand and water. Suction pumps were put into action as the struggle went on. Meanwhile, during these discouraging days of cave-ins and breakdowns, Mr. Reeves stood by with ready advice.

There is quite a large hole in the Bowie Creek area now. The flooding backwaters of the Trinity River finally brought about abandonment of the digging project, and the once enthusiastic anticipation has died down.—Died down? Yes, in all except one: I shall never forget the unchanging faith one man had in his own ideas and knowledge as he stood by the gaping gorge, spat a watery salute of Garrett snuff over the front of his well-filled blue overalls and said, "Well, it's in there, you just ain't dug deep enough."

South Texas Sketches

RUTH DODSON

Aunt Jane's Scares

IN THE "EARLY DAYS"—I mean those days before the telephone, the daily paper, the automobile—much of our leisure time was spent in conversation, and in the telling of stories of events in our own lives and in the lives of others. These stories often became legends that passed down from one generation to another. Of all the sorts of narratives with which we entertained one another, I believe "scares" were the most popular. But not all of these scares, these frightful experiences that many went through in the early days, were of the same character; some involved much danger, some much imagination. My great-aunt, Jane Burris, told me of two scares she experienced in those unsettled early days.

Shortly after she and Uncle Doc were married, not long after the Civil War, they were living in a little house near the Escondido Creek in Karnes County. Her uncle, Bill Butler, and his family lived about a mile away, on the opposite side of the creek. The men were away working cattle, as they usually were in those busy times. Late every afternoon the oldest Butler boy would come over on horseback to take Aunt Jane to spend the night at the Butler home. But one day it rained and the boy was unable to cross the creek, so Aunt Jane had to stay alone. That night it was too warm to sleep, she said, so she was sitting near the door, where she had only a curtain hanging. The large, vicious dog that she kept with her for protection was lying on the step in front of the door. All at once the dog charged, and she knew that someone was there. She didn't make a move, but depended on the dog. After a brief struggle the dog was silent; then she knew she must protect herself. She picked up the pistol that was on a table near by; it had only two cartridges in it—all the ammunition she had. When she audibly cocked the pistol, she heard someone just outside running. She jerked the curtain aside and shot in the direction the prowler was running, which was toward the corner of the wood fence that surrounded the house. At this corner there were two posts that spread apart, leaving a space through which one could pass. Aunt Jane said that she did not know whether or not it could have been she who shot the Negro found dead next day in the creek bottom, but that Uncle Doc always discouraged the idea that she could have been such a good shot.

Aunt Jane sat the rest of the night holding the pistol with the one load in it. Just at daylight, her Uncle Bill, who had returned home, came to see about her and was the first to see the dog lying at the door with his throat cut. The men, of course, made every effort to find the intruder, but were not successful —unless the dead Negro were he.

On the rare occasions when depredations were made along the border between Texas and Mexico, their stories were told and retold, with the result that people on ranches in that part of the country were always on the alert for raiding incursions. Especially were the women and children uneasy when left alone.

Aunt Jane told of a scare she had when she and Uncle Doc lived in La Salle County, not far from the Rio Grande. She said that one time she was alone with several small children, the oldest, John, a boy about twelve years old. Uncle Doc was away working cattle. Late one afternoon she saw her nearest neighbor and another woman coming horseback. They were riding fast; she knew something must be very much the matter. One of the women was riding a big, raw-boned horse, on a man's saddle—obviously all that had been available on short

notice. Facing a strong wind, this woman's sunbonnet had
blown off her head and was hanging down her back. She was
riding astride, and her long full skirt billowed out and all but
enveloped the horse. Aunt Jane ran to the gate to meet the
women; they stopped only long enough to tell her it was
reported a band of raiders was coming their way and she had
better hide, since her house was on a hill and could be seen
from a distance. They then rode on to carry the warning to
others.

Aunt Jane thought at once of a place to hide—perhaps had
already selected it in case it should be needed. It was a clearing in the middle of thick brush a mile and a half away. She
called John to get the horses and hitch them to the spring
wagon at once; a second child was sent to turn the milk calves
out; she and the rest of the children gathered up bedding, gro-
ceries, and cooking outfit and put them in the wagon as
quickly as possible. When they had everything ready, the children scrambled into the back of the wagon. Aunt Jane climbed
over one wheel and John over the other to reach the seat. She
said that when she picked up the lines her hands were trembling so she could hardly hold them. The horses, sensing the
excitement, started off in a brisk trot, but it wasn't fast enough
under the circumstances. She took the whip and brought it
down on one of the horses, then lashed the other one. When she
did this, the second horse stopped dead still. She had forgotten
that this horse balked if as much as touched with a whip. John
jumped out over the wheel, took the horse by the bridle, and
started him up again. He ran along, holding to the bridle, until
he had the horse in a trot; then, climbing in the back of the
wagon, he crawled to the front and took his seat by his mother's
side.

John had hardly settled himself when Aunt Jane felt
impelled to get more speed out of the team. All she needed to
do was to urge the one horse, then the balker would have kept
up with him. But before she realized what she was doing she

brought the whip down impartially, and the balky horse stopped as before. John jumped out and got him started again, then climbed back in the wagon, at the same time imploring his mother to put down the whip if she couldn't keep from using it on the balky horse. But Aunt Jane couldn't be prevailed upon to give up the whip. She said they traveled the whole mile and a half in just that way, with John jumping out and starting the horse, and her stopping him immediately after with a stroke of the whip.

They spent an uneasy night listening for anything that might sound like a party of bandits, but nothing happened. The next morning Aunt Jane made a fire and was cooking breakfast when Uncle Doc rode up. He stopped when he saw them, took off his hat and rubbed his hand over his head, and gazed at them, bewildered. Coming home, he had found the place deserted and the calves turned out, which indicated that the return was uncertain. He had seen the wagon tracks and followed them as quickly as possible, wondering uneasily what it all meant.

When Aunt Jane saw Uncle Doc she called to him and explained that they were hiding from bandits. "From bandits?" Uncle Doc was still puzzled. "What bandits?" he wanted to know. Well, Aunt Jane didn't know; all she knew was what their neighbor had told her, and she, apparently, had received the news from the woman who was with her—that bandits were expected to make a raid through the country. Aunt Jane said that Uncle Doc laughed until she thought he would fall off his horse; he was highly amused at the adventure. But he got down and had breakfast with them, then they packed up and went back to the ranch without the horse's balking one time— but Aunt Jane didn't use the whip on him.

It Cried at Midday

I DIDN'T MIND spending the dismal afternoon alone in the rambling old house where I was a guest. I had been born there. I had

grown up on the lonely ranch, now the home of my brother. So
the prospects of a few hours alone at the familiar place made
me neither happy nor unhappy. I would spend the time reading, I planned; I would not allow myself to become sad over
old memories.

After my brother's car disappeared down the road and
into the mesquite brush, I lingered on the front gallery, looking over the creek valley and to the gray hills beyond. But to
linger there was to invite reminiscences. So I went back into
the kitchen to have a cup of coffee that was still hot on the
wood range.

I had sat down at the kitchen table when Doña Jesusa, our
old Mexican neighbor, appeared at the outside kitchen door.

"*Pase*, Doña Jesusa," I invited. "You are just in time to have
a cup of coffee with me. How are you? I am glad to see you,"
I told her as she came in. We talked in Spanish.

"And I have much pleasure in seeing you. I heard that you
had come on a visit to your old home, so I walked the mile to
see you. But how my legs ache! I am so old now; I have little
strength. Ah, how much you grow to look like your mother; so
much like she did when I first knew her many years ago. I
almost fancy that I see her again." And the old eyes filled with
tears.

"Sit right here by the table and rest," I told her. "And here
is a cup of hot coffee. It is getting cold and damp outside, no?
I'll put some wood in the stove."

"Ay! Ay!" the old woman lamented as she sat heavily down
and slipped the black shawl off her head and low on her
large fleshy shoulders. "How *triste* everything about this place
is now. How much I miss my old neighbors, your parents."

"I sometimes come here for a little while, just to sit and
remember; to think of the times that are past and of those who
are gone—of your people as well as of mine. Tell me," she asked
challengingly, "you don't 'find yourself' here on the ranch now,
do you?"

I tried to smile the question aside, but the old woman looked squarely at me and insisted. "Now tell me the truth, you don't 'find yourself' here."

"Well, no, Doña Jesusa, I guess I don't 'find myself,' as you say. Many changes have been made in the old place." Then I sat down on the opposite side of the table, and I could see, through the window, that the fine mist was changing into a drizzle which the east wind would make uncomfortable for the old woman to be out in. I told her she must stay with me until my brother returned and took her home in his car. And I resolved to take the opportunity to try to learn something that had puzzled me for a long time. So while the old woman smoked loud-smelling, shuck-wrapped cigarettes and we both sipped coffee, I directed the conversation into the channel that I wanted it to take.

"Doña Jesusa," and my tone was confidential, "I want to ask you something. What have you ever heard in regard to this place being haunted? I am sure that the Mexicans have always thought it haunted, no?"

Her glance was appraising and a little distrustful; then, true to racial character, she evaded a direct answer by passing the responsibility back to me.

"Your mother told me that apparitions have been seen here; and that the mysterious cry of a baby has been heard. And not long before her death she told me that she had seen a woman in a ragged white dress standing near the outside wall of the dining room—right out there." The old woman indicated a location halfway down the north side of the house.

I recalled my mother's failing eyesight, her lonely days in her old age, and I thought: "Perhaps she did think she saw 'the woman dressed in white.'"

But I must use a more subtle method, I sensed, if I hoped to get from the cautious old woman the story that I felt might exist.

"Doña Jesusa," I began anew, "you know that this is a very

old ranch, this Rancho Perdido—this Lost Ranch. This house was built in 1872 on the site of an abandoned ranch house that had been built here before the Civil War. They didn't know it at the time of course, but later they learned that the northwest corner of the house rested on the lost grave of a baby, or a mother and baby; some of the old-time Mexicans had the legend. And they told that the baby had been heard to cry at midday—always at midday. But during the time that we have lived here it has been heard only once, as far as we know. Several members of the family heard it distinctly, but I was spending the day at another ranch, so missed hearing it. I was sorry, for I had hoped I would hear it sometime."

Doña Jesusa nodded silently. I waited patiently, hoping that she would share with me the dark thoughts that brooded in her eyes. She had worked for my mother through many middays and had had many opportunities to hear the baby cry, if it did cry. But she smoked silently on.

"But that is not all," I continued. "An old Mexican man, Martín Silvas, told me not long ago that when he was a boy he lived near this place; that was before any Americans came to this part of the country. He said that a Mexican family lived on that little hill just beyond the tank"—I pointed in the general direction—"and that late one afternoon they saw a woman dressed in white walking about this place, under the group of mesquite trees that grew here. She had her long black hair hanging, as if she had washed it and was letting it dry. When they investigated, they found that the woman had been no one of those in the neighborhood."

"The same one that your mother saw in the ragged white dress," Doña Jesusa affirmed. "And did none of you, in all the years you lived here, see or hear anything else?" the old woman wanted to know.

"Strange to say," I said, smiling at her, "my father saw something for which he couldn't account at the time. That was before I could remember, perhaps before I was born, but I

have heard him tell of it many times; and you know how accurate my father was."

"Yes, and a little hardheaded," she replied as she flicked
the ashes off the end of her cigarette.

"But the apparition that my father saw," I explained, "was
neither that of the woman in white nor of the crying baby.
It was of a woman in a dark dress with a shawl over her
head; and he saw only the woman's back. He was here alone;
it was about one o'clock, he said, and he was sitting on the
back porch reading. He raised his eyes from the book he
held, and as he did he saw the back of a woman, with a shawl
over her head, just as she went around the northwest corner
of the house. He thought it strange that she should be going
away from him instead of toward him. He got up and went to
the front part of the house, expecting her to appear there. He
thought, of course, that it was someone on an errand from the
little settlement down on the creek. He saw no one, and a
thorough search of the premises revealed no one. However, my
father didn't think that he had seen a ghost."

"What did he think he had seen?" Doña Jesusa wanted to
know, with a trace of sarcasm in her tone.

"Well, I have heard him offer the explanation," I told her,
"that it might have been a shadow—of a low-flying buzzard
or of a cloud; but whatever it was, it was no ghost, he insisted."

"Yes, that is the way your father was; he was a little hardheaded. And what about the baby crying?"

I knew she must have heard our version of the legend, but
she wanted to hear it again.

"As I told you, Doña Jesusa, I was not at home, but I
heard the story as soon as I returned. My mother told me at
once: 'We heard the baby cry today—the baby that is buried
under the house.' She said that they were all seated at the
dinner table—at midday—when every one of them heard the
protesting cry of a baby, just one wail that came from the
direction of the northwest corner of the house. They all

expected to see a Mexican woman, with a baby in her arms, appear at the open outside door of the dining room. But when she didn't come, one of the children got up from the table and went to see who their caller was. There was no one to be found. During the discussion that followed, the legend of the baby that cried at midday was recalled. My father tried to explain the noise as being that of some bird or animal; but the noise was never accounted for, convincingly."

The old woman deliberated while she rolled another cigarette, fumbled in the pocket of her full skirt for a match, struck it on the sole of her shoe, lit the cigarette and drew slowly on it. She looked out the window and announced: "It is raining harder; and it is getting late; I must be going."

"Oh, no, you are not to leave me here alone. You must stay till my brother returns so he can take you home in his car."

"You are afraid to stay here alone?" she asked.

"No, not afraid; of what should I be afraid? But *triste?* Yes. It makes one sad, no? to remember things of the past."

"Ay, ay," the old woman sighed.

"So you see, Doña Jesusa, my people can account for at least three apparitions. But the legend that Mexicans of the locality told years ago concerns only the woman in white and the baby that cried at midday; apparently we have added another character to the story, whatever it may be—the character of the woman with the shawl over her head. Do you suppose there is anyone living today who could tell the story of why this place is haunted, if it is haunted?" I asked. But the old woman sat absorbed in her own thoughts. She either didn't know or didn't want to tell me.

"Doña Jesusa," I said, trying once again to enlist the old woman's confidence, "do you think anyone will ever again see the woman with the shawl over her head; or the woman dressed in white, with her hair hanging; or hear the baby cry at midday?"

"Ay, ay. *Solo Dios sabe*—only God knows."

The Story of Casa Blanca

OF SPECIAL INTEREST to many old-timers in South Texas is the rebuilding of Casa Blanca. For no one knows how many years this rock house stood on the south bank of the Penitas Creek, about a mile from where the creek emptied into the Nueces River before it was overflowed by Lake Corpus Christi. A Robstown doctor secured a hunting permit for the site and reconstructed the one-room house on the foundation of the original, which was level with the ground. The new house is used as a hunting lodge.

No one knows the full story of the building of Casa Blanca. Title to the land surrounding it goes back to the Spanish grant allowed in favor of Juan de la Garza Montemayor and sons. Among the early-day Mexicans Casa Blanca was spoken of as Rancho Garzeño, or ranch pertaining to Garza. Tradition also says that it was headquarters of a large horse ranch operated by Garza. It is reasonable to suppose that it was the owner of the land who built the house.

Conflicting descriptions of the old house make it anything from an imposing stronghold to what it really was: a one-room house built after the Mexican style. Eighty years ago the four walls of the house were still standing, with the exception of a block or two of the stone that had fallen from one corner. Apparently the roof, which was gone at that time, had been built of lumber and was surrounded by a parapet about three feet high. The lumber waterspouts were still hanging to the wall.

There was evidence of fire's having burned the woodwork, but some of it, including the door, may have been removed and used in the construction of another rock house that was built some time later than Casa Blanca, not a great distance away. This was the Dix house, where the Duboses lived at one time.

As far as is known, no one, since the original owners, has ever lived within the walls of Casa Blanca. Legends of ghosts have hung around the place, but only of such ghosts as have been there for the express purpose of protecting the one or more buried treasures the place has been credited with. The oldest story is of a treasure that the owner buried in the gate of the corral when he took his family and left for Mexico and a safer home. Eighty years ago, however, there was no sign of the corral.

In the early 1870's a man by the name of Brewer bought a small tract of land that included the site of Casa Blanca. He built a small lumber house within a stone's throw of the crumbling walls, and brought his family to live there. Then legends arose around the reason for this family's selecting such an out-of-the-way place for a home. The Brewer family included several big, strapping boys, and an adopted orphan girl named Razzie. One legend said that the Brewers had come to look for the buried treasure—the big boys to do the digging. Another legend had it that Razzie was to come into possession of some money, and they wanted to be where they could spend it as they saw fit without any kind of interference.

A marriage was arranged between Razzie and the oldest Brewer boy. Razzie did come into some money, which the old man invested, in full or in part, in cattle out on the Rio Grande. (The Mexican man, Martín Silvas, who helped drive the cattle to Casa Blanca, was living when this was written but has since died.) Later, Brewer sold Casa Blanca and moved to another small tract of land up the creek a mile or two. In the late seventies the Brewers took all their possessions—all, that is, as far as anyone knew—and left the country. Sometime after 1879 a family named Brandis came and moved into the lumber house.

Then, one cold blustery night, the Brandis family was disturbed by the barking of their dogs. The next morning they found that someone had come in a wagon and had dug up something near the old rock house and carried it away. The hole that was left clearly showed the imprint of a box, they thought.

Whether the Brewers had returned for some of Razzie's money that they had buried, or whether some descendant of Juan de la Garza Montemayor had returned after such a long time, will likely never be known.

But whatever the treasure dug up that cold night, it was not the one buried in the gate of the corral; the location wasn't right for a corral. That treasure is yet to be found.

Two Ghost Stories of Military Life in the Southwest

KENNETH PORTER

ON MARCH 12, 1955, my wife and I, en route from Australia to the United States via Europe, were in Heidelberg at the Hotel Tannhäuser. In the hotel dining room we fell into conversation with two other Americans: an elderly woman, who proved to be the widow of General Lucius Roy Holbrook, and her niece. Perhaps because I mentioned that I was acquainted with Old Fort Clark in Texas, Mrs. Holbrook began to tell ghost stories, the first of which had Fort Clark for its locale. I asked permission to make notes, and the resultant manuscript was mailed later in the year to Mrs. Holbrook, who corrected and returned it. The notes are intended principally to indicate the time of the occurrences involved in the stories.

Fort Clark, Texas

When the Holbrooks were stationed at Fort Hamilton, New York, General Howard L. Laubach told them this story.[1] As a young officer he was assigned to duty at Fort Clark.[2] A little square one-story building at one end of officers' row was the only quarters available. The only reason this structure was vacant was that it was supposed to be haunted. The story, as told to Lieutenant Laubach by his commanding officer, was that a colonel who was formerly in command of the post had lived in the house.[3] He had a colored cook who was always accompanied by a big black cat. The colonel drank heavily

226

and when in his cups sometimes beat the cook. Eventually, after one such beating, the cook died. After that, people in the living room of the little house would hear footsteps on the ceiling which would come down the wall and halfway across the room, and then stop. People then began to *see* the cook and her cat. Finally, no one could be found willing to live there. A colored servant who was lodged there overnight without being told of the house's reputation was sitting on the porch next morning. He had heard the footsteps!

Lieutenant Laubach, for want of any other place to stay, moved into the little house. He had two dogs, one valuable, the other less so. For some time neither he nor they heard or saw anything out of the way. Then one night at 11 o'clock, as he was getting ready to inspect the guard, he heard footsteps across the ceiling which moved down the wall and came toward him to the middle of the floor. The dogs were so terror-stricken that they dashed through the screen window. The more valuable dog lost his senses and had to be tied up and eventually destroyed. The other could never be coaxed into the house again.

The lieutenant was about to be married and was concerned over the effect such visitations might have on his wife. His commanding officer repeated all the stories he had previously told, with some new ones added, in support of his belief that the bride would not wish to live there. There was, however, still no other place in which they could live, so the lieutenant reluctantly brought his bride to the "haunted house." To his relief, she never heard anything at all alarming.[4] Whether her presence "laid the ghost" for good or not the general did not know; at any rate, after leaving Fort Clark he never heard anything further about the "haunted house" he had once occupied.[5]

San Antonio, Texas

The year before World War I the Holbrooks were transferred to San Antonio.[6] It was very hard to get lodgings there.

However, they heard that the milk man always knew what houses were vacant, so they applied to him and he took them to Alamo Heights, to a pretty white stucco house with brown trimmings, verandah, yard, fence, and a barn with stalls for horses. It seemed strange that such a house should be standing vacant. They moved in with a splendid cook and a soldier who took care of their two horses. The garage was separate from the house and had a bedroom and toilet. The soldier slept in the garage. The other servants, all colored, slept in the house, in the basement.

Soon after they moved in, however, the Holbrooks' troubles began. One day the soldier said: "Mrs. Holbrook, your cook is going to leave." "Why?" she asked. "Because your house is haunted." When the Holbrook boys, then ten, fourteen, and sixteen years old, heard the story, they said they had known from the first that the house was haunted, because the other boys in school had told them so. They had also been told that there was a skeleton in the attic, but when they investigated they could find none.

The second day after they had moved in Mrs. Holbrook had been pulling out bureau drawers and had found letters from a woman who was a former occupant. "After what had happened," the letters said, "she and the children would not come back." Mrs. Holbrook then discovered little bugs crawling about. She called in the soldier. "What are these?" "Bed bugs," he answered. "You can't sleep in this house." "Maybe that's why the woman moved and won't return," Mrs. Holbrook thought. She went to the drugstore to find out what she could do. "You might as well move out," was the only advice they could give her. "But there's no other house vacant," she replied. Finally they gave her a solution to put in the cracks with a feather. The owner of the house offered to repaper and paint the house. The army offered to fumigate it. When this suggestion was made, Mrs. Holbrook realized that the house had been fumigated before and that this accounted for the indications that the window shades had been stuck to the window sills—to help make the house tight and fumigation more effective. When she mentioned this she was told that local custom required a house to be fumigated when anyone died in it. She wondered if some mysterious death, followed by fumigation, could account for the house's reputation. Despite the pessimistic views of the drugstore people, the Holbrooks were able to get rid of the bugs. The soldier offered to trade rooms with the cook so she would not be troubled by the ha'nts, and the cook moved out into the garage.

Then the soldier said: "I'm going to sit in the corner grocery and hear what they say about the house." He heard that the man who had formerly lived in the house used to have men in, against his wife's wishes, to drink and gamble. Mrs. Holbrook thought that perhaps this, rather than a death or bed bugs, accounted for the departure of the wife and children mentioned in the letter she had seen. Then she discovered that a little cocker spaniel sleeping on a screened verandah over the cook's room would sometimes scratch vigorously, producing a thumping sound. This, apparently, had been one of the things which had alarmed the cook. Mrs. Holbrook eventually learned that the trouble had all started when a Sicilian fruit seller told the cook that something terrible would happen to anyone who lived in the house. Mrs. Holbrook, when she found it out, refused to patronize the fruit seller any more. But it was too late; the cook, despite all explanations, finally left.

1. The Holbrooks were at Fort Hamilton, N. Y. from October, 1930, to December, 1933. Gen. Laubach was at Fort Wadsworth, N. Y. from May 7, 1931, to December 31, 1933. See *Cullum's Register*, VIII (1930-40), 91, 103.

2. Howard L. Laubach, born in Allentown, Pa., August 24, 1870, was graduated from the U.S. Military Academy and commissioned second lieutenant in 1893. He took up his duties at Fort Clark on May 31, 1894. *Cullum's Register*, Supp., IV (1890-1900), 554.

3. I have not attempted to identify the colonel.

4. Lieutenant Laubach and Katherine Hague were married **on** December 26, 1895. *Who's Who in America, 1946-47.*

5. Laubach would have had the opportunity to check on the "ghost" several years later, as from some time in 1910 to March 7, 1911, he **was** again stationed at Fort Clark. *Cullum's Register,* Supp., VI-A (1910-20), 661-62.

6. The Holbrooks were in San Antonio from July, 1916, to July, 1917. *Cullum's Register,* VI-A, 760-61.

Contributors

MICHAEL J. AHEARN wrote an article on his family's madstone while taking the course in life and literature of the Southwest at the University of Texas in the spring of 1958. He is going to follow family tradition by becoming a doctor.

JOHN Q. ANDERSON, student of the Southwest, author of many articles and editor of an important Civil War diary, spent his boyhood in the Texas Panhandle. He now teaches English at Texas Agricultural and Mechanical College.

RUTH DODSON has lived many years in the Nueces country of South Texas. On her father's ranch she came to know the language and ways of the *gente*, with whom she has maintained friendly contact all her life. Her longest contribution to the TFS annuals has been her study of Don Pedrito Jaramillo, the healer of Los Olmos. She has written a fine folk novel about Texas-Mexican cotton pickers which, it is hoped, will be published in the near future.

ARTELL DORMAN was teaching at Pyote, Texas, when she collected her stories about the Devil. She is working on beliefs about the Devil in Texas for her M.A. thesis, to be presented at North Texas State College, of which she is a graduate. At present she is teaching in the El Paso public schools.

JOHN HENRY FAULK grew up in South Austin. As a student of

Mr. Dobie's at the University of Texas he became interested in folklore, and with the aid of a Rosenwald Fellowship he recorded Negro sermons in and around Austin. After several years on radio and television in New York he has returned to live in Austin, not very far from his boyhood home.

EVERETT A. GILLIS teaches English at Texas Technological College. He has published a number of articles on folklore in the annuals of the Texas Folklore Society and elsewhere. He is a poet as well as a teacher and scholar.

MEREDITH HALE was formerly a teaching fellow in Spanish at North Texas State College. She is now living outside Dallas. "I Heard It on the Border" draws on her memories of life in El Paso some years ago.

WILLIAM HENRY HARDIN grew up in Coryell and Bell counties in Texas. After graduating from high school in McGregor, he joined the regular army. Now a retired officer, he lives in Austin and is a graduate student in the University of Texas.

GEORGE D. HENDRICKS teaches a course in life and literature of the Southwest at North Texas State College. He is the author of *The Bad Man of the West,* which has just gone into a third edition. Besides being a regular contributor to the annuals of the TFS, he has contributed to the *Journal of American Folklore, Western Folklore, Arizona Quarterly, Southern Folklore Quarterly,* and *Sing Out.*

J. R. JAMISON is the president of the bank in Dayton, Texas. He sent his article to Mr. Dobie, who sent it on to the editors of the Texas Folklore Society.

RICHARD LANCASTER is a student at the University of Texas. In the summer of 1958 he visited the Blackfoot Indians and wrote down a number of their stories, one of which is printed in this volume.

DONALD M. LANCE grew up near Mission, Texas, and received the B.A. degree from Texas Agricultural and Mechanical College in 1952. He is now working toward a Master's degree at the University of Texas. While taking a course in the ballad during the summer of 1958 he wrote the essay published here. At present he is teaching in Corpus Christi.

NORMAN (BROWNIE) MC NEIL learned how to play the guitar and sing *corridos* as a boy in San Antonio. After graduating from the University of Texas he spent a year in Mexico collecting and studying native songs. He wrote his dissertation on the Child ballads in the American Midwest. Now a teacher at the Texas College of Arts and Industries at Kingsville, he continues to study the music, life, and ways of Texas-Mexicans at first hand.

WILLIAM A. OWENS is known to members of the Society for his *Texas Folk Songs,* the annual publication for 1950. He is now professor of English at Columbia University, but commutes to Texas from time to time to work on the Oral History of Oil Pioneers. His most recent novel, *Fever in the Earth,* published by Morrow in 1958, grew out of this project. "Seer of Corsicana," another by-product of the project, first appeared in the *Southwest Review* for Spring, 1958.

AMÉRICO PAREDES knows the border country thoroughly. He grew up in Brownsville, where for a while he was a reporter for the *Herald.* In 1958 he published a book on the hero of a South Texas *corrido,* Gregorio Cortez—"*With His Pistol in His Hand.*" At the University of Texas he teaches balladry, creative writing, and southwestern literature.

KENNETH PORTER is professor of history at the University of Illinois. He has lived in Texas and has recently published a history of the Humble Oil and Refining Company.

GROVER ALLEN REYNOLDS was taking George Hendricks' course in southwestern literature at North Texas State College when he wrote the article printed here. At present he is a graduate student at the same college. He intends to become a teacher.

JOHN T. SMITH teaches English at Baylor University. While studying for the Master's degree at the University of Texas he took a course on the ballad under Mr. Paredes, who suggested that he work on *corridos* having to do with railroading. The result is the article in this volume.

WALTER FITZWILLIAM STARKIE was director of the British Institute in Madrid from 1940 to 1954. The article published in this volume he presented at the dinner held by the TFS during its 1958 meeting in Alpine. At that time he was a visiting professor of English at the University of Texas. He has lived with and studied Gypsies in various parts of the world and has written extensively on Gypsy ways and music. Among his books are *Raggle Taggle* (1933), *Spanish Raggle Taggle* (1934), *Don Gypsy* (1936), *In Sara's Tents* (1953), and *Spain: A Musician's Journey Through Time and Space* (1958).

FRED O. WELDON, JR., received the Master's degree in English at the University of Texas in 1958, presenting a thesis upon which his present article is based. After a year's newspaper work, he returned to the university, where he is currently a teaching assistant in English.

GIRLENE MARIE WILLIAMS was an undergraduate at the University of Texas when she prepared "Negro Stories from the Colorado Valley." For her term project in a course she was taking—that on life and literature of the Southwest, initiated by Mr. Dobie—she collected her stories from around La Grange, her home town.

Index

Singing schools, 153-60
Sinistrality, 69-87
Springtown, Texas, vigilante justice in, 201-8

Teasing, as form of humor, 58-68

Vigilante justice, 201-8

Whilden, Joe, 45-57
Wood, Will, 8-9

Zambra, Gypsy dance, 96-98, 102-5